LANGUAGE
AND
HUMAN NATURE

A Monograph in

MODERN CONCEPTS OF PHILOSOPHY

Series Editor

MARVIN FARBER
State University of New York at Buffalo
Buffalo, New York

Titles appearing in this series do not necessarily reflect the thinking of the editor or publisher.

The series has been developed to present *all* modern concepts of philosophy.

The following titles have either been published in the series or are in production and will be published soon.

1. ON SPACE AND TIME: Kant, Strawson, Heidegger — by Walter Cerf.
2. RADICAL CURRENTS IN CONTEMPORARY PHILOSOPHY — by David DeGrood.
3. THE MEASUREMENT OF VALUES: Behavioral Science and Philosophical Approaches — by Rollo Handy.
4. SOCIALIST HUMANISM: The Outcome of Classical European Morality — by Donald Clark Hodges.
5. THE PROMISE AND PERIL OF HUMAN PURPOSE: The New Relevance of the Purpose of Existence — by William Horosz.
6. LANGUAGE AND HUMAN NATURE: A French-American Philosophers' Dialogue — by Paul Kurtz (Ed.)
7. NATURALISTIC PHILOSOPHIES OF EXPERIENCE — by D. C. Mathur.
8. THE CONCEPT OF INTENTIONALITY: A Critical Study — by Vitendra Nath Mohanty.
9. AN EXAMINATION OF SET THEORY — by John L. Pollock.
10. PLATO'S DIALECTIC — by Lynn Rose.
11. POWER AND ITS MOULD: An Essay on State and Politics — by Nathan Rotenstreich.
12. PRINCIPLES OF EMERGENT REALISM: Philosophical Essays by Roy Wood Sellars — by Preston Warren.
13. THE METAPHYSICAL AND GEOMETRICAL DOCTRINE OF BRUNO AS GIVEN IN HIS WORK, DE TRIPLICI MINIMO—by Ksenija Atanasijevic, translated by George Vid Tomashevich.

LANGUAGE
AND
HUMAN NATURE

A French-American Philosophers' Dialogue

Edited by

PAUL KURTZ

State University of New York at Buffalo
Buffalo, New York

WARREN H. GREEN, INC.
St. Louis, Missouri, U.S.A.

Published by

WARREN H. GREEN, INC.
10 South Brentwood Blvd.
St. Louis, Missouri 63105, U.S.A.

Library of Congress Catalog Card No. 73-108782

Printed in the United States of America
6-A   (176)

SPONSORED BY:

The French Government

International Cultural Cooperation Committee
of the
American Philosophical Association

The American Council of Learned Societies

Philosophy and Phenomenological Research

AMERICAN COMMITTEE:

Paul Kurtz, *Chairman*
Marvin Farber
John Goheen
Herbert W. Schneider

FRENCH COMMITTEE:

Edouard Morot-Sir, *Chairman*
Raymond Polin
Paul Ricoeur
Henry Dumery

International Cultural Cooperation Committee: John D. Goheen, Chairman, Archie J. Bahm, Max Black, Lewis E. Hahn, Abraham Kaplan, Paul Kurtz, Karl H. Potter, Herbert W. Schneider, Wilfrid Sellars, Gregory Vlastos.

PREFACE

I.

The present publication contains the main papers presented at the French-American Philosophers' Conference, which convened at the State University of New York Conference Center, Oyster Bay, Long Island, October 18-19, 1968. The Conference was co-sponsored by the French Government and the International Cultural Cooperation Committee of the American Philosophical Association, and it was made possible through a generous grant from the American Council of Learned Societies.

The purpose of the Conference was to bring into encounter and dialogue philosophers from France and the United States. Recognizing that there was need for continuing dialogue, Professor Edouard Morot-Sir, French Cultural Counselor and Representative of the French Universities in the United States, contacted Professor John Goheen, Chairman of the International Cultural Cooperation Committee of the A.P.A. to see whether such a conference could be convened. There has been considerable communication between British and American philosophers, especially since the second world war, much less between French and American philosophers where both linguistic and philosophical differences often provide barriers. Although the works of Sartre, Camus, Merleau-Ponty and Levy-Strauss are known by many American philosophers, there is a real lack of knowledge about other kinds of philosophical research in France; similarly, French philosophers are not always well-informed about philosophical developments in the United States. It has been twenty years since the book, *Philosophic Thought in France and the United States,* edited by Marvin Farber, brought together French and American philosophers in a symposium involving the important areas of philosophic inquiry, thus bridging the gap between the two cultures.

With the need for a personal meeting between French and American philosophers in mind, the International Cultural Cooperation Committee of the A.P.A. proposed a small though intensive conference. The idea, however, was not to present different philosophical traditions in historical perspective, as is often done in similar conferences, but rather to deal directly with a philosophical problem thought to be central in both countries. A common topic of interest that seemed to emerge for both the French and the American organizing Committees was the philosophy of man—philosophical anthropology as it is called in France, or philosophical psychology as it is designated in the United States. Interestingly, the philosophers invited to contribute papers chose to focus on two problems in this general area—language and human nature; the former is at the center of the stage in America and the latter is considered crucial in France. In France, phenomenology, existentialism, Marxism and structuralism have been dominant post-war movements; in the United States analytic philosophy, logical positivism and pragmatic naturalism. No doubt one's philosophical position unavoidably influences the significance that one attributes to certain problems and the methods of approach that one employs to deal with them.

Although the philosophers taking part in the Conference were selected to represent the different points of view in their respective countries, they came not primarily as Frenchmen or Americans, but as philosophers, to deal cooperatively with a basic philosophical problem. Altogether there were some thirty participants. Six main papers were delivered, and there were six critical papers in response. In addition to the papers prepared beforehand, each of the participants was invited to write up and expand his remarks delivered at the Conference, including any further rejoinders or comments that he wished to make. What is here presented for the first time, includes, in addition to the main papers, the extended dialogue and exchange as prepared by the participants to the Conference afterwards.

I wish to thank the following for providing translations of various papers in this volume: Edouard Morot-Sir, Gerard Deledalle, Edward S. Casey, Wesley C. Piersol, Barbara Reid, and Hubert L. Dreyfus. I also wish to thank Mrs. Jane Holland for editorial assistance in preparing these papers for publication. We are grateful to the American Council of Learned Societies, the American Philosophical Association, and the French Government for providing financial assistance for the Conference. I wish to express my special appreciation to Professor Marvin Farber and the journal, *Philosophy and Phenomenological Research*.

PAUL KURTZ
Editor

II.

Congresses and conferences of all specialties respond to a natural need for communication and information in a world in search of a universal culture. Such a need for universality is even more the characteristic trait of every philosophical encounter which postulates as unity and ultimate limit, whether accessible or not, the existence of an eternal philosophy serving as the ideal common denominator of all the intellectual particularisms arising in a universe of cultural pluralities.

The French-American philosophical conference of October 1968 does not escape this historical necessity; but it presents, in addition, an original value which should be underlined and which sheds light on the texts which were presented and discussed during the Oyster Bay encounter. This conference was the first of its kind. First in what sense? We do not mean to say that for the first time relations have been established between French and American philosophers; to claim so would be to ignore three centuries of continuous and active cultural exchanges! But the originality resided in the very style of the meeting. There was a very real need for communication, certainly, but especially, and in a deeper sense, there was a need for confrontation which does not signify a desire for encounter between irreducible or divergent positions; this awareness of differences was animated by a spirit of dialogue and reciprocal understanding.

And this conference is concluded in the awareness of an enthralling problem—a problem which involves the existence of every philosophy, present and future: the diversity, or simply the duality of languages being compatible with the unity of the fundamental options for man, how is this methodological and semantic tension between the One and the multiple explained? The problem is raised; and the fact that it has been stated by the mere existence of the conference is reassuring for the future of philosophy, and also for the future of similar cultural encounters.

EDOUARD MOROT-SIR
Chairman, French Committee

CONTENTS

                                                              Page

PREFACE by Paul Kurtz and Edouard Morot-Sir vii

Part I. LANGUAGE

Section 1

J. Vuillemin: Expressive Statements 5
A. I. Melden: Expressives, Descriptives, Performatives 18
J. Vuillemin: Rejoinder to Melden 26
A. I. Melden: Rejoinder to Vuillemin 33
V. J. McGill: Comments on Vuillemin 36
Frederick B. Fitch: On Kinds of Utterances 39

Section 2

Wilfrid Sellars: Language as Thought and Communication . . . 41
Mikel Dufrenne: Comments on Wilfrid Sellars' Paper 63
Edouard Morot-Sir: Comments on Sellars 71
Joseph Margolis: Comments on Sellars 75
Edward S. Casey: Expression and Manifestation in Sellars
    and Dufrenne 78

Part II. HUMAN NATURE

Section 3

Raymond Polin: The Sense of the Human 87
ᵗack Kaminsky: Essence Revisited 113
Raymond Polin: Rejoinder to Kaminsky 119
Paul Kurtz: Human Nature and Value: Comments on Polin . . 121
Herbert W. Schneider: Comments on Polin 126
V. J. McGill: Comments on Polin 129
Joseph Margolis: Comments on Polin 132
Joseph J. Kockelmans: On The Basis of Moral Obligation . . . 135

xi

Section 4

Rcderick M. Chisholm: On the Observability of the Self . . . 140
Henri Lefebvre: Reply to Professor Roderick Chisholm
  and Comments 155
Chaim Perelman: Comments on Chisholm and Lefebvre . . . 164
Roderick Chisholm: Rejoinder to Perelman 167
Gilbert Varet: On the Observability of the Self according
  to Sartre 169
Donald Sievert: Chisholm on Substance 174

Section 5

Jacques Derrida: The Ends of Man 180
Richard Popkin: Comments on Professor Derrida's Paper . . . 207
Marvin Farber: On "Who We Are" as a Philosophical Question:
  Comments on Derrida 215
Peter Caws: On Self Reference: Comments on Derrida . . . 219
Wesley C. Piersol: Comments on Derrida 222

Section 6

Arthur C. Danto: Complex Events 225
Gilbert Varet: Complexity and Ambiguity; Some Observations
  on Arthur C. Danto's "Complex Events" 237
Edouard Morot-Sir: Comments on Danto 243
Gerard Deledalle: Conciliation 245

LANGUAGE
AND
HUMAN NATURE

Part I
Language

Section 1

EXPRESSIVE STATEMENTS

J. Vuillemin

It was at the same time, and yet independently, that a linguist, Professor E. Benveniste, who has been teaching linguistics in Paris for many years, and an Oxfordian philosopher, the late J. L. Austin introduced formally the same new idea, to a public already prepared to receive it by Wittgenstein's *Philosophical Investigations.* This was the concept which Austin named the performative, in which language is treated as action.

We can briefly characterize this concept of the performative as the way "to do things with words" and define it as an expression that produces a new state of affairs merely by being spoken or written. But we are dealing with a real performative only when certain definite circumstances give to an expression its proper authority or efficiency. This is a most important restriction indeed. Thus, when the President of an Assembly says "I open the session," the words perform something, but if just any citizen pronounced unofficially the same words, these same words would not possess any public effect, except to draw public attention to this somewhat uncontrolled character. Or, when Neville Chamberlain declared before the Commons that England was entering the war against Germany, this declaration was a proper performative and not a descriptive sentence, whereas when Aristide Briand proclaimed before the League of Nations: "I declare the peace on you," his declaration was not a performative, and may be not a descriptive sentence either, but only a piece of rhetorical bombast such as pompous orators will use. This means that the grammatical form of a statement, considered in a restricted sense, will not by itself commit the listener to interpret it in either way.

This last remark can be extended into a general rule of language and philosophical analysis. We would then be entitled to seek inside the same grammatical category of descriptive phrases a determinate category of utterances that, not being performative themselves, have nevertheless a performative-like function. I will try to show that this latter category, together with the performatives, offers an acceptable generalization of the new concept of language as behaviour.

5

I

Let us consider the two following language games.

First, let us suppose that, suffering from some ailment, I have called the doctor. As he asks me how I am feeling, I answer like a stoic philosopher and, what's more a stoical one, giving him such a description of my pains as would help the diagnosis. I then behave as a doctor who analyzes his own symptoms. In these circumstances, when I say: "I have a pain," a statement that for the sake of clarity I will from now on name D, my statement does not, by its way of meaning, fundamentally differ from the statement "I am walking." In these two statements, I describe my state of being or my behavior at the moment. My description is true, if and only if, I have a pain or I am walking. When another person speaks in my place and, for instance, the nurse says: "He has a pain," or, pointing at me: "He is walking," these new statements have the same truth value as the first, and knowing the truth-value of the former, we can without further information deduce the truth value of the latter. Basically, the pain is in this case considered as a behavior, in principle entirely objective and such that in principle other people have the same means as I have to verify the truth of the statement that describes this pain.

Second, in totally different circumstances, I can for instance say: "I have a pain," (this statement I will from now on call E) wanting simply to attract the attention of others to my present state of feeling or intending merely to ease myself by expressing my state. Now E is the normal way to utter: "I have a pain" and D seems only a derived and forced one. In the case of D one has indeed to struggle — a struggle that becomes harder as the feeling becomes more acute — to act as if he were experiencing the pain of someone else. Or, at least, he must throughout compel himself to live as if he were expressing at the third person this pain he feels in the first person, following the example of Caesar or of someone not so remote.

Leaving then D as roughly equivalent to the other instances of descriptive mood, let us compare E with these clearer instances, such as "I am walking" or what the nurse would say in my place: "He has a pain." When the nurse speaks, she cannot express my feeling. For this I must speak. On the other hand, when analyzed, the meaning of the statement "I am walking" seems to break in two parts, which exhaust it: "X is walking and X says "I am walking," where in the place of X, one should substitute my proper name. But this same analysis fails, if applied to the statement: "I have a pain." For the meaning of the statement "X says 'I am walking' " is no part of the meaning of the statement "X is walking," just as to say "I am walking" is by no means identical with actual walking. On the contrary the meaning of the statement "X says 'I have pains' " is part of the meaning of the statement "X has pains," supposing that in place of X one has to put my proper name, since expressing "I have pains" is admittedly a manner of having pains. In other terms, the words 'I am walking' are a piece of linguistic behavior, not of walking behavior, whereas saying the words "I have pains" — even if one lies or simulates — is a manner of behavior in respect to the pain.

In one case then, I feel immediately my act of saying as foreign to my statement. In the other my behavior seems to need expression and my mood depends in a certain obscure but undeniable way upon the fact that I am expressing it. Accordingly, despite their formal identity and notwithstanding the opinion of most philosophers, we have to think of the statements D and E as distinct.

One should yet object that this difference, although a genuine one, is purely accidental and reflects only how we are subjectively prepared to interpret the statements we are uttering or hearing. Let us then suppose, as most do, that what I will henceforth call the descriptive and the expressive language games are fused together, and let us consider the consequences of this hypothesis.

To construe the expression of pain on the description of pain means that, when I am uttering D, I cannot verify my statement except through the same objective and external symptoms that are accessible to others. In other words in this supposition, I have no particular and personal access to my pain that would escape the notice of others. Conversely, if one will construe D on E, he is necessarily involved with the difficulty of supposing that, in order to know the pain of another, I must project in him the data of my own consciousness as given in the understanding of E.

So we started by supposing an identity of meaning between D and E. This supposition resulted in the so-called quarrel between behaviorism and the philosophy of introspection which both lead to intolerable and inescapable conclusions. By *reductio ad absurdum,* one is then committed to distinguish within the one formal indicative statement (at least in Indo-European languages) two fundamentally different moods, the descriptive and the expressive.

Having thus started from a dialectic difference we will now proceed onwards and arrive at an exclusion proper. Philosophers actually agree that when uttering a statement, one both describes or indicates a state of affairs and also expresses an attitude, and this is an opinion I would accept for all its ambiguity. However, they sometimes go so far as to claim that the same statement can at the same time and in the same use have both the values of descriptive and expressive moods, and with this last claim I disagree.

In the *Principles of Mathematics*,[1] Bertrand Russell distinguishes the meaning a proposition contains and the meaning it implies. The meaning contained belongs analytically to the proposition, while the implied meaning belongs to it only synthetically. This distinction, I think, applies to our statements. In a descriptive statement like "I am walking," I assert explicitly a certain state of affairs and I express implicitly only an attitude of mind that is the assertive mood. If I were explicitly expressing my attitude, I would say rather: "I assert that I am walking" and this expressing mood cannot then be contained in my former statement but simply be implied by it. Conversely, in an expressing statement like E, I explicitly express my state of feelings and I assert only implicitly the state of affairs I describe. Were I explicitly describing what happened to myself I would speak objectively like a positivist or like Caesar answering the augurs:

> Caesar should be a beast without a heart
> If he should stay at home today for fear.

This tempts us to confuse the two moods and to believe their possible simultaneity results from the formal, but after all perhaps accidental identity between E and D. We might then say these moods obey some principle of complementarity, deeply rooted in the nature and in the circumstances of human communication. Let us suppose that, in describing something, I am — in Russell's meaning — acquainted with it, while my interlocutor is either unacquainted or accidentally unaware, and this is precisely why I want to communicate with him. Now, when I describe, the other can, in principle, verify my description, and become in his turn directly acquainted with the thing I have described. On the contrary I can express only what I have particular access to. I am able to express not the pains of others, but at most what I feel sympathetically for them. When expressing, I have acquaintance with something that the others have not and cannot have, not only "de facto" but also "de jure." If I am right, the complementarity of describing and expressing is the linguistic consequence of an ontological alternative of situations.

Primarily, we express our feelings; secondarily, we describe them. Conversely, we first describe at our so called sense-data, and secondly we express them. And despite the confusing identity of form it matters very much whether one utters D or E, just as it matters whether one says,

---

[1] Bertrand Russell, *Principles of Mathematics* (New York, W. W. Norton & Co., Inc., 1964): for instance chap. IV, § 55.

to take classical instances, "This is red" or "I am seeing a patch of redness."

Perhaps there a fundamental difference appears. A descriptive mood implies only the possibility of the corresponding expressive mood. For this possibility to be actualized, the attitude, which was only implicit before, must be made explicit. On the contrary, the expressive mood actually implies the corresponding descriptive one, because to express a state of feeling is always explicitly to describe it, since the speaker uses the system of his grammar. This is why the distinction between E and D is not so clear: their formal identity involves not only a possible, but an actual implication, which is dependent only upon the speakers awareness.

II

We have found that the same indicative form can either describe or express. We shall now try to overcome this ambiguity, replacing D and E in greater linguistic units or contexts. My thesis bears on a peculiar instability of the expressive mood in certain contexts; if true it would give a formal argument in favor of the principle of complementarity, that I hitherto tried to justify through semantical, rather than syntactical, considerations.

More precisely, an expressive mood cannot as such remain expressive but becomes descriptive: 1) when, having been used before as expressing in an independent clause, it becomes used in a dependent one; 2) when it falls into the scope of a question; 3) when it falls into the scope of an expliciting locution of mental operation or propositional attitude; and 4) when instead of the first person of the present tense, it is used in another person or in another tense.

At this point I will not give here any abstract theory, but simply an example of each case.

1) In the subordinate clauses, "If I have a pain," "when I have a pain," "although I have a pain," and so forth, the locution, "I have a pain" is necessarily used with a descriptive meaning.

2) When I ask, "Do I have a pain?", the locution can only be decriptive, if it ever fits any real situation. (Wittgenstein says, perhaps rightly, that, generally, such a question is sheer nonsense). In any case, asking if I have a pain aims, for instance, at clearing someone's doubt and then I describe myself in the state of suffering and I cease to express my pain.

3) I cannot maintain the expressive mood within the scope of certain modal operators referring either to a mental operation or to a proposi-

tional attitude. When I say: "I suppose that I have a pain," I can merely describe myself as I would describe someone else, but then I never express this pain. Also, when I say, "I believe that (or I doubt whether) I have a pain" — one can eventually ignore this construction as inconsistent with the semantical rules of our language — once more I am describing, I am not expressing.

4) The locutions, "You have a pain" or "I had a pain" are always descriptive, never expressive.

The formal conditions for an expressive mood to be used are then very restrictive. The expression must be an assertive independent clause, and only in the first person of the present tense.

From these restrictions formal arguments follow that will confirm the principle of complementarity. I shall explain this point by an example. Let us call A the phrase: "I suppose that I have a pain." When I utter A, it makes no difference whether or not I have a pain, since, in both cases, my utterance is enough to entertain my supposition. Then A is a function of D, not a function of E. The situation would again be of the same kind, when I say: "I believe that I have a pain." Indeed Wittgenstein is right to question the possibility of such an expression, but his doubts matter only if one construed the A-statement as a function of E instead of D. In other terms, calling now A' the expression derived from A when in A one substitutes E for D, we clearly see that, while occurrences of A-statements can often be found, we shall never find occurrences of A-statements because of syntactical incorrectness. Yet, if it is so, the principle of complementarity will work. Let us, contrary to the principle, suppose E synonymous with D. The phrases A and A' being sentences about beliefs, they are neither extensional nor intensional, in the language of Carnap. Therefore it is equivalent to say either that, as wholes, they have the same truth-value, or that the sub-sentences of which they are functions have the same isomorphic structure. But despite their formal identity, they differ and then have not the same truth-value, A' never being true. Consequently, D and E must be considered as having different isomorphic structures and *a fortiori* different meanings, and, in order to go from E to A, owing to the illegitimacy of A', it is forbidden to proceed directly, the only permissible way being through D.

III

The peculiarity of the expressive mood can then be formally marked. What are the consequences first from the linguistic and philosophical point of view?

For the linguist the expressive mood is an outburst of subjectivity into the language.

More precisely, what does this intrusion mean? In the normally indicative, descriptive mood, the speaker in the first person and in the present tense uses necessarily the system of oppositions of persons an tenses (not to speak of other oppositions explicitly or covertly involved in this part of language system). For instance, he opposes the first and the second person — and these two persons proper to the third pseudo person — and in the same way the present to the past and future tenses. In this sense, one may speak of the Ego, the I, as relative to the You. On the other hand, the same I involves, besides a present process of immediate acquaintance, a whole series of inferences and constructions working on memories and anticipations and giving it extension in time. Russell would say there that "I" is a description which uses an apparent variable.

If we now turn towards the expressive mood, we find two novelties. 1) Given the limitations that make this mood possible only in the first person and in the present tense, we exclude even the possibility of thinking of this expressive mood with other persons or other tenses, and hence prevent the system of oppositions from functioning normally as it does in the descriptive mood.
2) This same system of oppositions of persons and tenses with its morphological and syntactical peculiarities is both formally and intentionally used in the descriptive mood only, whereas, in the expressive one, owing to the grammatical structure of our tongue, it will be used formally, but not in any case intentionally. The breakdown of the bond between formal structure and intentional use results directly from the principle of the complementarity between expressing and describing. Either we describe and then we use the bond, or we express and then, since we are forced to use the formal structure, we can only mark the specificity of the mood we actually use by an act of abstraction touching this intentional use. We will then neglect systematically the system of meanings involved in the structure. In other words, we neutralize the system of oppositions, while formally using them.

This surprising duality of the first person finds echo in the problem of how to know our fellow men. We can dismiss both the realist, for whom the existence of others is given as a datum just as primitive as his own, and the solipsist, who claims such a preeminence for the Ego that the other persons are only its posits. In the descriptive mood, the I was privileged *de facto,* not *de jure,* and it was given merely in opposition and relatively to the You. On the contrary, in the expressive mood, the I possesses an inexpugnable position, characteristic of him *de jure,* not simply *de facto* and he must conceive himself as not being in a substitutive relation with any other. What I can describe, the others can share equally with me. What I can only express, the others cannot partake of. The first communication is equalitarian and reciprocally homogeneous. The second is unequalitarian and reciprocally quite heterogeneous. In terms of Romantic philosophy, the I must be posited in one class as relative and in another as absolute, these terms being merely a metaphysical and, I fear, a metaphorical paraphrase of a primarily linguistic situation.

IV

What are now the logical issues of these philosophical consequences? Let us compare the four classes of statements:

1) "I declare the session opened," when this phrase is uttered by the recognized and authorized President of an Assembly.

2) "I suppose that it will rain" — "I believe that it is raining."

3) "I have a pain."

4) "I am walking," "I am reasoning."

In all the four classes, one has to recognize two different sorts of self reflexivity.

The first is common to all these classes, inasmuch as each of the statements they contain involves the egocentric particular word "I." When we utter "I" in the discourse, we mean that the subject of the event process (to walk, to reason, to suppose, to believe, to have a pain, to declare) is the same as the subject of the utterance. (If the verb not only is in the present tense but indicates also an instantaneous and unique aspect of experience — as opposed to a lasting and recurring one — we should perhaps be satisfied with this specification.) Restrictedly, in this case, the empirical event of the utterance absorbs the content of the I. In order to name this event process in which the evanescent I occurs merely as brought by grammatical mechanisms and without any ontological commitment, we will have to utilize or invent, as Russell would do, a proper name which is in no way a function of I. Afterwards, we must locate the entity just named in the immediate space-time of the perception field. Lastly we add that the resulting state of affairs is the immediate cause of the utterance enounced.

In such conditions, a statement like "I am warm" becomes analyzed: "Warmth ——. Warmth causes immediately the utterance 'I am warm'," where "Warmth" must be understood as a proper name and where the blank must be filled in with the indication of a determinate spatiotemporal situation.

I am not sure that such an analysis — not to speak of the intrinsic difficulties of the causal theory of perception — is able to eliminate effectively the egocentric words. However, we can imagine the case to be solved, since, after all, this punctual "I" reduces to the *factum conscientiae,* being nothing but the reflexive and ultimate quality of whatever data we are given. In any case, as soon as the author of the action or the state described ceases to merge with the author of the actual utterance, that is with the mere event of the utterance itself, it seems more difficult to solve the subject problem, except by doing away with it. Perhaps the trick of the apparent variable will still give a solution, if any. One would for instance translate approximately the statement "I am walking" with the following conjunction: "$(\exists x). (\exists z).$ x is actually walking. z has been in such and such situation. The same causality chain binds x and z. x says $<p>$. where p is the utterance: 'I am walking'." But an ambiguity remains concerning p. Indeed, if we choose for p the raw utterance: "I am walking," "I" occurs again and it is doubtful whether this latter can be interpreted here like the former punctual one. On the other hand, if we choose for p the more precise translation "x is walking," our general translation turns out to be false, since nobody has ever uttered "x is walking," and we are at once embarked in all the intricacies of the quantification into a "referentially opaque context."

In what I have called the first kind of self-reflexivity as it applies to our four classes of statements, the grammatical subjects were, in a double way, referring both to the subjects of utterances and to the subjects of the processes that the utterances were about. More subtle is the second kind.

In the first class of statements, the situation is clearest. When I say, as my titles and the situation make it legitimate: "I declare the session of the Assembly open," or simply, leaving implicit the first words: "The session of the Assembly is opened," the statement enunciated by me is what induces the fact, for, while I declare the session open, the session is by force of my declaration effectively opened. The second kind of self-reflexivity appears here, that which is responsible for "doing things with words." *I* solemnly declare something and this something is in no way a picture of the process which my declaration is about, but is the process itself. I utter a statement, apparently referring then only to a statement-name, whereas at the same time *my* utterance refers to a state of affairs that without this very utterance would not exist.

In the last class of statements of the type, "I am walking," this second reflexivity is wholly absent. Hence, "I am walking" like "I am reasoning" are not to be reckoned as expressive, but as descriptive moods.

Between these two extreme cases, where the statement that I am uttering either describes an event without having any effect upon it or is this very event, the two other classes take place. In the second, ("I suppose-," "I believe-"), the second kind of self-reflexivity appears, inasmuch as the operation or the attitude expressed (not described) enters in determining the status of the clause introduced by the conjunction "that": it sets it up or it mitigates it, or whatever, and, here, the doing bears on the completive clause of the statement proper. In the third class of the type of E, the doing consists in a certain modification of the process by the statement itself, the linguistic expression being a very part of our behavior.

The first sort of self-reflexivity imposed the problem how to interpret the status of the egocentric particular words and eventually how to eliminate them and obtain a clean objective language. The second sort develops every kind of the most difficult problems that the logician has to solve. In the case of the performative, the distinction between use and mention eludes us, since what I declare (or mention), I also use, my saying causing the event. For the second class, of the type "I suppose-," "I believe-", even if we give up translating these expressions to obtain their synonyms (which would be too great a challenge), it is far from being certain that we can construe, corresponding to explicantia, explicanda that are atomic and extensional.

Now there only remains the third class to interest us directly. For most philosophers an utterance like E is an instance of an atomic and extensional proposition. Eliminating the I and the other characteristics that accompany it, such as the present tense and so forth, and thus transforming this statement into an eternal phrase, they want to, and believe they will obtain, after such an analysis, a neat report of an elementary state of affairs. Is this claim to be maintained or not? This is the last question we will deal with.

V

Allow me first to take a few steps on a side path.

We have found no formal criteria for our distinction between E and D at the level of the statements considered as the units of discourse. Now, in the realm of pure deductive logic, a similar situation arises also, as soon as one limits his study to the level of isolated propositions. Only at the level of deductive discourse, can one distinguish, for instance, two sorts of syllogisms, the Aristotelian and the Theophrastian. (In the Aristotelian sort, the logical bond between the three clauses belongs to the object-language and we have but one proposition, preceded by only one assertion sign: "If all men are animals and all animals are mortal, then all men are mortals." On the contrary, in the Theophrastian syllogism, the logical bond belongs to the syntax-language and links together three propositions, each of which is preceded by an assertion sign: "All men are animals. Now all animals are mortal. Then all men are mortal." The well known paradox of Lewis Carroll arises, if one ignores this distinction.)

It is puzzling that logicians, agreeing to the necessity of the distinction, nevertheless continue to maintain the myth of the proposition as unity of discourse. Regarding our topics, we notice that the question of what is the true unity of discourse is very closely bound to the question of assertion and then generally of moods. We missed a distinction between moods, because we were confined to the level of statements and therefore to a one-level language.

The sign of assertion is a part of a syntax-language and nobody could reason without standing at the same time on two different language-levels. Were we allowed to use an analogy here, we might presume that the expression of moods belongs to a meta-language, more or less clearly distinguished from the object-language. But in any case we see how using a language requires a sort of reflexion that will allow speaker and hearer to move continuously from the level of the propositions or the statements, whatever their nature, to the level of the discourse.

Now to our question.

For a sentence to be extensional the referring terms that occur in it must occur in such a way that its truth-value remains unaltered when one substitutes for these other terms having the same reference. For a sentence to be atomic, it must result from filling up a n-place predicate with n-adequate proper names. Naturally, what matters is not so much whether a particular sentence is or is not atomic and extensional. Taken for granted that one analyses it, the real point is that the parts of the thus broken up sentence are still referential and atomic.

Now, most positivists would consider E and D as analyzable. On Russell's pattern, they would roughly give for them an explication of the type: "Pain is here and now, this event is the immediate cause of the utterance: 'I have a pain'." (Here in the first part of the conjunction the word "Pain" would be a proper name; "is" a universal name of a specific relation; "here and now" again a proper name. But this analysis is peculiar to Russell's last philosophy and could as such lead us astray.) Let us only keep in mind that the first member of the conjunction is a sentence describing an event and that the word "Pain" occurs in it as a proper name.

A first objection arises against this explication, whether you choose as explicanda D or E. Expressing differs from betraying an emotion. From this point of view expressing and describing are both intentional and they obey conventional rules special to the uses of each tongue. I fear then that one cannot without a severe distortion of reality describe the relation between the event and the utterance about it as a causal relation. As Chomsky has shown us, the grammatical structure of the sentences cannot admit this oversimplification. All our four classes of statements fall under this criticism, because in all the first self-reflexivity occurs that is responsible for the duality event/utterance. Now with the intentionality we evoke the ghosts of contexts that are neither extensional nor atomic. Nevertheless taking into account the deep structure of language as given together with the behavior data of linguistic performances, one can still bring some comfort, perhaps illusory, to a lover of the causal theory.

More serious is the objection that depends on the second kind of reflexivity. The proposed explication supposes indeed a clear break between event and utterance: now, this break does not apply to a language game where one does express something. Here E and D separate. The expressive mood interferes intimately with the state it expresses. In short, it is behavior: not, however, as one is tempted to believe, merely external behavior, mainly characterized by its capacity to be objectively noticed and accessible to all individuals. It is rather what we in French call *conduite* in opposition to *comportement*. In such a conduite it seems *a priori* difficult or even impossible to dissociate the feeling expressed and the proper act of expressing. In the same vein, whereas D possessed directly a truth-value since it described a state of affairs independent of this description, E looks like a complaint — and about this conduct it would be more accurate to say it is right or wrong, sincere or affected, etc. — rather than true or false.

Things being so, E is not extensional. First it has not in the proper sense a truth-value. Secondly, contrary to D, the word "I" occurring in it cannot be replaced by another word with the same reference, insofar as its uses neutralize the equality of access to experience between I and You. On his part, D is extensional if the statements like "I am walking" are too.

Concerning the second question, E is not atomic. For E, not being analyzable in terms of our former conjunction, involves the blurring of the distinction between use and mention. In turn this blurring prevents a statement from being atomic, since it contains a complexity. In the case of semantical paradoxes of the kind "I am lying," one can analyze this complexity dissociating different linguistic levels. (When, for instance, the propositions about which I am lying belong to the n-th order, the proposition saying that it is false will belong to the $(n + 1)$th order.) But such a dissociation appears impossible in the case of E, as far as it would precisely suppose the dissociation between event and utterance and then reduce E to D. The expressive mood seems therefore to level indistinctly different language orders. While the first kind of self-reflexivity revealed in E an identification of the subject of an event with the subject of an utterance, the second kind bears on the more profound identification between the subject which behaves and the subject which expresses, and therefore, between the subjects of at least two levels of discourse.

Thus we started from performatives to reach a more comprehensive class of sentences, where language is used as action. This use seems to imply peculiar relations between the statement and the event the statement is about. In their turn these relations apparently present serious obstacles to behavioristic reductions.

All these consequences are perhaps bewildering at first glance. However, I am not a critic of the methods of analysis. I have merely tried to define their limits with some precision, distrusting all who mix up the conquest of science with its hopes and myths.

Perhaps an analysis of the expressive mood is possible in conformity with the strict canons of scientific language. For my part, I do not see how to perform it. I wish to avoid begging the question by a confusion between describing and expressing and to stress the difficulty and the amplitude of the task.

After all, we can communicate to other people our joys and our pains, but, notwithstanding our efforts, we are in the last resort alone to live them, even when we are expressing them.

COLLÈGE DE FRANCE, PARIS.

EXPRESSIVES, DESCRIPTIVES, PERFORMATIVES

A. I. MELDEN

The same sentence, under different circumstances, may be used of course in quite different sorts of ways, and not necessarily because any of the words or expressions occurring in it are multivocal. This is one of the lessons that can be drawn from Wittgenstein's repeated insistence that we give up the idea that meanings ride piggy-back on words and sentences, and that we look instead to their use in language-games — highly variable forms of activity within the context of which alone items of discourse are employed in communication. The chairman of an assembly is surely saying something when he says "The meeting is now open," but, unlike someone uttering these words in the course of a radio broadcast of the proceedings, he is not reporting an event that is taking place, but, rather, making that event take place. Again, "my shoulder aches" may be given as information in answer to the question of an examining physician; but, equally possible, the words may come out like a cry of pain that calls for the ministrations of an attending nurse. There are performatives no less than reports of fact, expressions no less than reports and descriptions of feeling. Indeed, there are, as we are reminded by Wittgenstein,[1] indefinitely many language-games, and ways of using sentences in what, very broadly, we call communication.

All of this is or should be familiar enough; but what is unusual in Professor Vuillemin's paper is the manner in which, first, he distinguishes certain expressive utterances from their grammatically indistinquishable "descriptive" counterparts, and, second, he links together expressives and performatives. I shall question a number of things he has to say on each of these matters, but there are, I believe, lessons to be learned from a close study of his remarks.

I

We are asked to consider two quite different language-games in which "I have a pain" may be used, in the one as a "description," in the other

---

[1] Ludwig Wittgenstein, *Philosophical Investigations* (Oxford, Basil Blackwell, 1958), sect. 23.

as an expression of one's state. Let me begin with the latter. In this case
we have a "statement," labelled "E," which serves to draw attention to
one's mental state, in the form of a complaint, perhaps to provide the
speaker with relief — in general, as "an outburst of subjectivity into the
language." Viewed in these latter ways, E is not, of course, a statement.
Indeed we are later told that it has no truth value, however truthful or
deceitful the speaker may be in uttering it.

This account will bring to mind a suggestion once made by Wittgenstein concerning the way in which one might have learned that "pain"
is the name of a certain kind of sensation:

> Here is one possibility: words are connected with the primitive, natural expres-
> sions of the sensation and are used in their place. A child has hurt himself
> and he cries, and then adults talk to him and teach him exclamations and,
> later, sentences. They teach the child new pain-behaviour.
> 'So you are saying that the word 'pain' really means crying?' — On the con-
> trary: the verbal expression of pain replaces crying and does not describe it.[2]

Surprisingly, it has been frequently supposed that what Wittgenstein is
saying here is (a) that the *only* way in which "pain" can enter a language is by serving simply as a replacement for crying, (b) that in
teaching a child how to use "pain," first in exclamations and later in
sentences, the child never learns that "pain" is the name of a sensation
and never learns how to describe and report his sensations of pain,
presumably on the ground (c) that in saying that the verbal expression
of pain replaces crying and does not describe it, the word "it" refers to
pain, whereas if the reply given by Wittgenstein to his imaginary interlocutor is to be even relevant to the question that is asked, the "it"
must refer to crying. Of course Wittgenstein held that "pain" is the name
of a sensation. Of course he held that however "pain" enters the language we use, we can and do describe and report our pain sensations:
Philosophical Investigations is full of remarks about the description of
our pain sensations.

Professor Vuillemin does not refer to this famous passage, but he certainly does accept some of the views concerning so-called pain avowals
which have been ascribed mistakenly to Wittgenstein on the basis of
misreadings of this passage. Indeed, he himself seems to share in this
misunderstanding of the views of Wittgenstein, for he appears to hold
the view that Wittgenstein rejected as senseless "I believe that I have a
pain" because he assumed that the subordinate clause could only function as an E-clause, i.e., as a sheer outpouring of one's feeling, in which
case "I believe that I have a pain" would be senseless. But why it should

---

[2] *Ibid.*, sect. 244.

be supposed he made this assumption unless it be supposed that Witt-genstein thought that "I have a pain" (assuming as indeed it seems one should that it is an utterance pertaining to a pain sensation) must be always and only an outpouring of feeling, I cannot imagine. In any case, Wittgenstein's rejection of the sentence as senseless has nothing to do with whether or not "I believe that I have a pain" should or should not be taken as a function of an E-sentence, but with quite a different matter, namely, the grammars (in Wittgenstein's sense) of "pain" and "belief." For what leads Wittgenstein to declare this sentence senseless is that pain is not an interior object that we can look for, peer at and observe with the view to resolving the doubt and acquiring the opinion, belief or knowledge that one does in fact have that object — the pain.

Wittgenstein certainly held the view, to which as I understand him Professor Vuillemin is sympathetic, that *a* natural way in which one learns to engage in pain-talk is by substituting a wailing cry of "Pain!" for a wail or a cry of pain. And no doubt "It hurts like the very dickens" is usually not information given, but a pain reaction. Not long ago Miss Anscombe told me about a suggestion Wittgenstein once made during a discussion, that many at least of our first person present tense utterances about such mental items as pains could be viewed profitably as *Äus-serungen,* as outpourings into verbal form of one's state of mind. But the fact that "I have a pain" can be such an *Äusserung* by no means implies that in uttering it, one is not saying something. Neither does it imply that what one says cannot be said to be true or false. Indeed, why should it be imagined that if one's utterance expresses one's feeling, it cannot also be a description of the feelings one has? If, struggling to restrain the cries of pain, I force the words out to an examining physi-cian that my ankle hurts like hell, is this not a statement of fact, infor-mation given, a description of my pains?

Professor Vuillemin, however, seems to be of the opinion that if "I have a pain" is descriptive, it cannot also be expressive. He appears in fact to hold the view that it can be descriptive only by being about something distinct from what ostensibly it would be about, were it being used expressively. For in his account of the utterance as descriptive, he asks us to imagine a language-game in which, stoically, one behaves towards one's pain as a doctor would who is bent on making a diagnosis; and this curiously, he takes to mean that in saying "I have a pain" one would be making a statement about one's behavior which does not differ "fundamentally" from "I am walking!" "Basically the pain is in this case considered as behavior, in principle entirely objective;" and what he means by "entirely objective" would seem to be indicated by what he goes on to say: ".... (I)n principle other people have the same means as I have to verify the truth of the statement that describes the pain." It is for this reason that he remarks that in the case of the "descriptive" use of the sentence "I have a pain" someone uttering it "must compel himself to live as if he were expressing in the third person the pain he feels in the first person" and, later on, "were I explicitly describing what happens to myself I would speak objectively like a positivist or like Caesar answering the augurs" about himself in the third person. And, unless I misunderstand him, it is this assimilation of the first person "descriptive" use of "I have a pain" to third person utterances about behavior that leads him to consider, in connection with the question of the distinctive character of the expressive use of this same sentence, the possibility of providing an analysis that eliminates the first person pronoun. Let me comment very briefly on several of the issues raised.

(1) It is surely strange, to say the least, to suggest that one cannot describe one's pain except by changing the subject, i.e., by talking about something else, namely, one's behavior. Certainly you and I are talking about the same thing when I say expressively, "I have a pain" and you, accusing me of being untruthful, say "You do not." Further, if my jaw pains me, most certainly I do describe the pain when I say that it is a dull, throbbing but intermittent pain. I am simply not talking about my behavior, but my pain, when I say in this way what kind of pain it is.

(2) I do not, of course, describe my pain when I say that I have a pain and offer this fact as my reason for appearing in the doctor's office. Am I describing anything at all? "Descriptive" seems to be philosopher's jargon for anything that has a truth-value. One can say that in this example one is stating a fact, offering information and giving a reason (or whatever), perhaps even that one is describing one's mental state. But this last is as forced as saying that one is describing the contents of one's room by stating what is certainly true about it, namely, that there are such and such objects in it. Listing or identifying the contents is not describing them.

(3) Much more important, however, is the fact that if I am concerned with the description of my pain (it is dull, throbbing and intermittent) or with my mental state (I am distressed, moody or in pain), it is not true in general that my attitude towards or my reaction to my pain is like that of a doctor making a diagnosis. I might, of course, speculate about what it is that ails me, but quite often I merely suffer. Pain-talk can be informative and descriptive without engaging in doctor or pseudo-doctor talk. There are many, many language-games in which the descriptions of sensations or of mental states occur.

(4) Suppose, however, that I am diagnosing myself or speculating about what ails me. It simply does not follow that, in saying "I have a pain," I am talking about my behavior. Neither is the attending doctor who grants that I am not pretending or malingering, and says reassuringly "I believe you. You must be in considerable pain." To suppose that he must be talking about my behavior is to confound the behavior that serves as *his* criterion of the pain he says I have, with the pain of which this behavior is criterion. In any case *I* have no criterion of the pain that I feel and report to him. What counts for my having a pain, *for the physician,* is what I say and how I act and comport myself. What counts for my having a pain, *for me,* is my pain; that is to say, I do not employ criteria in my own case.

(5) But in what way is one talking about one's behavior when one says "I am walking?" Does one have criteria here that assure one that one is in fact walking just as one does in the case of someone else? In an exceptional case this might happen: I have suffered paralysis, I am now making some recovery, and as I stand and hopefully cry out "I am walking" as I move one leg forward and begin to put my weight on it, I find that I am actually bringing it off. Here one can say that I find — even that I observe — that I am walking, and that on this basis I am able to tell that I am walking. But, normally, do I need to make any observation (as indeed someone else must) in order to tell that I am walking?

(6) But what is it that one would be talking about, in talking about behavior, if one were to speak "objectively" and "like a positivist?" Is the pain-behavior about which one would be speaking objectively, like a positivist, the movements of one's arms and legs as these swing about in quick jerky movements? Is the sound that one makes when in pain a recurring low-pitched sound? Suppose in fact that we supply a quite precise physical description of the movements and a quite precise specification of the pitch, etc., of the sound. To observe this much and no more is *not* to observe someone thrashing about or to hear him moaning in pain.

> I noticed that he was out of humor! Is this a report about his behaviour or his state of mind? ('The sky looks threatening': is this about the present or the future?) Both; but not side-by-side, however, but about the one *via* the other.[3]

Wittgenstein's remark is by no means transparent; but, whatever it amounts to, it is at least a warning against adopting too simple an account of the pain-behavior of others, which we observe, and on the basis of which we are able to say, usually with confidence, that they are in pain.

---

[3] *Ibid.,* **II,** v.

Indeed, unless I have quite misunderstood the line taken by Professor Vuillemin in the analogy he draws between performatives and E-sentences, one of the points he makes in this connection is a closely related one.

II

Consider the sentence "I declare the meeting open" uttered by the chairman and in the appropriate circumstances. Saying this *is* opening the meeting. As Professor Vuillemin puts it, what is said is not a picture of a process (unfortunately he calls this utterance a *statement* and speaks of it as referring to an event). This use of words he contrasts with "I am walking," when, presumably what one is saying agrees with some independently existing state of affairs. Now Professor Vuillemin attempts to draw an analogy between the expressive use of "I am in pain" and the performative. For just as the opening of the meeting is not an event independent of the chairman's uttering of the operative words (Professor Vuillemin muddies the water somewhat by saying that "the utterance refers to a state of affairs that without this very utterance would not exist"), so allegedly there is no "clean break between event and utterance" in the case of the E-sentence "I have a pain." This remark is immediately followed by other equally intriguing remarks. "The expressive mood interferes intimately with the state it expresses. In short it is behavior; not, however, as one is tempted to believe, merely external behavior, mainly characterized by its capacity to be objectively noticed and accessible to all individuals." And he goes on to say it seems "a priori difficult or even impossible to disassociate the feeling expressed and the proper act of expressing." What is here intimated is in my opinion important, albeit obscure. I shall offer several comments.

(1) Earlier I commented on Professor Vuillemin's unwillingness to concede that in uttering "I am in pain" one may not only be expressing one's pain but saying something that does have a truth value. There is a parallel point to be made here. For it is worth noting that many at least of the things that we say, about which we should not at all hesitate to concede that they do involve truth-claims, can also be viewed, in specific circumstances, as instances of doings or actions that go beyond the mere making of those truth-claims. For example, it may be that I have certain rights; but it may also be objectionable, in special circumstances, for me to say so. For this may well be, not only the making of a moral claim, but an indelicate reminder, or an unseemly or wilful

instance of standing on one's right. So the fact that an utterance may be true or false by no means rules out the fact that making the utterance is also an action of still another sort. More than one language-game may be involved in the utterance of a single sentence.

(2) A small point: "I am in pain" may be uttered as a complaint, no less than as an expression of pain, and if so it will be, of course, not merely similar to but in fact a performative. But if it is a complaint, stage setting will be needed. However, it may be, not a complaint, but a call for help or sympathy. Indeed it may be uttered as a natural (for a language-user) expression of pain.

(3) As an expression of pain, "I am in pain" is no mere string of noises or the sayings of what is the case. And whether or not there is anything like a purely contingent causal relation between the occurrence of the pain and the uttering of the sentence, there is clearly a conceptual connection between the idea of the sentence uttered expressively — as an expression of pain — and the pain. To recognize the utterance as an expression of pain is a sophisticated performance involving the application to the given case of the concept of pain, just as much as the recognition of someone writhing on the floor in pain is much more than seeing arms and legs etc. in motion. It is, as it was put in the passage cited from the *Investigations,* taking account of the pain *via* these movements. It is in this way that it is indeed "impossible to disassociate the feeling expressed from the act of expressing." But clearly a great deal more needs to be said about this very important matter.

(4) Finally, I want to enter a *caveat* about Professor Vuillemin's assimilation of expressives to performatives. The chairman who says "The meeting is now open" *is* opening the meeting, he is making that event happen. The man who groaning says (i.e., with expression) "I am in pain," is not making his pain happen, but expressing his pain. If you wish, both are not merely saying something, but in saying what they say they are also doing something else. But while there is no independent reality to which their doings correspond, the lack of independence derives from quite different sorts of considerations. There is an a priori connection between saying "The meeting is open" and the event that is the opening of the meeting, precisely because that saying *is* the opening of the meeting. But while there is a conceptual connection between saying expressively "I am in pain" and my pain, this is not for a parallel reason; for obviously my saying "I am in pain" is not my being in pain. My saying this could take place even though there is no such thing as a pain that I have. Still, it would not be possible to recognize this utterance as a complaint or as an expression of feeling without having an idea of

the kind of feeling that, ostensibly, is being expressed. Nevertheless, to notice that a pain is being expressed by the utterance, involves a different kind of sophistication from that involved in the recognition that the meeting was being opened by the chairman's utterance of his formula. For if nothing else, one could recognize that someone was using "I am in pain" expressively, but doubt that the speaker was in pain; but, given the appropriate external circumstances, one could not recognize that the chairman's utterance was being used performatively while doubting that the meeting was in fact being opened.

UNIVERSITY OF CALIFORNIA, IRVINE.

REJOINDER TO MELDEN

J. VUILLEMIN

I am afraid I have no time to discuss all the arguments which Professor Melden has developed. So I must leave them out except the main one, which concerns what I have called the principle of complementarity between the expressive and the descriptive statements. To explain why we disagree, I shall try to analyze first the principles which are admitted by Professor Melden to support his case, second the principles I am supposed to believe, third, through an inquiry into the philosophy of Austin, the principles that are really mine.

I

Professor Melden holds that there is no reason why an expressive statement should not be also a descriptive one. Conversely, in his opinion, there is no point in thinking that we could not do something (as a performance or as an expression) by uttering a simple declarative statement. To support these assertions, he seems to admit the following principles:

(1) Principle of descriptive meaning:
A linguistic utterance can give us some information only if it has a meaning. As being something abstract and conceptual, a meaning must or at least can contain some description. Therefore the expression, if it is a linguistic one, cannot be incompatible with the corresponding description.

(2) Principle of truth-claim for each meaning:
If an ingredient of description is necessarily part of a linguistic information, this information cannot be *a priori* deprived of its truth-claim, that is of its possible reference to a fact.

(3) Principle of the referential import of the meaning:
If two sentential utterances have different meanings, they are about different states of affairs. So, if a description can do something (for example, when I say I have certain rights), there are many language-games engaged together about one and only one state of affairs. Then the descriptive-statement cannot have a meaning wholly different from the meaning

26

of the corresponding performative- or expressive-statement, and the different language games cannot be mutually incompatible.

II

Because he probably thinks that I would agree with him on these principles, Professor Melden charges me with the consequences which follow from them as soon as one accepts at the same time my principle of complementarity.

He writes: "The fact that 'I have a pain' can be an Ausserung by no means implies that in uttering it, one is not saying something. Neither does it imply that what one says cannot be said to be true or false." And, "He (I) appears in fact to hold the view that 'I have a pain' can be descriptive only by being about something distinct from what ostensibly it would be about, were it being used expressively."

Consequently, in his opinion, I would have to allow to be true the three following assertions:

(1) The descriptive statement says something; being different, the expressive one says nothing.

(2) A descriptive utterance has a truth-value (symtomatically, Professor Melden speaks of a truth-claim), because it says something. Conversely, an expressive statement fails to have a truth-value, because it says nothing.

(3) If two utterances 'I have a pain' differ as E and D, they must necessarily be about distinct states of affairs.

III

Now I do not endorse these strange assertions, and as they can be viewed either as following from my principle of complementarity or as following from Professor Melden's three principles, nothing remains to me but to show why I do not accept these alleged principles and how one and the same prejudice is responsible for them. However, I must also confess that my paper was not sufficiently explicit, that nowhere have I given a definition or an explanation for what I have called the "moods," and that sometimes the words I have used could even have been misleading. For example, I denied that D and E had the same meaning. Only the context shows that I took here the word meaning in the large end loose sense of "linguistic meaning," the linguistic meaning containing together the proper meaning and the mood. In another context, I took the word in its proper sense, referring to Carnap's concept of isomorphic structure. Now this proper meaning does not contain the mood: it excludes it. To avoid all the ambiguities resulting from two different uses of the same word, from now on I shall use the word meaning only in his restricted senses as opposed to the moods.

This terminological point being taken as granted, what are then the principles which I recognize as mine?

Before discussing this question, let us remark that, concerning our point, the same situation arises for the relations between performative and descriptive and for the relations between expressive and descriptive. Doubtlessly, if by expressing some feeling we can sometimes do something instead of describing a state of affairs already given, this doing differs from the doing in the case of the performative. In any case, I always spoke of an analogy with or an extension of the performative, never about an assimilation. So I am in complete agreement with Professor Melden when he points out a peculiar difference between the performative—and the expressive—doing. But, to return to our point, the general principles involved in the problem of the relations between expression and description will not differ essentially from those involved in the problem of the relations between performance and description. Indeed there is nothing in the difference between the performative and the expressive doing (the first being a transitive one, the second an intransitive one), that could justify a difference in the treatment of the relation between the doing-statement and the corresponding descriptive-statement. In the following discussion, I shall not therefore dissociate the case of the performative and the case of the expressive statement. And that is why at this point I wish to refer to Austin.

In a paper written in 1956[1], Austin submitted to examination the theory of performatives he had given in his book *How To Do Things With Words*[2]. Concerning our question, I shall retain and quote three passages.

The first is clearly a criticism of Wittgenstein. "It's rather a pity," Austin says, "that people are apt to invoke a new use of language whenever they feel so inclined, to help them out of this, that or the other well-known philosophical tangle; we need more of a framework in which to discuss these uses of language; and also I think we should not despair too easily and talk, as people are apt to do, about the infinite uses of language."[3]

---

[1] See: John Austin, "Performative Utterances," *Philosophical Papers* (Oxford, Clarendon Press, 1961.)

[2] John Austin, *How to Do Things With Words* (London, Oxford Univ. Press, 1963.)

[3] John Austin, "Performative Utterances," *Philosophical Papers, op. cit.* p. 221.

The second quotation refers to the relation between performatives and events, when these performatives are "felicitous," that is when they succeed in performing their task, as the performatives seem to be required to do. Austin writes "Although these utterances do not themselves report fact and are not themselves true or false, saying these things does very often *imply* that certain things are true and not false, in some sense at least of that rather woolly word 'imply.' For example, when I say 'I do take this woman to be my lawful wedded wife' or some other formula in the marriage ceremony, I do imply that I'm not already married, with wife living, sane, undivorced, and the rest of it. But still it is very important to realize that to imply that something or other is true, is not at all the same as saying something which is true itself."[4] This refers to the same topic about which I wrote, referring to Russell's distinction between "to be contained" and "to imply."

Now to the third and most important point.

What does happen when the performatives are "infelicitous" (I promise without meaning to keep my promise, and so on.) Here, Austin seems to stand very near Professor Melden. He says: "There are questions that can only be decided by considering how the content of the verdict or estimate is related in some way to fact, or to evidence available about the facts. This is to say that we do require to assess at least a great many performative utterances in a general dimension of correspondence with fact. It may still be said, of course, that this does not make them *very* like statements because still they are not true or false, and that's a little black and white specialty that distinguishes statements as a class apart. But actually . . . the more you think about truth and falsity, the more you find that very few statements that we utter are just true or just false . . . 'True' or 'false' are just general labels for a whole dimension of different appraisals which have something or other to do with the relation between what we say and the facts. If, then, we loosen up our ideas of truth and falsity, we shall see that the statements, when assessed in relation to the facts, are not so very different after all from pieces of advice, warnings, verdicts and so on."[5]

This last remark could be interpreted as if all the distinctions made between performative or expressive utterances and descriptions were all at once blurred, the overlapping and the intermingling between them being the rule and resulting in an infinity of different uses of language.

Let us however study more accurately the question.

---

[4] *Ibid.,* p. 224
[5] *Ibid.,* p. 237

As Austin himself suggested it, even if we had to accept that all our sentential utterances do something, we would still find some differences between these very different kinds of doing and we would have then to pay more attention not to the *meaning* of an utterance, but to its *force*.[6] What he means by the force of an utterance perhaps becomes clearer if we seek for its grammatical counterpart. This counterpart is the notion of mood. Indeed, one cannot maintain this motion as such, since a same grammatical form can always disguise two or more different forces, but if one uses the word in its philosophical meaning without being committed to follow the suggested ambiguities of the grammar, the word *mood* I have used in my paper will be as useful as and, I think, more useful than the word *force*. At the same time, we shall see that Professor Melden had to accept his three principles only because he took no notice of this fundamental distinction.

Now, this distinction between the meaning and the mood of an utterance will clear up the difficulties I am charged with.

What have I then, owing to this distinction, to accept as general principles?

1) Principle of non-descriptive meaning:
Two statements which are formally identical can be different: however, both of them can convey some linguistic information or can "say something." That means that there is other linguistic information than descriptive information. My principle of complementarity would entail that an expression says nothing only if two sentences could not differ by their moods, being identical by their meanings.

2) Principle of the restriction of truth-values to the descriptive statements:
There are many kinds of abstract or conceptual structures or meanings, which, although they have the grammatical form of a statement, do not possess any truth-value. To have a truth-value is by no means a quality that would be attached to any sentential structure; it is only characteristic of the truly declarative or descriptive sentences, and one of the conditions for a sentence being truly declarative or expressive is that the state of affairs which the sentence is about is wholly independent of the statement which describes it. So, to make a sense is not enough to have a truth-value.

3) Principle of the referential neutrality of the meaning:
Professor Melden seems to hold that two statements having different meanings must be about two different things and therefore must be different. Well. But are we then forced to admit that two statements

---

[6] *Ibid.*, p. 238

which have the same meaning, are about the same state of affairs and have the same analytical content, cannot be different ones? In this case, two statements would have to be about two different states of affairs or have two different analytical contents in order to be different. This is the postulate one has to accept as soon as he blurs the distinction between meaning and mood.

Now, two statements can have, roughly speaking, the same meaning without being identical, if they differ by their moods. Compare, for example:

(a) Is the session open? (Interrogative mood.)

(b) The session is open. (Descriptive mood.)

The meaning of these two sentences is the same (and we could construe other cases with the imperative mood, the performative mood and so on). How would it be possible to do things with words without thinking, that is without using the same system of oppositions that is used in a declarative sentence? In this sense, all the sentences I can construe are describing, if by "describing" we mean not the whole linguistic meaning of the sentence, but only its conceptual structure (the proper meaning). Nobody confuses an assertion and a question: the sentences a) and b) do not differ by their content, but by a more subtle characteristic, the mood. Now, like all the constituents of a language, the moods form a finite and complete system of opposition, that gives each of them its own determination. The rules of this sub-system of the general system of language are as precise as, for example, the sub-system of the tenses or the sub-system of the persons. And it would be in the same way confusing, if I could mix up the moods, as if I could mix up the tenses or the persons.

To take an example outside the domain of the sentences, in the domain of concepts, what would one think of the following argument?

1) The words "hundred real thalers" have a descriptive meaning. The words "hundreds possible thalers" have another meaning, but, containing too a description, they can be used together with the former words, without any incompatibility.

2) The concept "hundred real thalers," being descriptive, has some reference. The concept "hundred possible thalers" would not be able to describe anything, that is it would not be a concept at all, if it had no reference.

3) If the concepts "hundred real thalers" and "hundred possible thalers" are really different, they must refer to distinct contentual meanings.

I would like to add something concerning the question: How is a description possible in the first person? In my paper, I said only that I was not sure that it would be possible to eliminate the egocentric particulars in such descriptive statements as 'I am walking.' In fact, I have tried in an unpublished article to show that this would be impossible. On this point I agree with Professor Melden. But to explain my arguments would be too long a story for the present paper.

College de France, Paris.

REJOINDER TO VUILLEMIN

A. I. MELDEN

Professor Vuillemin states in his reply to my comments that I seem to hold three principles. I do not of course state these principles. Presumably, the idea here is, therefore, they can be 'extracted' from what I do say. I am not sure, however, that I understand the principles as stated by Professor Vuillemin. Certainly I do not accept the contention that "as being something abstract and conceptual, a meaning must contain or at least can contain some description." One of my contentions, in fact, is that "description" is something rather special, by no means co-extensive in application with what can be said to be true or false. Hence I would want to reject part of what is involved in the second principle ascribed to me. And certainly I do not hold that "if two sentential utterances have different meanings, they are about different states of affairs." "This is scarlet" and "this is red" have different meanings, but both may be about the same thing and about its color; indeed they may be about the very same state of affairs, one being more specific than the other in saying what that state of affairs is. Most certainly I do not think, nor does anything I said imply, that "two statements having different meanings must be about two different things." "This is red" and "This is yellow" may be about the same object, e.g. a rose; but they do have different meanings.

However, it is much more important to turn to Professor Vuillemin's own views concerning the difference between the "content" (or "proper meaning") of sentences and their mood. What Professor Vuillemin appears to hold in the explanation he offers in response to my comments is that two utterances, one a question and the other a description, may have the same content but different moods by virtue of which one is a question and the other a description. Thus (1) "Is it the case that the session is over?" and (2) "It is the case that the session is over," have the same content indicated by the common element "that the session is over" but differ in mood, when the mood is indicated by something analogous to a quantifier that completes the sentence.

33

This is similar to a move made recently by Stenius[1], who follows, among others, Hare in *The Language of Morals*[2], and before him Wittgenstein[3], who speaks of a proposition or sentence-radical in the case of the same picture which can serve to represent how a boxer did in fact stand on a given occasion should or should not hold himself, etc., an idea that is involved, according to him, in Frege's talk about "assumption."

Professor Vuillemin's view differs of course from that of Stenius in that "description" is a term of mood, not content, and in taking this line he is, as I see it, on firmer ground. "Description" is something rather special. It is that in which a speaker engages or that which he offers, and so on. It cannot be identified with the alleged common element. But how shall we characterize it? Surely Frege's "assumption" suffers from the same defect. In what sense of "content" is there *the same content* involved in (1) and (2) above?

During the discussion I suggested that the content signified by the common part, "that the session is over" is as elusive a metaphysical entity as the proposition if we think of it, say as Moore did, as that which is expressed or signified by the complete sentence "The session is open." And this I think is the moral of Wittgenstein's talk of the picture of a boxer as a kind of proposition or sentence-radical. We can say that it is the same picture that can be used either to describe a state of affairs or to recommend a state of affairs, or etc., etc. But "same picture" does not mean that there exists a common material object —the picture—independently of the way in which we see the lines or deposits of ink on the surface. In the same way there is no common content—*if* this is thought of as a complex object signified by the sentence clause. If we think of the sentence clause in this way, then as I argued in the discussion of Professor Vuillemin's reply to my comments, the content turns out to be mysterious indeed.

Someone remarked during that discussion that Professor Vuillemin's view had the merit of accounting for the detachability of the content of a question and of dealing with it as something to which truth values can be assigned. Unfortunately it is not "that the session is open" but "The session is open" that is either true or false. Let this however pass and let me grant, for argument's sake, that from "Is it the case that the

---

[1] Erik Stenius, "Mood and Language-Game," *Synthese,* Vol. 17 (1967) pp. 254-274.

[2] Richard M. Hare, *The Language of Morals* (London, Oxford University Press, 1952).

[3] Ludwig Wittgenstein, *Philosophical Investigations* (Oxford, Basil Blackwell, 1958), p. 11.

session is open?" one can, in some sense detach "that the session is open." Now I do not wish to question the desirability of indicating *this* detachability in order to develop parallel logical devices for treating descriptives and interrogatives, or in order to throw light upon linguistic structures. But to suppose that because *such* detachability is possible, there must be some entity called "the content" signified by the detached sentence-radical is as questionable a bit of metaphysics as the supposition that because the same adjective may be attached to different things, there must be a common object—a universal—which these things somehow share.

University of California, Irvine.

COMMENTS ON VUILLEMIN

V. J. McGill

Professor Vuillemin in his brilliant essay, "Expressive Statements," makes a number of distinctions between descriptive statements and expressive utterances, and argues that the descriptive and expressive moods are always distinct, but related in a complementary fashion. Such linguistic findings have philosophical implications, e.g., that the uniqueness of the expressive mood, which is confined to the first person singular, can never, so far as he can see, be explained by behaviorism or "in conformity with the strict canons of scientific language."

There is a strong tendency to confuse the two moods with each other, he says, since the same indicative statements, e.g., "I am in pain," can now articulate the expressive mood, and now the descriptive mood, depending on the circumstances. "Primarily" we express our feelings, but if we say "I am in pain" in answer to a question our doctor has asked, or state a hypothetical, such as, "If I am in pain I take an aspirin," and in other cases which are cited, we take an outside-observer point of view toward our own pain, referring to it as others do and must, if they are to refer to it at all. The mood is descriptive. (A. I. Melden, in his contribution, has shown how doubtful it is that we ever take an outside-observer view of our pains.) In spite of the clarity of Professor Vuillemin's analysis a few doubts occur to me which I should like to express very briefly.

1) When I exclaim "I am in pain" (expressive mood), I explicitly express my feeling, and "I assert only implicitly the state of affairs I describe," and this apparently means that "the expressive mood actually implies the corresponding descriptive one." Accordingly, when I exclaim "I am in pain" (expressive mood) I *only imply* "I am in pain" (descriptive mood). It seems clear, however, that the first statement could not express the pain without "describing or indicating" it as pain. Vuillemin would of course admit this, and yet he states that the two moods remain distinct, that to express is not also to describe, i.e., "describe or indicate."

Nor is it easy to see how "the expressive mood actually implies the corresponding descriptive one," and "only" implies it, if "implies" is

36

taken in any ordinary sense, for what is uttered in the expressive mood, according to Vuillemin, cannot be true or false.

2) The conclusion that utterances or statements in the expressive mood have no truth value is itself debatable. The author insists it "would be more accurate to say it is right or wrong, sincere or affected, etc. . . . than true or false." My suspicion, on the contrary is that when people say that a man is feigning or insincere in crying "I am in pain," they would be quite willing to add: "What he is saying is false; he has no pain." And no one would regard the addition as less accurate, though some might think it less natural or less ordinary. To judge that there is insincerity, indeed, is to judge that there is falsity.

Vuillemin's suggestion that the cry of "I am in pain" is neither true nor false because it is like a complaint is more plausible. Yet this would mean that if a patient first said "I am in pain" (descriptive mood), and it was false, it would cease to be false if he repeated the same words in a complaining manner.

3) If the attempt is made to identify the meaning of the expressive mood with that of the descriptive mood, Vuillemin argues, the following difficulty develops: I must confess that "I have no particular access to my pains that would escape the notice of others." This might be questioned. If the identification means that the expressive mood is to be nothing that the descriptive mood is not, I still might be in a position to *describe* my pains, which others, merely because they are not so close nor as interested in the subject, would always fail to notice. This would be true, at least, if Vuillemin is right in holding that in using the descriptive mood we notice our own pains only as outside observers would.

On the other hand, if it is true that "primarily, we express our feelings, secondarily, we describe them," then we could not describe them without having previously expressed them. Now this is probably true ontogenetically: expression of primitive, unarticulated feelings precedes the description of these feelings. It is very doubtful where the kind of feeling expressed is articulated, which is the case Vuillemin is concerned with, since "I am in pain" (expressive mood) already describes the feeling which is being expressed. It seems clear, moreover, that we are often called upon to describe new complex feelings which we have never got around to expressing.

4) The expressive mood is unique, according to Vuillemin, in the respect that one can express only one's own feelings, never the feelings of others, whereas one can *describe* one's own feelings and those of others as well. This peculiarity of the expressive mood thus confirms

the privileged access to our own feelings which, he believes, can never be explained by behaviorism, or "in conformity with the strict canons of scientific language." It should be pointed out, however, that the mentalistic account of privileged access and the corresponding peculiarity of the expressive mood is not a satisfactory *explanation*. A behaviorism which does not spurn physiology might eventually do at least as well, especially since the centers for pleasure and pain have now been located, and other discoveries can be expected.

It is generally granted that epiphenomenalism is at least a *possible* theory of the mind-body relation, yet it implies that we would behave and talk just as we do in case there were no pains at all, in the customary sense of mental episodes. This is in accord with the usual scientific explanation of speech and other human responses; pains, as mental phenomena, are not stimuli. And excitations in the cortex discharging into certain efferent nerves would be said to constitute the independently necessary and sufficient conditions of my uttering "I am in pain" (expressive mood). A scientific explanation of the privileged access and the corresponding peculiarity of the expressive mood could thus hinge on the fact that the efferent pathways innervated in my brain proceed to my speech apparatus, but not to the speech apparatus of any other person.

5) The contention that expressing is always intentional, so that "expressing differs from betraying an emotion," is also puzzling. One would have thought that expressing a pain, especially if it is intense, would be just the kind of utterance which could be unintentional. But perhaps what is meant is that expressing is always *purposive,* so that "the relation between the event [expressed] and the utterance about it [could not be] a causal relation." Vuillemin does not argue for the claims involved here—that purposive explanation excludes causality and that expressing is always purposive—though given more space he would doubtless have given them strong support. But even if these claims were true, it is not clear that they would amount to a further distinction marking off the expressive mood from the descriptive mood, for statements in the descriptive mood can also be purposive.

If I have touched in these pages only on certain points of doubt or disagreement, I should like to say that the reason is that Vuillemin's essay is highly original and challenging.

SAN FRANCISCO STATE COLLEGE.

ON KINDS OF UTTERANCES

Frederic B. Fitch

There seems to be a tendency among natural language analysts to exaggerate the distinctions between various types of utterances, particularly between such types as descriptive, emotive, performative, and imperative utterances. Once these distinctions have been set up sharply and dogmatically, they can be used as a basis for claiming that traditional philosophers indulge in confusions that overlook these distinctions and therefore waste time on pseudo-problems. No doubt these distinctions do exist to some degree, but only with the vagueness that characterizes ordinary language and, I believe, without the deep cosmic significance that the natural language analysts seem to attribute to them.

In fact, I feel that it is more profitable to depreciate these differences and distinctions than to raise them like iron curtains separating different kinds of linguistic phrases from one another. After all, every utterance, of no matter what form, conveys information about the utterer, whether it is information that the utterer intended to convey or not. So, in an important sense, all utterances are descriptive utterances. Frequently, however, they are about the utterer only in the indirect sense of expressing beliefs or claims of the utterer, or his intentions, hopes, fears, or feelings. Nevertheless, the content can always be viewed, one way or another, as basically descriptive.

Consider the following example. A friend of mine was driving me home one day, and as we reached my house he said to me, "Pull the handle," referring to the handle of the car door. This statement of his illustrates the use of an imperative utterance to convey information regarding the mechanism of a door.

As another example, suppose that someone were to say to me, "Close the window." I would regard this statement as his way of conveying to me the information that he wished the window to be closed. If he were then to change his mind and say, "No, I take that back. Don't close the window," I would assume that he was now denying that he wished the window to be closed. It seems to be that the full content of an imperative

39

utterance is accounted for solely by the information conveyed, and similarly for utterances of other sorts.

Performative utterances are somewhat like imperative utterances, as when a chairman calls a meeting to order, or announces that a meeting is in session. Again it is clear that information is being conveyed. It is characteristic of performative utterances, however, that they confer special powers or duties on various persons, as when I say, "I hereby agree to be bound by this contract." But this fact about a performative utterance is already part of the information conveyed by the utterance.

If all utterances are treated as instances of descriptive utterances, as I believe they can be, then we do not need a special "logic of imperative statements," "logic of performative statements," and so on, as logics over and beyond, or basically different from the standard logic of propositions. A more coherent and unified method for applying logic to the contents of utterances then becomes possible.

YALE UNIVERSITY,
NEW HAVEN.

LANGUAGE AS THOUGHT AND AS COMMUNICATION

Wilfrid Sellars

My aim in this paper is to throw light from several directions on the intimate connections which exist between conceptual thinking and the linguistic behavior which is said to 'express' it. The position which I shall ultimately delineate and defend, though behavioristic in its methodological orientation is not, initial appearances to the contrary, behavioristic in its substantive contentions. It can, nevertheless, be characterized as an attempt to give a naturalistic interpretation of the intentionality of conceptual acts.

The early sections (I-IV) stress the essentially rule-governed character of linguistic behavior. I argue that a proper understanding of the nature and status of linguistic rules is a *sine qua non* of a correct interpretation of the sense in which linguistic behavior can be said to *be* (and not merely to *express*) conceptual activity. The second, and larger part of the paper (Sections Vff.) is devoted to exploring the sense (or senses) in which language can be said to 'express' thought. A distinction is drawn between three different contexts in which the verb occurs. It is argued that they involve radically different meanings which, if confused, blur the distinction between language as conceptual act and language as means of communication, and preclude the possibility of an adequate philosophy of language.

I

There are many interesting questions about the exact meaning or meanings of the term 'rule' in non-philosophical contexts. What, for example, is the difference between a 'rule' and a 'principle'? Are principles simple 'first' rules in that they are not special applications of more general rules? Or is the primary difference that rules can be arbitrary? Or are principles rules for choosing rules? Is the principle of induction, for example, a higher order rule for choosing law-like statements, themselves construed as extra-logical rules of inference? Though these questions are intrinsically interesting and relevant to the general topic of this paper, I shall not discuss them. For however the domain of norms and standards is to be stratified and botanized, the term 'rule' has acquired over the years a technical and generic sense in which it applies to general statements concerning that which ought or ought not to be done or to be the case, or to be permissible or not permissible — distinctions which can be put in many different ways.

For our purposes, then, a rule is roughly a general 'ought' statement. Such statements have been traditionally divided into hypothetical and categorical 'oughts,' or, as it has often misleadingly been put, 'imperatives.' The distinction between hypothetical and categorical oughts is an important one, though I believe that they are far more intimately related than is ordinarily taken to be the case.[1]

Hypothetical oughts have the form "if one wants X, one ought to do Y." They transpose a relation of implication between a state of affairs X and a doing of Y into an implication appropriate to practical reasoning. In spite of their crucial importance to a theory of normative discourse, I shall have nothing to say about them, save by implication.

As far as anything I have so far said is concerned, a categorical ought is simply one that is not, in the familiar Kantian sense, a hypothetical ought. I shall continue my division informally by calling attention to the most familiar variety of general categorical oughts, those, namely, of the form

If one is in C, one ought to do A.

Notice that although this proposition is conditional in form, it is not, in the Kantian sense, a hypothetical ought; and it is *as* contrasted with the latter that, even though it is conditional, it is called categorical. By application and the use of modus ponens one can derive conclusions of the form

S ought to do A

which not only are *not* hypothetical oughts, but are categorical (non-iffy) statements. Notice, by contrast, that from "If one wants X, one ought to do A," together with "S wants X" it is *not* correct to infer "S ought to do A."

The important feature, for our purposes, of general categorical oughts of the above form is that for actual existence to conform to these oughts is a matter of the agents to which they apply *doing A* when they are actually in the specified circumstance C; and this, in turn, a matter of

---

[1] For an exploration of this and related issues, see my *Science and Metaphysics* (London, Routledge and Kegan Paul, 1968), Chapter VI (especially sections XIV-XVII).

their setting about doing A when they *believe* that the circumstances are C.

It follows that the 'subjects' to which these rules apply must have the concepts of *doing A* and *being in C*. They must have, to use a current turn of phrase, the appropriate 'recognitional capacities.' Furthermore, for the rule itself to play a role in bringing about the conformity of 'is' to 'ought,' the agents in question must conceive of actions A *as* what ought to be done in circumstances C. This requires that they have the concept of what it is for an action to be called for by a certain kind of circumstance.

II

Importantly different from rules of the above form — which may be called, in a straightforward sense, *rules of action* — are rules that specify not what someone ought to do, but how something *ought to be*. Of these an important sub class has the form.

Xs ought to be in state φ, whenever such and such is the case
The purpose of such a rule is achieved to the extent that it comes to be the case that Xs are in state φ when such and such is indeed the case. This time, however, the conformity of actual existence to the ought does not, in general, require that the Xs which are, in a sense, the *subjects* of the rule, i.e. that to which it applies, have the concept of what it is to be in state φ or of what it is for such and such to be the case. This is obvious when the Xs in question are inanimate objects, as in the example.

Clock chimes ought to strike on the quarter hour.
Now ought-to-be's (or *rules of criticism* as I shall also call them), though categorical in form, point beyond themselves in two ways. In the first place they imply (in some sense of this protean term) a *reason,* a *because* clause. The exploration of this theme would seem to take us back to the excluded topic of hypothetical imperatives. In the second place, though ought-to-be's are carefully to be distinguished from ought-to-do's they have an essential connection with them. The connection is, roughly, that ought-to-be's imply ought-to-do's. Thus the ought-to-be about clock chimes implies, roughly,

(Other things being equal and where possible) one ought to bring it about that clock chimes strike on the quarter hour.

This rule belongs in our previous category, and is a rule of action. As such it requires that the item to which *it* applies (persons rather than chimes) have the appropriate concepts or recognitional capacities.

The distinction between ought-to-do's (rules of action) and ought-to-be's (rules of criticism) stands out clearly when the examples are suitably chosen. A possibility of confusion arises, however, when the ought-to-be's concern persons rather than inanimate objects. Consider, for example,

      One ought to feel sympathy for bereaved people

This example is interesting for two reasons: (1) It is a rule conformity to which requires that the subjects to which it applies have the concept of what it is to be bereaved. In this respect it is like a rule of action. (2) In the absence of a clear theory of action one might think of *feeling sympathy* as an action. Thus a casual and uninformed look might lead to the subsumption of the example under the form

      One ought to do A, if C.

It is clear on reflection, however, that feeling sympathy is an action only in that broad sense in which anything expressed by a verb in the active voice is an action.

Nor should it be assumed that all ought-to-be's which apply to persons and concern their being in a certain state whenever a certain circumstance obtains are such that the conformity to them of actual fact requires that the persons in question have the concept of this circumstance. The point is of decisive importance for our problem. To set the stage, consider ought-to-be's pertaining to the training of animals.

      These rats ought-to-be in state φ, whenever C.

The conformity of the rats in question to this rule does not require that they have a concept of C, though it does require that they be able to respond differentially to cues emanating from C. Since the term 'recognitional capacity' is one of those accordion words which can be used now in one sense now in another, it is a menace to sound philosophy.

On the other hand, the subjects of the ought-to-do's corresponding to these ought-to-be's, i.e. the trainers, must have the concept both of the desirable state φ and of the circumstances in which the animals are to be in it.

If we now return to the sympathy example, we notice another interesting feature. If we compare the ought-to-be with the corresponding ought-to-do,

      (Other things being equal and where possible) one ought to bring
      it about that people feel sympathy for the bereaved,

we see that the 'subjects' of the ought-to-be (i.e., those who ought to feel sympathy) coincide with the 'subjects' of the corresponding ought-to-do (i.e. those who ought to bring it about that people feel sympathy for the bereaved). It is the same items (people) who are the *agent*-subjects of the ought-to-do and the *subject-matter* subjects of the ought-to-be.

III

It is obvious, from the above considerations, that if *all* rules of language, were ought-to-do's we would be precluded from explaining what it is to have concepts in terms of rules of language. Now many rules of language *are* ought-to-do's thus,

(Other things being equal) one ought to say such and such, if in C

and as such they can be efficacious in linguistic activity only to the extent that people have the relevant concepts. It is therefore of the utmost importance to note that many of the rules of language which are of special interest to the epistemologist are ought-to-be's rather than ought-to-do's. For only by taking this fact into account is it possible to carry out a program according to which (a) linguistic activity is, in a primary sense, conceptual activity; (b) linguistic activity is through and through rule-governed.

Much attention has been devoted of late to linguistic *actions* [2] where the term 'action' is taken in the strict sense of what an agent does, a piece of conduct, a performance — the *practical* sense of action, as contrasted with the general metaphysical sense in which action is contrasted with passion. The topic of linguistic actions, whether performatory, locutionary, illocutionary, perlocutionary [3], or perhaps, elocutionary is an important one. Indeed, it is important not only for a theory of communication, but for epistemology, for there are, indeed, linguistic *actions* which are of essential interest to the epistemologist: thus asking questions and seeking to answer them. On the other hand it can scarcely be over-emphasized that to approach language in terms of the paradigm of *action* is to make a commitment which, if the concept of action is taken seriously, and the concept of rule is taken seriously, leads to (a) the Cartesian idea of linguistic episodes as *essentially* the sort of thing brought about by an agent whose conceptualizing is not linguistic; (b) an inability to understand the rule-governed character of this conceptualizing itself, as contrasted with its overt expression. For if thought is analogous to linguistic activity to the extent implied by Plato's metaphor 'dialogue in the soul,' the idea that overt speech is *action* and its rules *rules of action* will generate the idea that all inner speech is *action* and *its* rules *rules of action,* which leads to paradox and absurdity without end.

---

[2] I have in mind particularly John Austin and his students. The best statement of this approach is to be found in Austin's *How to do Things with Words* (London, Oxford University Press, 1963.)

[3] For an explanation and defense of these distinctions see Austin's *How to do Things with Words.*

I propose, instead that the epistemologist, while recognizing that language is an instrument of communication, should focus attention on language as the bearer of conceptual activity. This is not to say that the two aspects can be separated as with a knife. Indeed, by pointing out that ought-to-be's imply ought-to-do's we have already recognized that language users exist at the level of agents. Roughly, to be a being capable of conceptual activity, is to be a being which acts, which recognizes norms and standards and engages in practical reasoning. It is, as Kant pointed out, one and the same reason which is in some of its activities 'theoretical,' and in some of its activities 'practical.' Of course, if one gives to 'practical' the specific meaning *ethical* then a fairly sharp separation of these activities can be maintained. But if one means by 'practical' *pertaining to norms,* then so-called theoretical reason is as larded with the practical as is practical reasoning itself.

IV

Even if it be granted than many of the linguistic oughts which are of special interest to an epistemologist are ought-to-be's, the fact that ought-to-be's and ought-to-do's are conceptually inseparable might be thought to preclude a linguistic approach to conceptual abilities. Clearly *primary* epistemic ought-to-do's (and by calling them 'primary' I mean simply that they are not the unfolding of ought-to-be's, whether as primary they are categorical or hypothetical), pertaining to the systematic use of linguistic abilities and propensities to arrive at correct linguistic representations of the way things are, presuppose the possession of concepts by the agents to which they apply. And since all ought to-be's unfold into ought-to-do's which, in their turn, presuppose concepts, the outlook for linguistic theory of concepts would seem to be dark indeed. Yet the fundamental clues for a resolution of the problem have already been given.

To fix our ideas, let us consider an example which, though simplified to its bare bones contains the essence of the matter:

> *(Ceteris paribus)* one ought to respond to red objects in sunlight by uttering or being disposed to utter 'this is red.'

This *ought-to-be* rule must not be confused with (fictitious) *ought-to-do* rule,

> *(Ceteris paribus)* one ought to say 'this is red' in the presence of red objects in sunlight

The latter presupposes that those to whom it applies have the concepts of 'red' objects,' 'sunlight,' and, even more important, of what it is to *say* 'this is red.' In other words, they must already have the conceptual framework of what it is to do something in a circumstance.

The distinction between *saying* and *uttering,* or being disposed to utter, is diagnostic of the difference between the 'ought-to-do' and the 'ought-to-be.' It might be objected that to use language meaningfully is to *say* rather than merely utter. But to merely utter is to parrot, and we need a concept which mediates between merely uttering and saying.

Notice that the ought-to-do which corresponds to the above ought-to-be, namely

> One ought to bring it about *(ceteris paribus)* that people respond to red objects in sunlight by uttering or being disposed to utter 'this is red.'

presupposes that *its* agent subjects have a conceptual framework which includes the concepts of a red object, or sunlight, of uttering 'this is red,' of what it is to do or bring about something, and of what it is for an action to be called for by a circumstance.

On the other hand, this ought-to-do does *not* presuppose that the subjects in which the disposition to utter 'this is red' in the presence of red objects in sunlight *is to be brought about* have any of these concepts.

But what of the objection that the *subject-matter* subjects of the ought-to-be coincide with the agent subjects of the ought-to-do and hence that they too must have the concepts in question? The answer should be obvious; the members of a linguistic community are *first* language *learners* and only potentially 'people,' but *subsequently* language *teachers,* possessed of the rich conceptual framework this implies. They start out by being the *subject-matter* subjects of the ought-to-be's and graduate to the status of agent subjects of the ought-to-do's. Linguistic ought-to-be's are translated into *uniformities* by training. As Wittgenstein has stressed, it is the linguistic community as 'a self-perpetuating whole which is the minimum unit in terms of which conceptual activity can be understood.

Furthermore there are radically different kinds of linguistic ought-to-be's: not only word-object ought-to-be's (or, as I have called them elsewhere, language entry transitions) [4], but also the ought-to-be's formulated by formation and transformation rules.

---

[4] "Some Reflections on Language Games," *Philosophy of Science,* Vol. 21, No. 3, 1954 (Reprinted as Chapter 11 in *Science, Perception and Reality*). It is important to note that a full discussion would refer to may-be's (or permitteds) as well as ought-to-be's — otherwise the concept of 'free' as opposed to 'tied' (stimulus bound) linguistic activity, essential to any account of the functioning of a conceptual system, would be left out of the picture.

The oughts governing utterances as perceptual responses to the environment are not ought-to-do's — though, as the pragmatists have emphasized, perception as an element in enquiry occurs in a context of actions, epistemic and otherwise. Similarly the oughts governing inference are not ought-to-do's. Inferring is not a *doing* in the conduct sense — which, however, by no means implies that it is not a *process*. Again, as the pragmatists have stressed, inference as an element in enquiry occurs in the context of action, epistemic and otherwise.

A language is a many-leveled structure. There are not only the ought-to-be's which connect linguistic responses to extra-linguistic objects, but also the equally essential ought-to-be's which connect linguistic responses to *linguistic* objects. There could be no training of language users unless this were the case. Finally, there would be no language training unless there were the uniformities pertaining to the use of practical language, the language of action, intention, of 'shall' and 'ought,' which, as embodying epistemic norms and standards, is but one small (but essential) part of the conceptual structure of human agency.

One isn't a full-fledged member of the linguistic community until one not only *conforms* to linguistic ought-to-be's (and may-be's) by exhibiting the required uniformities, but grasps these ought-to-be's and may-be's themselves (i.e., knows the rules of the language.) One must, therefore, have the concept of oneself as an agent, as not only the *subject-matter* subject of ought-to-be' but the *agent*-subject of ought-to-do's. Thus, even though conceptual activity rests on a foundation of *conforming* to ought-to-be's of *uniformities* in linguistic behavior, these uniformities exists in an ambience of action, epistemic or otherwise. To be a language user is to conceive of oneself as an agent subject to rules. My point has been that one can grant this without holding that all meaningful linguistic episodes are *actions* in the conduct sense, and all linguistic rules, rules for doing.

A living language is a system of elements which play many different types of roles, and no one of these types of role make sense apart from the others. Thus, while the mere concept of a kind of vocalizing being a response by a human organism in specified circumstances to a certain kind of object does make sense in isolation, this concept is not as such the concept of the vocalizing as a *linguistic response*. For to classify an item as linguistic involves relating it to just such a system as I have been sketching. 'Word' goes not only with 'object' but with 'person,' 'ought-to-be's,' 'ought-to-do's' and much, much more.

V

Within the framework sketched above, I propose to explore the idea that insofar as it has conceptual meaning, language is essentially a means whereby one thinker can express his thoughts to others. Now the term 'thought' has a wide range of application, including such items as assumptions, the solving of problems, wishes, intentions, and perceptions. It is also ambiguous, sometimes referring to *what* is thought, sometimes to the *thinking* of it. To limit the range of my paper, I shall concentrate on thought as belief, and since the latter term shares the ambiguity indicated above, I note that for the time being at least, I shall be concerned with believings rather than things believed.

The following characterization of the state of believing something will serve to get the discussion under way

Jones believes that-p = Jones has a settled disposition to think that-p.

It would be foolhardy — indeed downright mistaken — to claim that this formula captures 'the' meaning of believes, and even more so to put it by saying that 'a belief is a settled disposition to think that something is the case.' For, as with most, if not all, of the words in which philosophers are interested, we are confronted with a cluster of senses which resemble each other in the family way.

To say that the senses of cognate expressions bear a family resemblance to one another must not be taken to imply that they present themselves as a family, nor even that they constitute a family. Aristotle seems to have thought that philosophically interesting concepts present themselves to us as families in which, with a little effort, we can discern the fathers, mothers, aunts, uncles, and cousins of various degrees. In some cases something like this may be true. But the matter is rarely so simple, and there is more than a little truth to the idea that the families are 'created' by reconstruction (hopefully rational) or regimentation rather than found.[5]

If the above account of belief gets us started, it does so by confronting us with the equally problematic concepts of *disposition* and *thinking that-p*. Before stepping into these quicksands, let us ostensibly make matters worse by turning our attention from *believing* itself to the more complicated concept of the *expression* of belief. For sound philosophical

---

[5] Equally dangerous are such mephorical contrasts as those between 'paradigm' and 'borderline,' 'shadow' and 'penumbra.' All suggest a sequential strategy according to which, once we find the thread, we know how to begin and what kinds of difficulty to expect.

strategy calls for the examination of concepts as they function in larger contexts, rather than subjecting them to scrutiny in splendid isolation. By taking elusive concepts together, one may limit the degrees of freedom which enable them separately to elude our grasp. If beliefs are to be construed as dispositions, this strategy would have us seek to relate the sense in which beliefs are 'expressed' to the sense in which the dispositions of things and persons are manifested by what they do. This suggests the schema

x expresses Jones' belief that-p $=$ x is a manifestation of Jones' settled disposition to think that-p.

If the right hand side of this attempted explication were clearcut and unambiguous, substantial progress would have been made. But it isn't; and our only hope is that a spark of clarity may result from rubbing unclarities together.

A first unclarity concerns what it is for a disposition to be 'manifested' by a doing, and how the class of doings by which a given disposition is manifested is to be delimited. If the 'disposition' is of the familiar kind to which we refer by such expressions as 'an angry disposition' or, perhaps, by such a term as 'humility,' then it would seem that, depending on circumstances, any of a wide range of episodes could be its manifestation. Indeed, there is a sense in which, depending on circumstances, any of a wide range of episodes could count as a 'manifestation' of Jones' belief that-p. But, to characterize belief that-p as a settled disposition *to think that-p,* is, if sound, to narrow things down in an interesting way. For to do so, is to introduce a conceptual tie between the designation of the disposition and the kind of episodes which can be said, at least in a primary sense, to 'manifest' it.

For if we ask what episodes manifest a disposition to V, when 'V' represents a verb which stands for a doing (e.g. 'laugh') the answer must be, in the first instance, episodes of V-ing (e.g. laughing). We have consequently committed ourselves to the idea that it is episodes of *thinking that-p* which are, in a primary sense at least, manifestations of Jones' disposition *to think that-p;* and consequently that it is episodes of thinking that-p which are, in a primary sense, manifestations of Jones' belief that-p. This gives us the schema

x is a primary manifestation of Jones' belief that-p $\rightarrow$ x is a thinking that-p.

But now our troubles really begin. For there is a *prima facie* tension between 'being a thinking that-p' and being a 'manifestation' of anything. The latter term carries with it the implication of 'making something manifest,' i.e., apparent, (roughly) perceptible, observable. But, we are tempted to expostulate, what need be less 'manifest' than an episode of thinking that-p.

It might be thought that all we need do is replace 'manifestation' by a term which lacks this implication. And there are, indeed, such terms at hand — thus 'realization,' 'actualization.' The statements

    episodes of thinking that-p are *realizations* of the settled disposition to think that-p

    episodes of thinking that-p are *actualizations* of the settled disposition to think that-p

trip easily off the metaphysically trained tongue. But they are ruled out by our strategy. For the concept with which we are concerned is that of the *expression* of a belief, and 'expression' clearly has the same implication of 'overtness' or 'perceptibility' as does the 'manifestation' to which our initial intuitions have led us.

The boulder may have slipped, but perhaps it has not rolled to the bottom. Our task may ultimately prove to be like that of Sisyphus, but perhaps we are not yet forced to make a new beginning. To continue is to look for a way of making coherent the idea that episodes of thinking that-p are the primary *expressions* (with all that this implies) of the belief that-p.

To do so within the allotted space however, I must abandon the leisurely dialectic which consults intuition at each stage of the argument, and instead must draw upon the familiarity of standard philosophical moves. In terms of this new strategy, the obvious move is to espouse a form of logical behaviorism according to which, in first approximation, 'thinking that-p' is, in its most episodic sense, to be equated with 'candidly and spontaneously uttering "p"' [6] where the person, call him Jones, who utters 'p' is doing so *as one who knows the language to which 'p' belongs*. I need not remind you of all the troubles which beset this move. Some of them will be taken into account as the argument moves along. But since, in any case, my strategy remains in a broad sense dialectical, the fact that the above equation suffers from serious inadequacies need not prevent it from playing an essential role in the argument

The phrase 'candidly and spontaneously' is intended to sum up an open-ended set of conditions without which the suggestion can't get off the ground. Jones' thinking that-p obviously cannot be a quoting of 'p' or uttering it on the stage in the course of acting. The qualifying phrase also clearly rules out the case where Jones is lying, i.e. using words to

---

[6] Similarly, 'wondering whether-p' would be equated with 'uttering "p?"', 'wishing that-p' with 'uttering "would (that) p"' and 'deciding to do A' with uttering 'I shall do A.'

deceive. Somewhat less obviously it is intended to imply that Jones is not choosing his words to express his convictions. He is neither lying nor speaking truthfully. In a sense, as we shall see, he is not *using* the words at all.

According to the behavioristic position we are now considering, thinking that-p is, in its *primary episodic* sense, thinking-out-loud that-p. As thinking-out-loud, an utterance of 'p' is not directed to an audience. It is not, as such, a social act. Explicit performatives (e.g. 'I promise') are clearly out of place in utterances which are, in the desired sense, to be thinkings-out-loud. Nor is it appropriate to characterize thinkings-out-loud in terms of the categories of illocutionary performance — at least those which require an audience (e.g. 'statement,' 'avowal,' 'argument') [7] — even though exactly similar utterances would, *in a context of 'communication,'* be appropriately so characterized.

VI

It is important to realize that the ways in which we classify linguistic expressions are not only bound up with the jobs they do, but with the purposes for which the classification is made. Since these purposes tend, for obvious reasons, to concern the role of language as a means of communication, i.e., as that by which we give information, warn, make statements, predict, describe, etc., we should not be surprised, our behaviorist will tell us, if expressions which, as candidly uttered in *noncommunicative* contexts, are thinging-out-loud, are classified in a way which is conceptually tied to communication, and, hence, to functions of quite a different order of complexity. One needs only think of the difference between the purely logical characterization of 'it is not raining' as the 'negation' of 'it is raining,' and characterizing it as the 'denial' of the latter, or note the social implications of classifying a word as a *referring* expression.

Thus the ways in which common sense, and not only common sense, classifies linguistic expressions, and the verbs which it uses to describe what people do with them, are heavily weighted in the direction of linguistic *performances* in a context of *communication*. That it is legitimate to view language in this way is not to be doubted. Indeed, it is philosophically important to be clear about the categories in terms of which the variety of ways in which language functions in inter-personal exchange

---

[7] We can grant that a thinking-out-loud that-p might be a constituent of a reasoning-out-loud or a deliberating-out-loud on a certain topic.

are to be understood. But there is a danger that exclusive concern with this perspective will obscure those connections between thought and language where the latter is *not* functioning as a means of communication.

The point is not that there are failures of communication, e.g. the supposed hearer may be an inanimate object mistaken for a man or a foreigner. It is not even that there are soliloquies, if by this is meant cases of 'talking to oneself.' It is the more radical point that thinking-out-loud is a form of meaningful speech which doesn't consist in talking *to* anyone at all, even oneself, and hence is not, in any ordinary sense, *talking*.

VII

But before I develop this point let me return to the formula we were considering before this digression on the orientation toward contexts of communication of the categories in terms of which common sense, linguistics, and many philosophies of language approach linguistic behavior. The formula was

x is a primary expression of Jones' belief that-p
= x is a primary manifestation of his settled disposition to think that-p (i.e. is a thinking that-p).

The implications of the term 'manifestation' (and, for that matter, of 'expression') led us in the direction of a logical behaviorism according to which the relevant sense of 'thinking that-p' is 'thinking-out-loud that-p.' Thus reinterpreted, the formula becomes

x is a primary expression of Jones' belief that-p
= x is a primary manifestation of Jones' settled disposition to think-out-loud that-p (i.e., is a thinking out-loud that-p).

It will be remembered that the point of this behavioristic move was to assimilate the sense in which an episode is a primary *expression* (implying overtness) of a belief to the sense in which an episode of, for example, a piece of litmus paper turning red is a *manifestation* (implying overtness) of its disposition to turn red.

It should be noted in passing that in the case of the litmus paper we seem required to expand the characterization of the disposition into

disposition to turn red, *if put in acid.*

This generates the suspicion that if we are to continue with our strategy, we must similarly expand our analysis of 'Jones believes that-p' into

Jones has a settled disposition to think-out-loud that-p, if . . . .

If what? There many pitfalls here, though we can, perhaps, cover them up temporarily with something like 'if the question whether-p arises.' To do so, however, would immediately confront us with a more serious difficulty. For it simply isn't the case that if a person believes that-p, he utters 'p' let alone thinks-out-loud that-p, whenever the question whether-p arises.

Confronted by this fact, we are strongly tempted to abandon our strategy and say that if a person believes that-p, then (other things being equal) whenever the question whether-p arises, he tends to *think* (*not* think-out-loud) that-p; to which we might add that if the circumstances are appropriate he may *express* his thought by uttering (saying?) 'p.'

VIII

On the other hand, if, however, we are to continue with our original strategy, we must resolutely put aside the temptation to draw the kind of distinction between *thought* and its *expression* which this formulation implies, and continue with the intriguing idea that an uttering of 'p' which is a primary expression of a belief that-p is not merely an *expression* of a thinking that-p, but is itself a *thinking,* i.e., a thinking-out-loud that-p.

Yet the preceding remarks do remind us that we must take into account the fact that there is a sense of 'express' in which we can be said to express our thoughts by *using* language for this purpose. Thus, we express our thought that-p by *saying* 'p.' Can we sophisticate our logical behaviorism to do justice to this fact?

Let us take a closer look at the words 'thought' and 'express.' First the latter: it will be noticed that the reference to observability implied by the term 'manifestation' in the context 'manifestation of the disposition to think that-p' was absorbed by the behaviorist into the phrase which describes the disposition. Thus, '*manifestation* of the disposition to *think* that-p,' became, in effect '*actualization* of the disposition to think-*out-loud* that-p.'

Thus the behaviorist's formula becomes, in effect,

x is a primary expression of Jones' belief that-p
= x is a manifestation of Jones' settled disposition to think that-p
= x is an actualization of Jones' settled disposition to think-out-loud that-p (i.e., x is a thinking-out-loud that-p).

It is only too clear that by pushing this analysis of the context 'expression of belief' in this direction the behaviorist has lost contact with the idea that people *express* their beliefs by *using* language. The point can be put simply — indeed bluntly — by saying that the concept of the *actualization of a disposition* is not, as such, the concept of an *action,* whereas *expressing their beliefs* is something people *do.*

The statement

   Jones, by saying 'p', expressed his belief that-p

requires an interpretation of *saying p* as an action which is undertaken by Jones *in order to express (to someone)* his belief *that-p*. If we suspect that Jones is lying, we could equally describe him as saying "p", but we would then go on to say something like

   Jones, by saying 'p', *pretended* to believe that-p.

In neither case could Jones' saying 'p' be construed as a case of *thinking* (even 'out loud') that-p. Thus were Jones speaking truthfully, the thinking immediately involved, if any, would be of the sort described by such formulas as

   Jones thought that saying '. . .' would express his belief that-p

   Jones intended to express his belief that-p by saying '. . .'

or, in the case of lying

   Jones intended to pretend to believe that-p by saying '. . . .

Thus, granted the validity of the concept of thinking-out-loud, the thinking-out-loud which, were it to occur, would be immediately involved in the situation formulated by

   Jones, by uttering '. . . ,' expressed his belief that-p

would be *not*

   Jones thought-out-loud that-p

but rather

   Jones thought-out-loud that saying '. . .' would express his belief that-p

or, where Jones is lying,

   Jones thought-out-loud that he would pretend to believe that-p by saying '. . . .'

Needless to say, the latter thinking-out-loud would be self-frustrating in the presence of the audience he intends to deceive.

IX

   If we leave behaviorism aside for a moment, we can add a new dimension to the discussion by noting that the term 'express' in contexts pertaining to thought has two radically different senses. The difference can be brought out by relating these senses to two different contexts, namely,

   (1) *Jones* expressed his thought (belief) that-p by saying . . .

   (2) *Jones' utterance* of 'p' expressed his thought that-p

I shall call the former the 'action' sense of express, and the latter, for want of a better term, the 'causal' sense. Both, as we shall see, are to be distinguished from a third sense illustrated by the context

Jones' utterance of 'p' expressed *the* thought that-p

where the phrase '*the* thought that-p' stands for an abstract entity, a thought in Frege's sense (i.e., in one sense of this term, a 'proposition'). I shall call this the logical (or semantical) sense of 'express.'

Although my ultimate aim is to show how a logical behaviorist might draw these distinctions, my initial move will be to discuss them in more traditional terms. I shall, therefore, construct a regimented (I dare not say idealized) model according to which, in the course of learning to speak a language, a child acquires the capacity to be in mental states which are *counterparts,* in a sense to be analyzed, of the utterances which come to belong to his repertory of linguistic behavior. The idea can be blocked out in two steps:

(a) A mental episode which is a thinking that-p is correlated, in a certain linguistic community, with a piece of linguistic behavior which stands for (expresses in the logical or semantical sense) the thought (proposition) that-p

(b) In the initial stages of the child's mastery of the language, whenever it has a thought that-p, this thought is manifested in a purely involuntary way by the corresponding verbal behavior.

As our model for understanding the sense in which the uttering of 'p' is the involuntary manifestation of a thinking that-p, let us take the instinctive connection between a pain and a piece of unlearned pain behavior. The fact that a connection between states A and B of a child is, in some sense, *learned* rather than *instinctive, acquired* rather than *part of its initial equipment,* by no means entails that either A or B is under the child's voluntary control. Not all learning to *do* something in a broad sense of 'do' consists in the addition of new behaviors to the stock of things that are under one's voluntary control.

The key feature of our model is that the acquired connection between the mental act and the verbal behavior is not to be construed on the action model of 'using the behavior to express one's thought.' Thus, verbal behavior is not in our child's voluntary control in that, although, *once the language is learned,* a necessary and sufficient condition of the child saying 'p' is that it thinks that-p, the saying is the involuntary manifestation of the thinking.

Notice that the model allows the child a rich vocabulary, including the language of intention and resolve as well as the language in which matters-of-fact are stated. It also allows that the child learns to verbalize about verbal behavior and even about the mental acts of which its verbal behavior is the involuntary manifestation.

X

We are now in a position to weaken our model and still make our point. We need not suppose that the child remains a chatterbox. We can suppose it to acquire the ability to keep its thoughts to itself in the sense that it can effectively tell itself to keep quiet, without ceasing to think. We can grant that to this limited extent its verbal behavior becomes under its voluntary control. When it is thinking without speaking, we shall say that it is in a keeping-its-thoughts-to-itself frame of mind. When not in this frame of mind, it thinks out loud. [8] Thus, 'Thinking out loud' remains the primary form in which thinking occurs. The child's keeping its thoughts to itself can be compared to the opening of a general switch which breaks (or, to mix metaphors) short circuits the initial acquired connection between thoughts and verbal behavior.

At this stage, the child has no conception of locutionary acts (e.g. predicting, telling) as verbal behavior which can be engaged in whether or not one is thinking the corresponding thoughts. It has no concept of *saying "p" without thinking that-p*.

On the other hand, it is perfectly capable of having concepts of *actions* involving thinking out loud. Thus, wondering out loud about the weather; "I shall wonder out loud about the likelihood of rain." It is important to see that this by no means entails that there is such a thing as an action of *thinking out loud that-p*. Even in our more sophisticated framework there is no such thing as an *action* of thinking that-p, though there is the action of *deliberating* (i.e., deliberating out loud) what to do. By granting, as we must, that it can conceive of actions consisting of thinkings out loud, we admit a further sense in which its verbal behavior (*as* thinkings out loud) would be under its voluntary control.

The child's verbal behavior would express its thoughts, but, to put it paradoxically, the child could not express them.

Notice, also, that although its linguistic behavior would be meaningful, and we could say of each of its utterances what, specifically it meant, e.g.

Jones' utterance meant 'it is raining,'

It would, on our assumptions, be incorrect to say, for example

Jones, by uttering '. . .' meant (to convey) . . .

---

[8] The concept of 'thinking out loud' appropriate to this model should not be equated with thinking-out-loud as construed by the behavioristic position we have been considering. The latter does not recognize 'mental episodes' in the sense required by the present model.

For the latter supposes that Jones has the concept of an action of uttering '. . . .' as a piece of linguistic behavior which could exist independently of its being the "spontaneous verbal expression" of the corresponding mental act. There being no such action as bringing about a specific mental act, there could be no such thing as bringing about a thinking out loud for the purpose of conveying a thought.

In other words, just as our regimenting fiction enables us to draw a distinction between a sense in which a mode of verbal behavior can *express* thoughts without being *used to express* them, so it enables us to distinguish between the context

utterance of E (in L) means - - -

and the sense of 'means,' closely related to 'intends,' which involves the context

Jones, by uttering E, means (to convey) . . .

The familiar saw that words have meaning only because people mean things by them is harmless if it tells us that words have no meaning in abstraction from their involvement in the verbal behavior of language users. It is downright mistaken if it tells us that for an expression to have a certain sense or reference is for it to be *used* by people *to convey* the corresponding thought. Rather, we should say, it is because the expression has a certain meaning that it can be effectively used to convey the corresponding thought.

XI

Let us now return to the initial accounts we gave of belief and its expression. The first thing to note is that if we were to reformulate them in terms of our model we would get something like the following schema

Jones believes that-p = Jones has a settled disposition to think that-p, if the question occurs to him whether-p, and, indeed, to think out loud that-p, unless he is in a keeping-his-thoughts-to-himself frame of mind.[9]

We also get the following formulae with respect to 'expression of belief':

x is a primary actualization of Jones' belief that-p → x is a thinking that-p (and, indeed, a thinking out loud that-p unless he is in a keeping-his-thoughts-to himself frame of mind.)

_____

[9] The 'if the question occurs to him whether-p' condition can be taken to cover all cases in which, where the alternatives 'p' and 'not p' are relevant to his course of thought, he thinks that-p, even if the question whether-p is not actually raised.

x is a primary expression of Jones' belief that-p → x is a thinking
out loud that-p.

Thus, where Jones is in a thinking out loud frame of mind, the verbal
behavior is both an *actualization of* and, in the 'causal' sense, an *expression of* his belief, both a *thinking* and an *expression of thought*.

XII

But what will our logical behaviorist say to all this? Clearly he will be
unhappy about our uncritical acceptance of mental acts as covert inner
episodes. What moves might he make? He may well accept our initial
formula

Jones believes that-p = Jones has a settled disposition to think
that-p.

But he will emphasize the 'settled,' which we have not yet done, and will
call attention to the fact that it presumably contrasts with something. It
is not obvious what the contrasting adjective should be, but it, too, should
apply to dispositions. Let us, he suggests, try 'proximate,' drawing on
the contrast between 'settled' and 'near the surface.' Another appropriate
contrast would be provided by 'short term.'

Objects, as is well known, can have causal properties which are not
so to speak, immediately available. Thus iron attracts filings, *if* it has
been treated in a certain way. A *proximate* disposition can roughly be
characterized as one which is immediately available.

Our logical behaviorist, consequently, suggests that

Jones believes that-p = Jones has the *settled* disposition to have
short term, proximate dispositions to
think-out-loud that-p, if the question
whether-p arises, and he is in a thinking-
out-loud frame of mind.

In other words, our logical behaviorist construes the contrast between
fleeting thought episodes and settled beliefs as falling *within* the broad
category of dispositions, and hence construes the 'covertness' of thoughts
as simply a special case of the covertness of dispositions. Flammability,
he reminds us, is not a covert flame.

Many features of our previous discussion can be fitted into this framework, once its distinctive character is understood. Thus, the behaviorist
substitutes for the previous account of the child's candid and spontaneous verbal behavior as the expression (in the 'causal' sense) of classically
conceived *episodes* of thought, an account according to which a

thinking-out-loud that-p

is simply an 'actualization' of a

short term proximate, disposition to think-out-loud that-p.

In the non-behavioristic model we stipulated that the child be unable to verbalize without thinking the appropriate thought, in other words, that only if it has the mental act of thinking that-p does it utter 'p.' In the behavioristic reconstruction framework, the corresponding stipulation would be that all utterances of 'p' be thinking-out-loud that-p.

Both stipulations could be formulated in the same words, thus 'the child utters "p" only in the course of thinking out loud that-p.' But the two concepts of thinking out loud are radically different. In the non-behavioristic model, the phrase 'thinking-out-loud' referred to thoughts together with their verbal expression. In the behavioristic reconstruction it is to be taken as an unanalyzed expression which means roughly the same as 'candid' spontaneous verbal behavior,' but serves, by its hyphenated mode of composition, to emphasize that the basic meaningfulness of candid, spontaneous verbal behavior is *not* to be construed in terms of its being the reverberation at the tip of the tongue of covert episodes which are thoughts properly speaking, in accordance with the schema

x is candid, spontaneous verbal behavior = is an expression [10] of thought

XIII

It is important not to confuse logical behaviorism with what might be called logical physicalism. I mean by the latter the view which denies that, to quote Chisholm, "when we analyze the kind of meaning that is involved in natural language we need some concepts we do not need in physics or behavioristics." [11] Chisholm thinks that to deny the need for such an irreducible concept is tantamount to trying to "analyze the semantics ... of natural language in a physicalistic vocabulary of a behavioristic psychology with no undefined semantical term and no reference to thoughts." [12]

In the essay which led to the correspondence from which I am quoting, I had argued that the concept of meaning which belongs in the context

E(in L) means - - -

is not to be analyzed in terms of a reference to 'thoughts.' Thus I rejected any analysis along *either* of the following lines

E(in L) means - - - = *candid and spontaneous utterances* of F
                                        causally express thoughts pertaining to - - -

---

[10] 'Expression' in the causal sense, i.e., a manifestation at the 'surface' of a covert process which is its cause.

[11] *Minnesota Studies in the Philosophy of Science,* Vol. II, p. 523.

[12] *Ibid.*

$$E(\text{in } L) \text{ means } \text{-- -} = \textit{speakers of } L \text{ use } E \text{ to express their}$$
$$\textit{thoughts pertaining to} \text{ - - -}$$

where 'thought' is to be taken as referring to classically conceived inner episodes or mental acts.

On the other hand, though I denied that 'means' in the sense appropriate to the context 'E(in L) means - - -' is to be analyzed (defined) in terms of a reference to thoughts, I also argued that it cannot be analyzed in physicalistic terms. From Chisholm's point of view this was a blatant attempt to have my cake and eat it. As he saw it, to *admit* that "to analyze the kind of meaning that is involved in natural language" we need a distinctively semantical term ('means') which *cannot* be analyzed in physicalistic terms, but *deny* that the explication of this distinctively semantical term requires a reference to *thoughts* has all the appearance of paradox.

The correspondence went on at some length, and although some progress was made, the issue was never really joined. As I now diagnose the situation some ten years later, the cause of this failure was my inability to clarify adequately two points:

(a) The exact nature of statements of the form 'E(in L) means - - -'
(b) The exact relation of the concept of *meaning* to that of *thought*.

The space which remains is too short to do anything more than indicate the moves I should have made.

My basic move should have been to clarify along the lines of the present paper the distinction between the contexts

person expresses

and

utterance expresses.

My second move should have been to give a more adequate clarification of the concept of meaning as it occurs in the context 'expression (in L) means - - -' (as contrasted with the context 'person, by uttering E, means - - -.') At the time of the correspondence I was unable to do much more than offer the rather cryptic suggestion that statements of this form are (a) *sui generis,* (b) *convey* (rather than *describe*) how the subject expression is used, by exhibiting an expression in the hearer's active vocabulary which has the same job — the idea being that by rehearsing his use of the latter, he will be able to grasp the use of the former. As I have since argued,[13] to say what an expression means is to *classify* it by the use of a sortal predicate the application of which implies that the expression in question does the job in its language which

---

[13] Most recently in *Science and Metaphysics,* Chapter III.

is done in the speaker's language by an expression from which the predicate is formed. Thus, roughly

    'und' (in German) means *and*

has the form

    'und's (in German) are ·and·s

where ' ·and· ' is a sortal predicate of the kind in question.

But above all I should have made it clear that in my view the fundamental concept pertaining to thinking is thinking-out-loud as conceived by our logical behaviorists.[14] This is not to say that I agree with him in rejecting the classical conception of thoughts as inner episodes in a non-dispositional sense. Rather I accept mental acts in something like the classical sense, but argue that the concept of such acts is, in a sense I have attempted to clarify, a derivative concept.

Finally, I should have emphasized my total commitment to the thesis that the concept of thought essentially involves that of intentionality in the following sense. To say of a piece of verbal behavior that it is a thinking-out-loud, is to commit oneself to say of it that it *means something,* while to say of it specifically that it is a thinking-out-loud that-p, is to commit oneself to say of it that it is a piece of verbal behavior which means *p.*

Thus, at the primary level, instead of analyzing the intentionality or aboutness of verbal behavior in terms of its expressing or being used to express classically conceived thoughts or beliefs, we should recognize that this verbal behavior *is already thinking in its own right,* and its intentionality or aboutness is simply the appropriateness of classifying it in terms which relate to the linguistic behavior of the group to which one belongs.

University of Pittsburgh.

---

[14] The priority in question, to use Aristotle's distinction, is in the order of knowing as contrasted with the order of being. As an analogy, notice that concepts pertaining to things as perceived by the senses are prior in the order of knowing to concepts of micro-physical particles, whereas, (for the Scientific Realist) micro-physical particles are prior in the order of being to objects as perceived by the senses.

COMMENT ON WILFRID SELLARS' PAPER

Mikel Dufrenne

Professor Sellars presents us with a personal, subtle and nuanced mode of reflection. I shall not attempt to discuss his paper in detail, or even to refute it, but shall rather try to understand it: to repeat it in my own way by transposing it into a language which is more familiar to me. For language is a means of *communication* — communication of a *thought* — only if it is a *common* language, belonging to a *community*. And just as national communities are often divided into social classes possessing their own subculture or sub-language, the community of philosophers, or of scholars, is often divided into different schools, each of which also has its language which must be translated in order to be understood.

Sellars' reflection bears on language *(le langage)*. We should be fully aware that it does not deal with "tongue" *(la langue)* in the sense in which linguists understand this term; Sellars treats speech *(la parole),* that is, speech behavior *(le comportement parlant)*. It seems to me that the general intention animating this reflection is to posit and then surpass the traditional duality of language and thought. Thought is defined as conceptual actuality; Sellars examines it as act, not in its product: he does not elaborate a theory of concepts any more than a theory of conceptualization (and he does not try to determine, for example, the way in which the concept is linked with the word and the use of the word in certain statements). Conceptual activity is tentatively defined as "recognitional capacity": "The concept of *doing* A and of *being* in C," which is simply consciousness of a situation as calling for an action and of this action, which can be an act of speech *(une parole)*. Thought is therefore defined in terms of consciousness.

Surpassing the language-thought duality is possible only if, with Sellars, one considers speech or speech behavior. For if language is considered from the standpoint of linguistics, that is, as tongue, one must conclude that it is exterior and anterior to the subject who learns it by interiorizing it. In other words, Sellars' enterprise presupposes a subject capable of speech — one who knows how to speak. In this regard, if there is a duality of tongue and subject, the subject surpasses this duality by appropriating the tongue: his "mother tongue" understood both as the tongue of his mother and the mother of his thought.

The language-thought duality remains in the behavior of this subject. How can it be surpassed? How can the two terms be identified with one another in a relation which at first opposes them? There are several possible responses to this question. First, the relation can be conceived dialectically as affirming the unity of contraries; but this solution only poses the problem without solving it. Next, the relation can be seen as one of reciprocal engendering: then it must be explained how thought and speech are accomplished together in the act of expression stemming from a certain origin. This is the standpoint of phenomenology, at least in Merleau-Ponty's conception: "Our view of man will remain superficial so long as we fail to go back to this origin, so long as we fail to find, beneath the chatter of words, the primordial silence, and as long as we do not describe the gesture which breaks this silence." [1] I would orient myself along these lines, for this description of a primary speech, which is doubtless poetic speech, might enable us to kill two birds with one stone: to clarify the common advent of consciousness and speech and to throw some light on the origin of language as a system of not wholly arbitrary signs. Professor Sellars proposes still another response; he discerns two relations between language and thought: that of identity and that of expression, depending on whether it can be said of linguistic behavior that it *is* "conceptual activity" or that it *expresses* it. This is an apparently paradoxical solution: it is difficult to say both that language is thought and that it is an instrument — a means of communication — serving thought. It is conceivable that the difficulty might be removed if language were analyzed into speech and tongue — into the language which I am and the tongue I use in order to communicate. Yet the difficulty would not be removed, for the tongue itself is not like other instruments, which are exterior and simply available; we do not say "I speak *with* French," but "I speak *in* French," or "I speak French." The tongue becomes ours, adheres to us in the use we make of it; and this is precisely because it is not foreign to thought, indeed because language is thought. Perhaps we must both distinguish between these two relations of identity and expression, and surpass this distinction: it may be the vocation of language to permit thought to take its distance, to elect to be independent or pure, and capable of inventing new languages or new symbolisms; but at the origin, thought is taken up in speech, and doubtless never completely detaches itself from it.

---

[1] Maurice Merleau-Ponty, *The Phenomenology of Perception*, trans. Colin Smith (London, Routledge and Kegan Paul, 1962), p. 184.

Let us turn now to a closer look at Mr. Sellars' txt. It consists of two apparently unrelated parts whose link is difficult to see: the first, which deals with linguistic rules, specifies the notion of an identity of language and thought; the second proposes an analysis of the notion of expression.

I

I must admit that I was at first quite surprised by the first part. Dealing with "linguistic rules," Sellars manages the *tour de force* of not mentioning the word "grammar" (in spite of an allusion to the rules of formation and transformation) nor the word "lexicon" (in spite of an allusion to the word "red"). But I was mistaken in my surprise, for this is not a question of tongue, but of behavior, in which rules, instead of being stated, are interiorized. If the behavior of the speaker submits to rules, it is no doubt because the tongue itself consists of rules: it is an institution both arbitrary and binding, and it can be defined as a system of laws. Yet Sellars is not interested in the nature of the tongue as an object, but rather in the way in which it is spoken and in the relation of discourse with thought: in the behavior of the individual who has this tongue at his command.

Mr. Sellars does not examine the finality of this behavior (one speaks *in order to* say something) or its freedom (one *chooses* to speak rather than be silent, and one *chooses* one's words); although he does evoke the intention to communicate, what he studies is the "rule-governed character" of this behavior. Here I should like to note in passing that this character should perhaps be studied in relation to an activity which continually produces new forms of discourse and which can always transgress the laws of language, destroying the system. It is perhaps a rule to say "this is red" in the presence of red objects in sunlight, but what is to prevent me from saying "this is purple?" Who will prevent the poet from resorting to a metaphor? There is no law that cannot be contorted or violated, and this privilege cannot be denied the speaking subject.

What is the situation, then, concerning these rules? Mr. Sellars defines them as "oughts" which are categorical, not hypothetical. These are obviously not moral duties, in the sense of the German *Sollen,* but practical duties, stated in such propositions as "One ought" or "You must." These duties do not involve a moral subject, and may not apply to any subject at all. Sellars distinguishes, indeed, between "ought-to-do's" and "ought-to-be's." The former concern the activity of a subject who has something to do in a given situation and who is conscious of this. The latter concern rather an object, in which one looks for a certain state by reason of its nature or its function; for example, clocks ought to tell time. But can one, in this second case, talk of a rule? I would rather speak of "condition" in a broad sense; it is the condition (that is, the nature) of a clock to tell time; or: a clock is only a clock on the condition that it tell time. In other words, a law of essence — to use Husserl's term — is not a rule; a rule is always a rule for an action and therefore always addresses itself to a subject capable of activity.

Yet Sellars insists on giving a place to the ought-to-be's alongside the ought-to-do's. He first observes that the former can also involve a subject, for example when we say that "one ought to feel sympathy for bereaved people"; translation: it is of the nature of a decent soul to feel compassion for the bereaved. He then observes that ought-to-be's can give rise to ought-to-do's: the clockmaker ought to build clocks which ought to tell time (at least if he wants to sell his clocks: here the imperative is hypothetical). Such "rules of action" also apply to the trainer of those lower animals which constitute the delight of behaviorism, or to the educator who deals with human subjects, e.g., in order to teach them sympathy for the bereaved, or the correct use of language.

For language — or rather tongue — must be learned. Once learned, it constitutes a manner of being for the subject, the property of a nature informed by culture. It is in this sense that one can speak of being, and of ought-to-be's: in order to speak, *you must* (one ought to) have been disposed to speech, just as a certain animal is disposed by training to respond to a certain stimulus. We can see that the ought defines here a condition, from which a practical rule, a rule of the social game, can be inferred: culture must be transmitted, the child must be taught to speak, the rules of action which govern the use of speech must be inscribed in his being in the form of knowledge *(savoirs)* or habits.

But perhaps this condition of speaking man, who has had to appropriate his native tongue, is not entirely the effect of his socialization. For man to speak, he must be originally capable of language, and no behaviorism will help a trainer to make an animal speak. It is here, it seems to me, that Sellars separates himself from the elementary behaviorism according to which linguistic acts would be automatic (though acquired) responses to stimuli — a behaviorism which contains echoes of logical atomism, as the example "this is red" attests. What Sellars justly introduces to complicate this overly simple schema is three-fold: the idea of consciousness: one must be conscious of things in order to speak about them; the idea of self-consciousness: "one must have the concept of oneself as agent"; and the Aristotelian notion of disposition: one must be disposed to speak in order to speak, one must master language in order to have it at one's disposition. And what Sellars assembles under the term conceptual activity, or more simply, thought, are these very traits of verbal behavior.

From this point on it can be said that speech is thought. But Sellars only identifies these *after* having distinguished them. And perhaps one must ask oneself whether they are not *first* mingled. Even a corrected behaviorism makes its task of posing the most difficult problem too easy. It gives itself a world and a language which are already constituted — a world in which one knows that there is red, a language in which one knows that there is the word "red," and in addition, a subject supposed capable of using one to say the other. I wonder whether the true philosophical problem is not once more that of foundation or origin (understood in a phenomenological, not a chronological, sense); that is, whether reflection should not go back towards an unreflected prior to the distinction of subject and object, of world and language, in order to try to show how the object (the red) is constituted simultaneously with the perceiving subject who becomes himself capable of thinking at the same time that he becomes capable of speaking (by re-inventing on his own the use of the word "red").

II

It is not in this direction that Wilfrid Sellars orients himself. He presupposes thought, or the thinking subject, and in the second part of his paper, he asks himself how language can express thought in order to communicate it. Within thought itself, he distinguishes form and content, and he first considers form alone, that is, belief; his strategy consists of defining belief as disposition and his problem is to try to determine how this disposition is expressed by language. The title of the second part (sections V-XII) could be "Thought as Language" rather than "Language as Thought."

This further recourse to the notion of disposition (the disposition to think, not to speak) leads Sellars into a dialectic: "My strategy," he says, "remains in a broad sense dialectical." Yes, and even in a specific sense: this is the dialectic of the interior and the exterior so often encountered in Hegel. For what is a potential which is not realized? A disposition to think must manifest itself by the fact of thinking, and this thought must manifest itself as thought "out-loud." But here *speech* is not speaking, but *uttering:* it is simply the means of giving body to thought, and not of communicating it; discourse is neither a dialogue nor a monologue, it is only the manifestation of an interior state.

We are once again in the behaviorist perspective; but Sellars is always on guard against the reductionist element in behaviorism which is tempted to reduce thought to the phenomenon of verbalization. To think out loud, Sellars observes, is still, or already, to think. And it is possible that this thought is also striving to communicate itself: language then becomes again the means of communication which permits me to say, or also to dissimulate, what I think or what I believe, thus to be sincere or deceptive.

Hence Sellars fully recognizes the distinction between being and doing — a distinction that seems to me to be more justified here than when it was used to define linguistic rules. In one case, I am what I think; in the other, I say what I think. There result two very different meanings of the word "expression" which are distinguished in terms of the distance taken by thought in regard to language: in one instance, thought identifies with language; in the other, thought uses language. In other words, sometimes expression is spontaneous — and Sellars even says "involuntary" — and sometimes it is premeditated. In French, this distinction can be conveyed by the difference between *"s'exprimer"* (to express oneself) and *"exprimer"* (to express).

Sellars adds a third sense of the word "expression," terming it the "logical (or semantical)"; this no longer takes into account the veracity of the speaker, but rather the verity of the statement: the statement must be correct in order to say truly what it means.

This analysis is assuredly interesting and necessary. And Sellars underpins it by showing that the verbal behavior of the child is not immediately under his control: the child expresses thoughts without knowing that he expresses them; or rather, he discovers that he expresses them, and then learns to express them deliberately: "It is because the expression has a certain meaning that it can be effectively used to convey the corresponding thought." Here again, Sellars complicates the behaviorist schema in order to preserve the rights of the subject, that is, the interiority of mental acts: for the subject, he says, expresses himself, i.e., thinks out loud, only if he in fact thinks something and does not intend to keep his thoughts to himself. The whole debate between logical behaviorism and Professor Sellars bears on the exact sense of the syntagma: to think out loud. To think out loud is indeed to think, and this presupposes a disposition to think: it may be an act, but it presupposes a being.

I can only endorse the interest of these distinctions, whose importance Mr. Sellars stresses in his introduction. But I wonder if the proper understanding of language does not invite reflection to surpass them, or rather to locate itself just short of them, that is, short of the old distinction between language and thought. If, as Sellars says so well, "verbal behavior is already *thinking in its own right*," perhaps there is a common root for the three senses of the word "express." To express is to be at once thinking and speaking. For thought is nothing other than the possibility of putting oneself at a distance from things in order to name them and to possess them symbolically instead of being taken up, and possessed, by them. This power is revealed — is expressed — in its exercise, that is, through acts of speech in which the subject affirms himself as subject: he is what he does. In other words, thought does not precede speech; it is nothing interior or internal. As Wittgenstein says, thought does not naturally lead us to conceive of some "queer process." [2] Thought exists entirely *in* behavior, the behavior of a concrete individual — "Mr. X," as Wittgenstein says — that is, in linguistic operations: "The function must come out in *operating* with the word." [3] In brief, speech expresses thought because it is thought in act.

Yet just as language separates us from things, it can separate us from itself: it makes possible a movement of reflection which introduces a gap between thought and its expression, and which authorizes us to consider language as an instrument in the service of thought: thus I can be silent or speak according to whether or not I wish to communicate, and I can say or hide what I think. And I can also *want* to think something; I can will that my discourse have a sense, that it be neither absurd nor nonsensical, and that it tell what is true. But perhaps the two norms of veracity and of verity, which jointly imply the dualism of thought — understood both as the intention animating speech and as the intellect controlling discourse — and of language are both already proposed by the immediate experience of language. On the one hand (with respect to the second sense of the word "express"), if thought is identified at the outset with speech, an act of speech is immediately addressed to someone; it aims at the universal and claims truth. Sellars indeed isolates "a language which does not function as a means of communication," even from self to self; a language which is *speaking and not talking*. But can one conceive of a speech which is so unreflected that it does not reflect back *(se réfléchisse)* on someone? How does one speak even in a low voice, or even remaining silent, without hearing oneself speak? This hearing *(entendre)* is understanding *(entendement)*, that is, thought. Language is a means of expressing oneself which is inseparable from the consciousness of expressing oneself; it is in this that it differs from all

---

[2] Ludwig Wittgenstein, *Philosophical Investigations,* trans. G. E. M. Anscombe (London, MacMillan, 1961), par. 196; Wittgenstein underlines "process."
[3] *Ibid.,* par. 559; I underline "operating."

other spontaneous means of expression. Allow me to quote Wittgenstein again: "A misleading parallel: the expression of pain is a cry — the expression of thought, a proposition." [4] Moreover, the monologue, even the interior monologue, is always a latent social act: to express oneself is also to address oneself to an absent other; a solitary discourse is not a solipsistic discourse. Even if the child coincides with his speech, even if he does not have the thought that-p without thinking out loud that-p, it is always to someone — to himself or to an imaginary interlocutor — that he says "p".

By the same token, however, this thought, which at once constitutes itself and experiences itself in speech, strives to be true. First, it wants to be heard by the other, by all others: it assumes the form of universality, that is, the form of the true. Secondly, speech always has a content. To say "this is red" is to think that this is red. Thought can be true because language can say the world, thus installing us in truth: in a certain commerce with the world according to which we are in the world as present to it, at once blended with it and distinct from it.

Thus everything is given with language or with the fact of expression — all of the dimensions of thought: consciousness of the world, consciousness of self, consciousness of others, and thought's claim to truth. But how is language itself given? Man gives it to himself, but he has first to be man in order to give it to himself. I am grateful to Professor Sellars for having shown that man has to be capable of language. If the development of man and of culture is only understood through language, language in turn is only understood through man. And the idea of disposition as the power of a [human] nature should remain at the disposition of the philosopher.

But even if language itself is true, if it can say or express the world, and if this saying is not the sovereign act of a Kantian subject imposing its laws on nature, then we must also presume the world's disposition to *be said* (in very different ways, e.g., as logical language accords with the logic of the world, or as the poetic word conjures up the presence of the perceptible). The origin of language perhaps lies in this power of *Physis* (Nature). But Professor Sellars did not undertake a metaphysics of language; it would thus be unjust and vain to *op-pose* to him a question which he does not himself pose and which probably has no verifiable answer: "How is language possible?" *

UNIVERSITY OF PARIS, NANTERRE.

---

[4] *Ibid.*, par. 317.
* Translated by Edward S. Casey.

COMMENTS ON SELLARS

EDOUARD MOROT-SIR

The remarks suggested to me by this remarkable philosophical effort "to give a naturalistic interpretation of the intentionality of conceptual acts," in the very words of Wilfrid Sellars, are not criticisms aimed at particular points in the text—they reply rather to methodological perplexities which seem to me to be inevitably raised by the problem behind this reflection: what is the current epistemological standing of the word "thought" in the language of a philosopher?

1) Professor Sellars explores the epistemological possibilities of a traditional distinction in the psychology of language between exteriorized thought and interior thought, and he seems to think that the concept of "thinking-out-loud-that-p" can serve as the basis of a naturalistic interpretation of conceptual activity. I doubt that such a distinction can provide a solution for traditional philosophical difficulties. In the first place, the classic duality of language and thought is purely and simply eliminated—does this not suppose the problem to be thus solved? Moreover, the possibility or the impossibility of an interior language which is non-realized and non-explicitized can be examined, and I am not predicting the reply which the psychology of language could make today. Whatever the reply, it would neither justify nor invalidate a naturalistic approach and solution to the problem of thought and language; that is, to the problem of the signification of the distinction made by common sense between language and thought. Furthermore, the psychological sense of this duality of exterior and interior should be specified: for example, if we give it a spatial value, then to what do the concept of thinking-out-loud and that of interior episode correspond exactly, anatomically and physiologically? We should leave the field of psychology for that of biology, and admit right from the beginning that the solution to the general problem of the common distinction between language and thought can only be given by the progress of biology. This would perhaps be sufficient justification for a naturalistic approach, but it would also turn around to say that naturalistic philosophy

71

should patiently await the success of a scientific problematics and that meanwhile silence would be the golden rule! I do not deny the legitimacy of such an attitude, but I then wonder if it is worthwhile to distinguish between logical behaviorism and logical physicalism. This will be the subject of my second remark.

2) This is a question I should like to ask Professor Sellars, for I admit that I do not see clearly the difference between these two philosophical strategies, unless secondary distinctions are introduced into the methodological field which is the property of every naturalistic trend. And then I was struck by a word used by Professor Sellars: he seems to qualify the whole of his logico-linguistic analysis as *strategy*. What is the epistemological status of strategy as intellectual or linguistic (according to the vocabulary one chooses to use) process? Does strategy precede theory in the succession of events of knowledge? If so, what is the theory from which it is derived and which justifies its choice? If not—and such an attitude would be conceivable—what are the practical values which make one strategy preferred to another? The answer could be: this strategy is the only one enabling a valid solution in reference to logical and linguistic conventions. The problem of the epistemological status of the word "strategy" is, it seems to me, of capital importance, for its solution, if it is possible, would result in the legitimacy of philosophical discourse and thus of the language used by Professor Sellars to speak of thought and language. I have here the impression, furthermore, that we must go back to the distinction, which is today classic among logicians, between language and metalanguage, since the fact of this duality can, it seems to me, be useful in replying to the general question posed by W. Sellars in his paper, and in order to renew the philosophical approach of naturalism. But forgive me for introducing this possibility of philosophical strategy without justifying it. I simply believe that its use would eliminate the *sine die* rejection of the solution of the problem of the distinction and relation between language and thought. And this indication leads me to my final remark:

3) One can well understand Professor Sellars' preoccupation and the importance of the research to which he invites us. One could even conceive of a complete discourse applied to the ensemble of what we call "nature" and rid of the word and of the concept of thought. And this would perhaps be the criteria of every scientific effort, or in other words, the epistemological criteria of all scientific research. And inversely, the philosopher would be characterized by the need to use the word "thought" in duality with the word "nature" such as the latter is used by scholars according to a particular field of application.

More than once while studying Professor Sellars' text I had the sensation of an occult presence of Descartes who, as we know, believed that science could be founded on the duality of mind and matter, and that this duality could be founded on a permanent intellectual experience—that of "I think." And it is revealing that in the last pages of his paper Professor Sellars raises the problem of belief, which is exactly the Cartesian question of *Cogito*. We therefore arrive at the following situation: if we refuse Cartesian duality such as it is proposed to us in the Metaphysical Meditations, how can the duality of language and thought continue to have meaning? Or should we simply concede that Cartesian duality has no epistemological, and therefore philosophical interest? I admit that at this crossroads I feel like the traveller lost in the forest evoked by Descartes in part three of the *Discourse on Method,* when he gives the rules for what is traditionally termed tentative ethics. But this Cartesian advice remains valid today: follow a path to its end, obstinately, not knowing whether or not you will find your way out of the forest. I am afraid that the strategy of logical behaviorism has as its consequence to remain patiently at the crossroads while waiting for someone to come look for you, this someone being one scientist or another. But on the other hand, it is no longer possible today to be Cartesian as Descartes was in the first part of the seventeenth century. And I come back to the question: if we must give up the substantialist interpretation of the duality of thought and extension, and with it the pure experience of a thought which is opposed to matter, must we then reject Cartesian epistemology, say that the word "thought" in the spiritualist or idealist style derived from Descartes and such as it is expressed by three centuries of French philosophy is a word which has become outmoded, and accept a physicalism which, according to tastes, can integrate or exclude Cartesian duality? There is perhaps a third solution: to admit that relational duality of thought and matter, and consequently of thought and language, is currently undergoing a new phase of interpretation which should be defined on the basis of a dialectic, and no longer a naturalistic strategy. Professor Sellars would hope to integrate the concept of intentionality with logical behaviorism. I would readily approve if he were willing, at the same time, to recognize that this intentionality is nothing other than the reference to the following dialectic situation: language, as a concept, implies two non-linguistic notions—the signified and the signifying—and from this implication the two dualities of nature and language and of language and thought are derived. And it is this dialectic situation which keeps me from defining thought in terms of "thinking-out-loud."

I realize that I am proceeding here by affirmations and that this dialectic strategy which I oppose to naturalistic strategy would have to be, if not justified, at least explained in detail. To give my reader an idea, I am thinking, with reference to dialectics, of that residue which remains in any idealistic philosophy after it is rid of all of the implications of substantialist metaphysics which hide its true face. Am I so far from Professor Sellars? I wonder. His effort to mark distances in relation to a strict logical physicalism seems to me to be symptomatic of the desire to escape a pure analytical ontology.

NEW YORK CITY.

COMMENTS ON SELLARS

Joseph Margolis

If I understand Wilfrid Sellars' rather difficult paper, I do agree with him that it would be absurd to hold that children, in learning a language which we suppose they do not antecedently possess, may correctly be characterized in their initial *training* in terms which entail or imply that they already possess the language they are to learn. I believe that this is the key theme of Sellars' distinction between "ought-to-be's" and "ought-to-do's" and his central claim that "ought-to-be's imply ought-to-do's," though the implication does not necessarily apply to all subjects of such "ought-to-*be's*" (for instance, clocks, animals, infants learning language). I take this to be the point of Sellars' linking of his thesis that language is inherently rule-governed and the thesis that "a rule is roughly a general ought statement," usually thought of in terms of "rules of action" but which Sellars wishes to construe as covering "rules of criticism" as well ("ought-to-be's"). Both of these claims are, however, much too elliptical to be pursued in depth—though *what* a rule of language is and *what* the sense may be in which one *ought* to-do or to-be, relative to given rules of language, are fine questions that Sellars' analysis does not attempt to supply. On the other hand, in keeping with Sellars' penchant for a so-called dialectical development of a philosophical issue, the apparatus of "ought-to-do's" and "ought-to-be's" may very well be intended to be abandoned, once the force of the originally exposed absurdity is grasped.

I suppose my sense of strain in reading Sellars' account amounts essentially to this: the apparatus is not itself satisfactorily introduced, so that one may decide whether it is literally to be defended (in which case, the elliptical issues mentioned are precisely the ones to be developed) or whether it is merely a heuristic device for appreciating what, elsewhere, is stated in a single sentence and what is, in any case (given the absurdity mentioned), beyond dispute. Sellars himself says, very usefully here, that, with respect to the training and learning of children, with regard to language (and analogies of various sorts may surely be constructed for other skills), "we need a concept which mediates between merely uttering and saying." The schematic rule, "ought-to-utter" (or, "ought-to-respond-by-uttering," that is, a rule of criticism), is intended by Sellars to fix the required ingredient in an adequate account of the learning of a language.

Sellars goes on, as he says, "within the framework sketched," to give an account of language as "essentially a means whereby one thinker can express his thoughts to others" and of "the more radical point" that "meaningful speech," utterances in "non-communicative contexts," may express one's thoughts, without being, "in any ordinary sense, talking." The second thesis is an extremely puzzling, but central, claim. It may be useful here to say that Sellars construes a child's learning of a language (before it has mastered the language) very much in the manner in which Wittgenstein is often taken to speak about one's learning (verbal) pain behavior—in both of which the "verbal behavior is not in our child's voluntary control." His solution is that there must be a stage in which "the saying is the involuntary manifestation of the thinking." And hence it is that he holds that, though the child's verbal behavior "would express its thoughts," the child itself "could not express them." (I may say, in this connection, that *if* a child may learn to report his pain—the vexed question that Wittgenstein's remarks reinforce—then a child has not learned this verbal behavior until he *can* report his pain. The parallel regarding learning to express one's thoughts is obvious.)

Sellars' argument is ingenious and seemingly simple. But there is, I think, a deep circularity in the account. Sellars *introduces* a suppositious episode of an uttering that-p, that is not assimilable to a use of such an utterance in communicative contexts, and that is, nevertheless, a thinking that-p. From this, as far as I can see, he concludes that there *is* "a form of meaningful speech" (thinking-out-loud) that "is not in any ordinary sense, talking." But though, *given* Sellars' heuristic strategy for fixing what is needed to understand the linguistic training of children, the invented episode may be (shall we say, "dialectically") required, we have no independent and affirmative evidence by which to assess the claim (and alternative accounts may be at hand). The fact is that so-called "non-communicative contexts" (for masters of the language) are, surely, no more than communicative contexts *manqués*; these will not support the required intermediary step. Also, one wants to know what contributes relevantly to the plausibility of holding that, in the initial stages of a child's learning a language, its "thought is manifested in a purely involuntary way by the corresponding verbal behavior," "that only if it has the mental act of thinking that-p does it utter 'p'." For one thing, the pain analogy does not help, since *learned* pain-behavior (even if involuntary) is designed to replace or supplement *unlearned* pain-behavior; but what might be meant by the *unlearned* expression of a child's thought? And for another, *given* that a child's *general* verbal behavior sufficiently resembles the behavior of those who have mastery of the language, we *begin* to say that the child uses language to express its thought (much as in the full-fledged model that Sellars has in mind); it is only in a courtesy sense that a child in training may be said to be thinking-out-loud when it utters discrete verbal (or, rather, word-like) fragments; we ascribe to it thought when we ascribe to it speech. But if this is so, then neither Sellars' non-behavioristic nor his behavioristic construction captures the distinction of learning a language; for he says (non-behavioristically) that *"only if"* the mental act occurs does the child "utter 'p'," and he says (behavioristically) that *"all* utterances of 'p' " are thoughts that-p." But it is only when the *global* pattern of a child's would-be verbal behavior (in *this* sense, then, intermediary between uttering and saying) meets the rule-like conditions of speech, that we say that the child is speaking or talking. The context is a communicative context, even if speech is not directed to anyone. And, in any case, the utterances taken distributively could not possibly help us to make sense of a linkage between a child's thought and its expression; such connections would have to be viewed contingently, precisely (and ironically) because all *rules* can be violated. The advantage of the alternative here sketched, on the other hand, is that it avoids altogether what is surely a dubious and undefended apparatus of unanalyzed mental states and episodes.

Temple University
Philadelphia.

EXPRESSION AND MANIFESTATION IN SELLARS AND DUFRENNE

EDWARD S. CASEY

Symptomatic of our language-conscious times is the fact that two of its most eminent philosophers, working quite independently of one another, make language a focal point of their wide-ranging interests. Yet both Wilfrid Sellars and Mikel Dufrenne refuse to follow certain tendencies in their respective traditions which would reduce language on the one hand to its use in "action" (in the Austinian sense) and on the other to existential commitment (in the Sartrian sense). Sellars reminds us that language has a "causal" (genetic-explanatory) and a "semantical" aspect in addition to an illocutionary dimension; and that mental acts, which must be considered in any thorough analysis of language, cannot themselves be construed as actions. Dufrenne is anxious to establish both a *telos* (rationality) and an *archē* (Nature) for language; he also wants to show its transcendental character.[1] Similarly, both thinkers are agreed that an understanding of language must move beyond "description" to a dimension which is *de jure* prior and which could be called "genealogical" in Husserl's sense of this term: phenomenologically or conceptually originary.[2] In this respect, Dufrenne and Sellars not only reaffirm the difference between the order of knowing and the order of explanation but tend to emphasize the latter: hence the importance of speculative metaphysics in the one case and of theoretical ("regimented") models in the other. It is no accident that Sellars should make the child's acquisition of language a pivotal point in his discussion, or that Dufrenne should refer to "the power of *Physis*." Sellars' concern with *Nomos*, seen most clearly in his treatment of "ought-to-be's" or categorical "rules of criticism," rejoins Dufrenne's insistence on the *being* of man: a being that proceeds ultimately from *Physis* as his origin. Though Sellars does

---

[1] See Mikel Dufrenne, *Language and Philosophy,* trans. Henry B. Veatch (Bloomington, Indiana University Press, 1963), ch. III, esp. p. 73.

[2] See Edmund Husserl, *Formale und Transzendentale Logik* (Halle, 1929), ch. 5-7; *Erfahrung und Urteil* (Hamburg, 1964), Introduction.

not undertake a "metaphysics of language" in the present paper, one could say that the metaphysical question is always on his own horizon of "scientific realism"—as is the transcendental question concerning the possibility of language. Thus Sellars says quite explicitly that "sound philosophical strategy calls for the examination of concepts as they function in larger contexts, rather than subjecting them to scrutiny in splendid isolation."[3]

One such "larger context" conspicuously overlooked by both Sellars and Dufrenne in their discussions of language is that of semiology or theory of signs. The effects of this oversight may not be ultimately destructive, for most semioticians from Peirce to de Saussure would agree that language is itself the paradigmatic semiotic system. But a certain lack of clarity does result from this act of (perhaps conscious) over-looking—an obscurity centering about the notions of expression and manifestation. Adopting as a model Husserl's theory of signs as it is given in the first of the *Logische Untersuchungen,* I would like to explore, in a comparative and critical way, the joint themes of expression and mani-festation as they appear in Sellars' and Dufrenne's contributions above and in other related writings.

Husserl makes a preliminary and crucial distinction between signs understood as "indications" (*Anzeichen*) and as "expressions" (*Aus-drücke*). Indications, which form the basis for communication, are conceived as acts of "manifestation" (*Kundgabe*) by means of which certain given items are taken as designating other items not directly present to apprehension. The indicative sign, through its "manifestation-function," motivates the sign-interpreter to presume the existence of the realities designated. In the case of non-linguistic indicative signs, we have the familiar phenomenon of natural designation: smoke indicating fire. When linguistic signs are used indicatively, they typically function as manifesting the psychic states that accompany or underlie explicit linguis-tic expression. As such, indicative signs do not possess or refer to a "meaning" (*Bedeutung,* which Husserl does not distinguish at this point from *Sinn*).[4] Nevertheless, indication is essential to communication, since it is a necessary factor in all interpersonal discourse. We shall return to this point.

In Husserl's theory, an *expression* is a "meaningful sign" (*bedeutsam Zeichen*). Such a sign is not found outside the realm of language; hence

---

[3] From Sellars' article *supra,* section V. References to this article and to Du-frenne's will be made by section number in parenthesis.

[4] See, however, *Ideen I,* par. 124 for a later distinction between the two terms.

an expression is a linguistic sign *par excellence*. Even if the indicative sign (or more precisely, the indicative function of signs) is necessary for communication, an expressive sign lies at the core of language understood as a phenomenon of meaning. Though Husserl admits that the "communicative function of language" is the role which language as a whole is "originally called to fulfill,"[5] the expressivity of linguistic signs can be isolated in its purity—indeed, *must* be if we are to discern its essence. Like Sellars, Husserl believes that we can capture expression in "non-communicative contexts" (VI), that is, independently of being pronounced or addressed to anyone (oneself or others). The communicative element in language, crucial as it is, can be "bracketed" in order to discover the nature of expression. Sellars provides the rationale for this project: "there is a danger that exclusive concern with [the communicative] perspective will obscure those connections between thought and language where the latter is not functioning as a means of communication" (VI).

Dufrenne doubts whether such a project, pursued in common (though quite differently) by Sellars and Husserl, is possible or even advisable. Communication is not merely the ultimate use of language, but is inseparable from its essence: "Man speaks in order to communicate something."[6] Every act of speaking, even speaking silently to oneself, is "a latent social act: to express oneself is also to address oneself to an absent other; a solitary discourse is not a solipsistic discourse" (*supra,* II). For Dufrenne, the man who speaks communicates not only with others, but also with himself: "the man who thinks communicates with himself in a silent monologue."[7] Dufrenne arrives at this position by expanding the notion of communication to include not only manifestation, but also information, meaning, and significance.[8] Thus what Husserl and Sellars would restrict to the province of expression, Dufrenne places in communication itself. This move represents a fundamental shift in orientation; language does not exist so much to express meanings *per se* as to make meanings accessible to others. This explains why Dufrenne does not hesitate to characterize language as "an instrument in the service of thought," as a "means of expressing oneself" (II). Yet, as Sellars has written elsewhere, this is a potentially dangerous claim: "Serious errors creep into the interpretation of both language and thought if one

---

[5] E. Husserl, *Logische Untersuchungen* (Halle, 1913), I, par. 7.

[6] *Language and Philosophy*, p. 71.

[7] *Ibid.*, p. 72.

[8] *Ibid.*, p. 71; see also *Le poétique* (Paris, Presses Universitaires de France, 1963), ch. 1.

interprets the idea that overt linguistic episodes express thoughts on the model of an instrument."[9]

It must be realized, however, that Dufrenne and Sellars are in accord on one basic point: language may express thought by being itself thought in act. Sellars' contention that "verbal behavior is already thinking in its own right" (XIII) is echoed in Dufrenne's assertion in *Language and Philosophy* that "language is, if you wish, a tool, but it is a tool that thinks on its own account."[10] The latter admission seems to take much of the force out of Dufrenne's instrumentalist view of language, or at least to limit it narrowly. I take this common insight of Sellars and Dufrenne to be a significant addition to the prevalent view that verbal behavior is an *action;* some of it certainly is—e.g., "deliberating" in Sellars' example—but much of it can only be conceived as a mental *act* in its own right: that is, as spontaneous thinking.

The form this direct "candid" thinking takes is crucial. Is it an act of *manifestation,* as both Sellars and Dufrenne hold?[11] The same question arises when the term "manifestation" is replaced by "actualization." In either case, the basic metaphor is that of the appearance at the phenomenal "surface" of a "covert" mental process.[12] Sellars' notion of "thinking-out-loud" is a central example of manifestation; as he specifies elsewhere, "in thinking-out-loud covert conceptual episodes proper are, so to speak, coming to the surface and finding their appropriate expression in speech."[13] What Husserl would call the "manifestation-function" of indicative signs is taken by Sellars to be "the primary form in which thinking occurs" (X); thus it is made basic to any understanding of expression. Dufrenne similarly gives a major role to manifestation in language: language manifests an "impersonal intelligence," and it "reveals" the speaker to himself.[14] What are we to make of the idea of manifestation or revelation within language?

---

[9] W. Sellars, *Science, Perception, and Reality* (New York, Humanities Press, 1963), p. 188. It should be noted that Dufrenne writes in *Language and Philosophy* that "in its origin language is really not a tool"—or at least it is "not a tool like other tools" (p. 79).

[10] *Language and Philosophy,* p. 87.

[11] Sellars, *supra,* V; Dufrenne, *Language and Philosophy,* p. 74 and p. 87.

[12] Cf. Sellars, *supra,* XII, fn. 10; here Sellars does limit this sense of expression to its "causal" type; yet this seems the most fundamental of the three types discerned.

[13] W. Sellars, *Science and Metaphysics* (London, Routledge and Kegan Paul, 1968), p. 75.

[14] *Language and Philosophy,* p. 74 and p. 87.

Husserl's answer, to which I would subscribe here, is that a foreign element is being introduced into pure expression whenever we speak of "manifestation." An indicative use of signs is substituted for their purely expressive role. In the latter role, *nothing* is manifested or revealed, for nothing *needs* to be. The reason is that in the ideal solitude of pure expression the speaker is already fully revealed to himself; in fact, he coincides with his psychic states, which he experiences "simultaneously" (*im selben Augenblick*) with the production of language itself.[15] At this level, nothing is manifested because nothing is communicated—to others or to oneself. Thus Husserl disagrees with Dufrenne that language is inherently and thoroughly communicative; as expressive, it is essentially pre-communicative or even non-communicative. And he would hold against Sellars that the spontaneous and solitary production of language does not have to be conceived as a thinking-out-loud; for "out-loudness" is not necessary to the full comprehension of expressive language. The silence of interior monologue is not a-typical, as Sellars maintains; it is not merely a question of keeping one's thoughts to oneself: one is still *expressing* these thoughts. But such expression, as the very enactment of the thoughts, need not take the explicit form of a phonic ex-plosion; expression can be—indeed, ideally *only* is—complete in non-communicative, non-manifesting silence.

Perhaps the underlying ground for this ultimate difference between Husserl and both Sellars and Dufrenne lies in the Husserlian view of intentionality. Instead of restricting intentionality to the semantic dimension in Sellarsian fashion, Husserl characterizes it as prevading *all* expressive acts. In his nomenclature, a "meaning-intention" must "animate" (*beleben*) the phonic complex (i.e., the word understood as an "acoustic image" in de Saussure's term) in order that expression take place. Without this act of animation, one has only the phonic element—which, taken by itself, is precisely the basis of mediation, indication, and thus communication. In fact, it could be shown that the special attention given to this phonic component of expression has led philosophers and linguists alike to over-emphasize the role of communication in language.[16] One way of circumscribing this perennial and ultimately pernicious tendency is to stress instead the intentional character of expressivity— where "intentionality" means more than mere "aboutness" or even (as in Sellars' view) the "appropriateness of classifying [verbal phenomena] in terms which relate to the linguistic behavior of the group to which

---

[15] Husserl, *Logische Untersuchungen,* I, par. 8.
[16] See Jacques Derrida, *De la grammatologie* (Paris, Minuit, 1967).

one belongs" (XIII). Rather, intentionality must be seen in its full richness as the very *life* of expression, as its animating force: in this view, "pure expressivity will be the pure active intention (mind, psyche, life, will) of a *bedeuten* animating a discourse whose content (*Bedeutung*) is present to it."[17]

YALE UNIVERSITY
NEW HAVEN.

---

[17] Jacques Derrida, *La voix et la phénomène* (Paris, Presses Universitaires de France, 1967), pp. 43-44.

Part II
Human Nature

THE SENSE OF THE HUMAN

Raymond Polin

Ethics is a practical theory of man. It is the philosophy of man, of men, in relation to their actions. Ethical systems in the past have always affirmed, explicitly or implicitly, a certain doctrine of man, which they sometimes called, in the manner of Hobbes, who liked to go straight to the heart of the problem, *De Natura Humana.*

But the sense attributed to the human constitutes a fundamental choice; it does not result from a discussion, but, alone, makes possible discussion, which has in turn the goal of making this view of human nature clear and conscious. This is the first act of a freedom asserting itself; the first moment of a practical philosophy. It does not have to be based on a previous demonstration. Or, rather, it should be based on an entire philosophy and all of its practice, for its justification comes later. Its truth stems from its consequences rather than of its premises. This is why philosophers have most often confined themselves to studying the logical sequence of its consequences. But we must enter the circle and we can only enter it via a decision without evidence. We have chosen to enter it through the analysis of human nature considered as a fundamental principle, although we risk giving clarity at the cost of arbitrary temporariness. Nothing can be reasoned immediately; not even the evidence of a reason. The reasons must be progressively forged.

Practical, ethical and political philosophy is a philosophy of man, of men; its principles should determine the sense of the human.[1]

I

De Natura Humana

When it comes to determining the sense of man, practical philosophy since Kant has been increasingly faced with a new difficulty. This difficulty is well illustrated by the Kantian effort to postulate a meta-

---

[1] We return to my book, Raymond Polin, *Ethique et Politique* (Paris, Sirey, 1968).

physics based on ethics instead of deducing, in accordance with tradition, an ethics based on metaphysics. Man is thought of more and more exclusively as an actual freedom, an acting freedom, and less and less as a nature. And, if it is possible to construct the theory of a nature, whether viewed in its perceptible determinations or in its metaphysical determinations, what becomes of a theory of actual freedom? How can we construct the theory of man as defined by the practice of freedom, which is carried out with a view to a theory, and in order to give it a sense? And yet this is the very condition in which the necessary philosophic reflection on man takes place. We see that it would be senseless to give in to the immediacy, the irreflective nature, the impulsive spontaneity of our desires and our passions under the pretext that the theory of man is made true only at the time that the act is achieved, and achieved in complete success. The practical theory of human freedom is the theory of powers and intentions — without it man's action would not be what it is and would not take on an ultimately intelligible meaning.

Neither shall we allow ourselves to be limited by the refusal, which is greatly in fashion, to recognize in man a nature whose main characteristic is to be identified with his freedom. Whoever speaks of nature in effect implies the existence of a structure given to the nascent state *(natura, natus)*, its spontaneous development according to a certain established form, in the manner that a plant grows (the gradual completion of an order which is inherent in it). In relation to man, nature represents an order which is exterior to him, which is characterized by its exteriority, and upon which he depends without mediation.[2] As concerns that which is thus exterior to him, he can grasp with his hands, take and possess. He can utilize, transform, and master. But, if we recognize that man has a nature, we admit that he is reciprocally integrated with and reduced to this structure of exteriority. He in turn can naturally be grasped, then utilized, mastered, possessed. We then see that he is entirely dependent upon a given which is nevertheless for him the exterior in itself. We see that man resides, just as the animal, entirely within a given, and consequently within a past, his past.

Yet how could a nature of this sort be attributed to man, since he exists entirely in his freedom and for his freedom; since he is what he does, his act, his work, as he is always beyond what he has been, beyond that which would constitute his nature? We know how Jean-Paul Sartre, proceeding from the idea that man is a "free being," particularly stressed the fact that human freedom precedes the essence of man.[3] Freedom

---

[2] Hegel, *Grundlinien der Philosophie des Rechts* (Berlin, 1821), Paragraph 4.
[3] J. P. Sartre, *L'Etre et le Néant* (Paris, Gallimard, 1943), p. 61.

cannot be described as an isolated faculty of man or as a property which belongs, among others, to the essence of the human being. This is to say that there is no single concept, no single definition which is universally valid for all men.[4] It is impossible to find in each man a universal essence which would be human nature, and proceeding from which man could be explained. In other words, his nature, for a man, is everything that he grasps of himself as having been. But he is never his past, except in the form of "néantisation." He is always free, with a total freedom which continually excludes all nature.[5] If existentialism is a humanism, is it not a humanism without men?

Questioning the existence of a human nature while not questioning a human reality raises, however, a false problem. The opposition between human freedom and human nature had been evident to philosophers, at least since Kant, but the latter had indicated the solution to it when he proposed the formula: man is a being whose nature is to do freely his nature. Thus is suggested, in effect, not a nature whose determinations would suffice to make man grow and live like a plant, but a nature which in principle, so to speak, is the form of the fundamental aptitude to do freely its nature. It is the power of freedom which is already obviously the nature and the essence of man, even if it does not permit foreseeing and defining the future of every man or the history of the human race.

Philosophers of freedom will unite in recognizing, in effect, that we cannot speak of human nature given as a substance, and that we must denounce a substantialistic definition of human nature.[6] But a philosophy of freedom does not necessarily exclude — it is quite the opposite — a functional definition of human nature. Such a functional definition implies that what is given and that what is universally definable in every man, as his essence and his nature, from the time he was born and came into existence, is the function of freedom, the ability to become, the power to create. This nature is not determination, but a condition of human existence, the capacity to move, in a movement of creative transcendence, towards a point beyond the self which it conditions, but does not determine. What is given is the faculty of creation, which is the faculty to become man; what is not given is creation itself, in its act and in its work. What is not given is the use which will be made of it.

If the history of man is not given, this does not prevent his functional

---

4 J. P. Sartre, *L'existentialisme est un humanisme* (Paris, Nagel, 1946), p. 67.

5 J. P. Sartre, *L'Etre et le Néant*, p. 65.

6 Ernst Cassirer, *Essay on Man* (New York, Doubleday, 1956), p. 53.

nature, his native and essential function of freedom, from being given. The true problem, then, is not that which might be raised by the existence of a human nature, but the problem of the sense taken in its function of freedom, which is its function as man.

Moreover, the true difficulty which Sartre encounters lies here, not in the definition of a human reality — he has never ceased to locate a human reality, nor to make himself very distinct, if not very clear, on what he means by it — but in the definition of the freedom with which he identifies it. As long as, using a type of argumentation which could be called transcendental, he bases the existence of a freedom on the so-called evident fact of nothingness, Sartre keeps to defining freedom by "nothingization," and imprisons it on the ineluctably indetermined finality of nothingness. Let us not dwell on the highly contestable nature of the reality of nothingness. Let us merely note that, because it is absolutely "nothingizing," because it is total, Sartre's freedom loses the privilege of Hegelian *"Aufhebung"* of being at once going beyond preservation, negation and creation. Because it is "total," it becomes unsuitable for serving as a means to action and as a motor to history. It has as its sole work nothingness, and, at this point of indetermination, it could be confused with nothingness. If it is no longer anything it can be taken for anything at all. The function of freedom, since it becomes capable of all senses, escapes any determination of a sense and, despite Sartre's verbal denials, it risks falling into gratuitousness, absurdity, nonsense. The least that can be said of it, in any case, is that it is indefinable inasmuch as it is total.

Furthermore, we cannot question without paradox either the fact of a human species or the universality of its definition. The criteria are numerous and far exceed the human presence of a natural power of freedom, of a potential functional freedom.

Indeed, it must be admitted that no one, in fact, ever errs regarding the extension of the concept of man. We know of no animal which can be taken for a man, nor of any man who can be taken seriously for an animal. We shall not linger on the problem Sartre lightly brought up, of determining what common definition of man could apply both to man in the state of nature and to bourgeois man. But there is no congenital cretin so deformed, no demented person reduced to such a rudimentary existence, as no longer to be a recognizable member of the human species. And they are in effect recognized as such by social as well as by legal customs. *"A fortiori"* the child, or even the occasional child-wolf of legend, poses but a problem of maturation and of education. There is no human being so defective, or so little human, that he is not such in a manifest and evident fashion.

A comprehensive definition, sufficient to establish a classifying description, does not pose any problems either. Without even having to resort to a criterion of heredity, science, just as simple common sense, can define perfectly well the distinguishing exterior characteristics of the human species, within the framework of a rational system of classification of animal species. Such a definition indicates, without any possible confusion, a two-handed mammal, able to stand upright, whose skull is of characteristic facial angle and capacity, and who has a cerebro-spinal system of a unique degree of development and complexity. In fact, modern scientists are more hindered than helped by the huge gap which separates the characteristics recognized in the human being and the characteristics peculiar to a particular animal. In their search for a continuous animal evolution, they are always trying to discover intermediary species and even the borderline species, which would be the first human species and of which it could also be said that it is the last animal species. They have not succeeded. When organic vestiges presented by paleontology are too minimal to permit a hypothesis, a last, but decisive criterion remains: the marks of work accomplished by human hands, the presence of an artificial work, the traces of a civilization, the testimony of a freedom.

Despite the apparent diversity of historic traditions, philosophers also quite agree among themselves on the basis of a definition of man, but dispute, rather, regarding its interpretation. Even those who do not accept a definition of a dualistic and substantialistic character can hardly escape, in effect, a bipolar definition — the pole of life and the pole of freedom (or, as we often say, of the spirit); the pole of self-immanence and the pole of self-surpassing, of transcendence in act. [7] The human being is an original totality in which life and freedom play, with regard to one another and in a reciprocal fashion, the roles of matter and of form. The perfectly integrated unity of the two is an ultimate achievement. But, in this common ground of human existence, the biological manifestations of desire and the works of freedom will usually dominate alternately. These are not two substances which are opposed, but two functions in reciprocal interaction,[8] which are nourished from the same source of vital energy and which engender one another reciprocally in a joint dialectic.

---

[7] Cf. our *Création des Valeurs* (Paris, Presses Universitaires de France, 1944), chapter XIII, I.

[8] Ernst Cassirer, *Essay on Man*, p. 53.

The former is all self-preservation, spontaneous adaptation and immanence of the given, desire to remain in one's being, to absorb what is, to make oneself master of it. But even when this force of life predominates, it is inseparable from the function of freedom; the mind, as Hegel would say, dwells there in itself and in a hidden form: tendencies and desires are already forms in themselves of freedom.[9] This, then, is already a specifically human life, as it expresses a freedom which is still contained in itself and it is evidenced in large part on the level of the affective, the desire and the passions. Consciousness of it is, if not reflective, at least sensed. This human animal is already no longer a simple animal. His predominant passions, fear and glory, are already the passions of man.[10] This man of desire is capable of participation in a moral life and in a political community. A certain type of human order and an ethic of obedience correspond to the predominance of desire.[11]

The function of freedom tends, for its part, to order human existence and its world in an entirely different fashion, no longer in regard to the past and the given, but in relation to a future in whose creation it participates. In it, human existence becomes intention and the accomplishment of values projected beyond it, self-preservation and self-transcendence in one's work, consciousness in act making itself at the same time that it is becoming consciousness of itself. One becomes capable of reflection, of reflection in speech, which is the speech of one's work; one aspires to express oneself in an ordered discourse, intelligible to oneself and liable to be understood and recognized by others — at best, by all others, in the form of a reasonable language. By concentrating what others have termed spirit around the creative force of freedom, we can see, in a single movement, that freedom finds in the power to say no but a mere instrument, that the spirit does not constitute the ascesis of life,[12] that freedom, both in its form in itself and in its form for itself, is human life itself. But, corresponding with the predominance of freedom is the positive creation of a work, the establishment of a new order which aims to be intelligible, universal.

Thus we review the traditionally characteristic traits of a "human nature": freedom, speech, consciousness of oneself and of the future, reason. But, as soon as all substantialistic signification is removed from these very traditional, very banal attributes, as soon as they are made functions, their importance becomes purely formal and negative. Through

---

[9] Hegel, *Grundlinien der Philosophie des Rechts*, Paragraph 11.

[10] M. Merleau-Ponty, *La Structure du Comportement* (Paris, Presses Universitaires de France, 1942), p. 218.

[11] Cf. *Creation des Valeurs*, chapter XV, III.

[12] Max Scheler, *Situation de l'homme dans le monde* (Paris, Aubier, 1951), p. 72.

them, we can know what a man is not — a God, or an animal, or a thing, an object which is possessed and which can be used and abused. However, there are not sufficient elements to determine positively what his sense is and whether the human has a uniform and necessary sense. Speech, as freedom, is the instrument of any end, of any realization, just as is reason, for reason can be understood as a simple rational method, a simple coherent calculation for thinking and acting, and, in a larger sense, as the method of a metaphysical constitution of the world and of oneself. None of these attributes, as essential as they may be to the human, can dictate a choice from among the possible values of man. None of them is sufficient to establish a value of man which they would necessarily imply and which would be self-evident. The essence of the human — freedom, consciousness, speech, reason — is not sufficient to determine, or to make determinable, either his value or his sense. A choice must still be made.

This choice can be a lucid one. The more lucid it is the more human it is. But it can be simply experienced in the exercise of a freedom still in itself which is evidenced even in its most immediate passions.

It would be necessary to establish, not the substantialistic elements of a human nature, which can always be surpassed by the exercise of its freedom, but the sense of the function of freedom; the sense and the value of the human. This is no longer a question of the determination of a universal essence but of a creation of values, of a creative decision, of the assigning of a meaning to a transcendence in act, of a plan of work and, consequently, of a practical theory.

II

The sense of the human is not based on a scientific observation with which all would unanimously agree. The determination of the sense of a human existence only has bearing on an already complete and entirely given being when this being is a dead person. And this appreciation, which has lost its practical reach, remains hypothetical, for it pertains to a realization which is neutral in itself, whose sense, always subject to requestioning, must be indefinitely supposed, interpreted and appreciated anew.[13] If it is a question of a living being, this appreciation affirms the sense and proposes the value of a being yet to be made and who will result from an accomplishment to be realized.

To determine the sense of man is to assign each time to his function as man a specific end, to treat him as a value, the polar value around

---

[13] *Création des Valeurs,* Chapter XXIV.

which the world of men and the constellation of their values should be ordered in relation to him. It is to establish the significance he should take on in relation to all other things, thereby constituting a moral and metaphysical option, and even the fundamental presupposition, the first value of a metaphysics, at the same time that it constitutes one of the decisive values of reference in relation to which every practical creative attitude can be defined. For every definition of man, in this strong sense, there is a corresponding conception of the world and an effort to make it true, a certain value which man should assume in it and a certain 'sense of the function he should fill there. This is why every great definition of man aspires to announce a period in his history and the sense of the work which he should accomplish in it, even if it usually only succeeds in summarizing a period of his history and understanding the task he has accomplished in it.

Whatever major definition of man is considered, we realize that man as such is defined by vocation and, so to speak, by the profession which he assigns himself. His function as man takes on a meaning in relation to the value he proposes to actualize and to which he feels bound by an obligation. A definition of man is fundamentally a moral definition, as it is affirmed as a value and imposed as a duty. Man is, for himself, that unique species of being whose distinguishing characteristic is that in him his existence is inseparable from his value and that it depends on it; to be a man is to be obliged to have value, it is to exist for a value, to exist to have value. It is, at the least, to be capable of value, capable of obligation, capable of morality.

This idea of capacity, of a given which is merely potential, in which is contained an aptitude open to a certain type of thought and action, and which is not the germ in which an ulterior development is inscribed and determined in an immanent fashion, permits us to preserve a sense to the concept of the free man. The notion of 'faculty' [14] has often been treated with disdain or considered outmoded; but in fact, it is chiefly its caricature which has been criticized,[15] while the notion itself, in flexible forms and under various names has never ceased being used to describe the initial "given" by which man is recognized: powers, aptitudes, func-

---

[14] Still recently, M. Heidegger, "Dépassement de la métaphysique," in *Essais et Conférences,* translated by Andre Preau (Paris, Gallimard, 1958), p. 87.

[15] Let us note, moreover, that Locke himself, who willingly used the concept of faculty, already specified that it had to be understood in the sense of potential aptitude, and that by faculties he designated, not distinct beings but certain manners of thinking or acting which had sense only in relation to an agent (*Essay Concerning Human Understanding,* Book II, chap. XXI, article 17).

tions, factors, qualities, traits. It has the merit, if necessary, of permitting us to attribute to this given merely a purely formal and functional sense which is suitable to a given which is simply potential, and even to a nature whose distinguishing characteristic is, according to the Kantian formula, to do freely its nature.

We shall assign ourselves the task of reviewing the study of the characteristic aptitudes of man, viewed in a purely functional form, and of studying the sense of everything that might concern his practical existence. We shall take as a guiding line the idea that, if each of the four traditionally recognized traits — freedom, consciousness of self and of the future, speech, reason — remains in itself formal, negative, and strictly indeterminant, the convergence of the four, on the contrary, orientates the elaboration of a value and a sense of human reality.

Man is not born free, he is born capable of freedom. What he brings with life, at the time of his birth, is a simple power of negation which he will learn, in a slow and uncertain fashion and perhaps, but not necessarily, to use. Freedom thus conceived is not describable in terms of being any more than in terms of nothingness. It is an act of going beyond all "givens," of escaping all determination; in other words, it is transcendence in act. Man is not free; he frees himself; in any case, he can have this power. He frees himself first by resistance to and refusal of himself, of the given and of others, by reacting in an unpredictable fashion to the influences he is made to undergo, by surpassing the determinations to which he is subjected, by making himself other than what the pressure of the given, by itself, would determine him to be. This power of negation begins to become act when man becomes able to speak and able for a reasonable motive, whatever it may be, to say no. The first experience and the first test of a liberation reside in the power to say no, even at the cost of life and for values created for oneself. This is the Hegelian experience of the formation of man, who triumphs over his animality and frees himself by prefering to life, as a biological value, invented values, a vanity, a prestige.

In this power of negation could be seen but a power of destruction and annihilation, or the principle of a death struggle among men. This would be to forget that this negation, which is transcendence in act, is not a negation for nothing, but an act of transcending, of going towards a beyond which one creates for oneself and imposes upon oneself, of which one is oneself the author and the sole responsible party. All of the effectiveness of negation, refusal, abandonment and rupture comes from affirmation, from creation of an "other," which is yet but a vain value which remains to be entirely made and to be made real in an accomplishment. The progress of creation is carried out in a permanent going and coming between a creation of values which is creation of a nothing, of an entirely unreal project, of a future which is not yet, and the effective and efficient transformation of a "given," the order of which is, alternately, undone and remade, destroyed and recreated. Negation is only freedom only because it is creation. Man is not freed towards nothingness and by means of annihilation any more than he is freed towards the being or is made free by it; he is freed in the process of a positive creation.

Neither can there be any question of attributing an absolute character to this creation, or a divine, so to speak, act of an absolute freedom — so absolute that it would be unconditional and unlimited. This would be like asserting that creative action consists of a succession, without continuity, of radical creations produced in each instance from nothing, like instantaneously disappearing flashes of lightning. According to such a myth, we would have to say that by denying the given and rising above it, man would be delivered of all attachments which are exterior and anterior to him; by transcending himself and treating what he has just been as nothingness, he would discover himself in his dizzying freedom; but it would be freedom of a nothing and for nothing. On the contrary, freedom does not reside in a radical discontinuity, in a sort of ontological hiatus, but in the positive, but limited act of an imperfect, entirely human act. Creation does not reside in a nihilistic negation, however total it may be, but in the laborious elaboration of an accomplishment which is freed little by little from a certain given and which, in its imperfect newness, preserves and surpasses the anterior given, according to the classic schema of Hegelian *Aufhebung*.

This is why, as the tradition descended from Hegel asserts, every man is entirely in what he does. He becomes with the advancement of his accomplishment and only continues to exist by pursuing it. He is not freed from the accomplished realization except by the next realization. He is not preserved except by surpassing himself. As such, our freedom constantly allows every man to refuse, whether it be at the risk of his life, a historically given situation or an element thereof. From this effort of liberation which takes place in history and develops throughout the indefinitely repeated advancement of a project of value towards its realization, is born what will form the second experience and the second marked by an essential unpredictability. The human resides in this newmarked by an essential unpredictability. The human resides in this newness; humble innovations, which do not surpass the simple formation and education of oneself; striking innovations which revolutionize the styles of living of a whole group of men. The sum of all of these radical inventions constitutes little by little through integration, in an unceasing accumulation of preserved and surpassed realizations, an entirely human world which serves as a mediation between man and the natural raw given. Civilizations, non-natural accomplishments of men, serve as proofs, as sufficient testimonies to the existence of a human power to create. In this indefinite repetition of finished accomplishments into new accomplishments, a civilization, devoid of a sufficient natural inertia to be, is preserved only if it is constantly re-invented and transformed into a history. The human force of freedom, which is carried out in a dialectic of every man with his civilization, is a creator of history; there would be no history without creative freedom. Man is capable of history, the history of the creation of his works, inasmuch as he is capable of freedom. All of the history of men is the history of their freedom.

We are thus radically opposed to philosophies which, as is implied in Freud's thought, concentrate man in his past, in his "archeology," and reduce him to being but a destiny. For us, if man is not without given conditions, he is, he tends to be, he must be, in his future and through his freedom. Despite his abandonments, his failures, and his downfalls, and even with them, he exists in a history.

To affirm that man is capable of free creation is to recognize that nothing is either definitively or totally given, that no order is ever ineluctable, that the sense of things and of oneself always remains to be made and remade, at the same time as one's own civilization and one's own history.

The historical signification of man begins, indeed, with the affirmation of his creative freedom. But freedom is not a sufficient definition of man — if freedom as such is a value it only has the value of a mean; it is the universal mean for all values. It is the form of all possible functions which are characteristically human, but it is not sufficient to define any of them as necessary. This is because it can be freedom for any sense, for any value, for any obligation, according to any law. Only freedom as such can furnish man with a definition which is, in spite of everything, negative.

However, if freedom is not an absolute power to create, but a finite and limited power, is there not, by virtue of this finitude, this limitation, the indication of a human sense, or, at least, the orientation towards a properly human sense?

There is, in effect, an inherent limit in the idea of freedom, which distinguishes it from the power of radical creation which is sometimes called, for lack of a better term, divine, because we would find ourselves in the presence of the pure indeterminate. We can never call freedom this power of absolute creativity without having recourse to mystery and without leaving philosophy for theology. There is no freedom as such. A freedom is a relation. Freedom only takes on meaning in relation to a given, and more precisely, in relation to a given which is defined by its order. We do not speak of freedom without supposing that we are freed in relation to something; in relation to the ordinal structures of this thing. The concept of freedom remains hollow and empty (so much so that it can be filled with the divine, which is totality of sense, as with the indeterminate, which is absence of sense) as long as it is not liberation to an order. The order in question, and whether this order is a particular one or a universal one, is of little importance. Every freedom only takes on meaning according to the meaning of the order from which it is freed.

The idea of order is no less essential to the idea of freedom than it is to the idea of theory. The study of the relations of order with freedom joins the study of the relations of order with theory.

For the Ancients, as for all those for whom the idea of a perfect universal order which is full of meaning is predominant, the concept of freedom is a minor concept: freedom is often defined as the development, the accomplishment of that which is, in accordance with the order which is like a germ within it and which is immanent in it. In this sense freedom is combined with the necessary becoming of the being. Or the concept of freedom is sometimes limited to that which develops in accordance with the order immanent in it, and does not encounter any obstacles or oppositions which are exterior to its own being. One can talk, in a derivative sense, of the freedom of the citizen in the City. This definition of freedom can be in accordance with the strictest necessitarianism, as in Hobbes. It can result, as in Descartes, in the affirmation that man is never more free than when he judges under the constraint (which is within him) of the evidence or, as in Spinoza, in the definition of freedom as an understandable necessity. In any case, such freedom is good freedom.

Philosophers themselves unanimously condemn bad freedom, which would be deviation from order and which would engender the corruption or the destruction of order. By whatever name it is called — arbitrariness, caprice or license — this bad freedom, which is freedom in appearance only, only causes, moreover, the development of the forces of disorders which are immanent to order itself. It does not represent a liberation, but the appearance of that part of evil which is inherent in order.

Or order can be considered as given only in its principles or in its form; it is imperfect, fluid, or in the act of becoming, and it depends on men to realize effectively this order, either continuously, by each one of them in the City (this is how Locke or Kant would conceive it), or in the gradual development of men (as Hegel would have it). Freedom consists of the power to make real the essential order inscribed in the nature of things and of men; it is a power of effective realization, but it remains a free power, linked with an obligation, and not with a necessary determination. At the same time, and reciprocally, this same freedom, which is capable of constructing a real order in accordance with the essential order, can be considered as the end of this order. While freedom is obligated to the law, the law consists in an obligation to freedom. Freedom is a result of the fact that man's relation to order does not consist of a necessary determination, but of an obligation. This means, here again, that freedom has no meaning except in relation to an order and by virtue of an order.

Finally, as we have chosen to show, when no previous order is given, either in the form of a divine presence, or in the form of an ontological structure, or in the form of immanent and essential necessity, or in the form of historic determination, or in the form of law, freedom takes the form in which it asserts itself as a veritable first beginning, as a power sufficient to be determined exclusively by itself and which takes all of its effectiveness from itself alone. It appears as a creative freedom; that is, as a freedom in the full sense of the term, which not only chooses, but invents the terms of its choice, which is capable of being freed from all previous given order and, by transforming it, of surpassing it and of adding to it, from itself, a radical innovation. But, as it risks falling into pure indetermination and becoming freedom of a nothing and for nothing, as it risks being deprived of all meaning and degenerating into insignificant gratuitousness, nonsense, and the absurd, freedom is freedom for an order, in view of an order to be established or imposed, beginning from a set of given conditions.

The innovation which freedom creates can only be recognized as innovation if it participates in a new order, if it serves as a reference for an order, if it provides its coordinates. That is to say that a creation is not recognized as such except when it is the creation of an order. The relation between freedom and order is maintained, but freedom for an order, freedom creating order, preserves its pure character of integral freedom, as it itself gives the principles of this order, which is an order to come and to be made. Freedom exists only in relation to the future.

Not only does freedom for order escape caprice and arbitrariness, but it maintains a meaning in the creation it accomplishes. What is essential to the idea of order, and all the more when it is a case of a plan for order, is not an ontological structure, but the presence of an understandable and justifiable meaning. Order is signification, because it is conceived essentially as a system of comprehensible relations; relations full of the meaning of the elements of order in relation to one another and to the whole. An order without meaning would not be conceived and justified as an acknowledged order.

Thus creation, through the order that it establishes, strives for an intelligible system. It seeks itself out and gives itself a meaning which will fully satisfy those who understand created order. Through order, the act of creation is thus founded at the same time that it is understood. Freedom is not founded on itself, as has sometimes been said; it is not for itself its own foundation, but is founded on the intelligibility and the effective understanding of the task it seeks to accomplish. The order which free creation is obliged to project and to accomplish is, then, an order of which there would be an intelligible theory. The imperative which can be drawn from the analysis of theory in its relations with practice,[16] "Act in such a way that your work may have an intelligible theory," is the essential and characteristic obligation of man in his capacity of man.

The powers traditionally recognized as being characteristic of man — speech, consciousness of itself and for the future, reason — take their signification from this creative function of order and sense, for which they serve as the instrument.

First of all, this human freedom that strives to create in order to establish an intelligible order is not only freedom for consciousness but consciousness by freedom. Consciousness of itself is at the end of its task. It is not consciousness which is hidden freedom progressively uncovered, but freedom which is consciousness in itself entirely directed towards its end, which should be consciousness for itself. Freedom is intension of consciousness for oneself and for the future. It exists, man exists, for the future, for a future which is his accomplishment, his order. The time to come is the temporal dimension of freedom. Whereas the animal resides entirely in his past, in his heredity, whereas the thing is nothing before or beyond its present, man is much more in the work to be made than in the accomplished work, which only takes on meaning in relation to the next intention. The most impor-

---

[16] R. Polin, *Ethique et Politique,* p. 37.

tant always remains to be done; there is always something more to be done as long as one does not renounce oneself. Whether it is thought, desire or action, the future counts indefinitely more than the past. Man's life is made of waiting, desire, hope or fear, as the future is the only field open to this freedom. The affective echoes attached to this orientation towards the future have been complacently presented as fundamental experiences. Let us merely note that this orientation does not lead to any effective consequence which is necessary and suitable to characterizing the human; one can react by ardor and hope as well as by anguish and worry. Risk and adventure are no less human values than surety and security. The outcome always remains to be invented and realized. But, across the multiple projects through which freedom advances, is made, and sometimes unmade, persists this striving for a future which is more ordered, more intelligible.

Speech provides the means and already the first manifestation of reflective freedom. Through speech, we attain distance in regard to ourselves at the same time that the acquired consciousness of ourselves becomes all the more lucid and clear as we become better able to make it explicit through words. We rely on the permanence of discourse through which we express ourselves in order to stretch and break the ties by which immediate and confused sensed existence binds us.

Some philosophers have complacently stressed the dialectic of expression which takes place between the self and its language, and which always maintains the distance and inadequacy of the one in relation to the other. But, instead of reflecting retrospectively and morosely on the essential and inexhaustible obstacles to the communication of consciousnesses, we should stress, in the perspective of a philosophy of action, the accords which actually are established despite the unavoidable persistence of all of the ignorances, all of the ambiguities, all of the misunderstandings, and in spite of their ineffaceable persistence. This inadequacy to be reduced indefinitely, this unsurmountable distance to try to surmount, this obscurity which is never entirely enlightened — all of this is the field constantly proposed for human action. This inadequacy is essential to existence because it forms the relationship, the distance between freedoms irreducible among themselves inasmuch as they are freedoms. These long-distance accords through the uncertain, the ambiguous, the unknown, the obscure, make up all of the thickness and the density of human relations and provide the opportunities for their fecundity.

We can justifiably stress the fact that we are never more, for ourselves and for others, than what we can express effectively in a language.

Speech, in the dialogue which it makes possible with others, is the condition of the establishment of our truth; it alone gives our acts a meaning which we can assume. Despite the current idolatry for the sensed thing, speech alone engages us. Even in its imperfect aspects, this inadequacy is the sign of a freedom; speech is an act of freedom by its very nature. By permitting us to take on distance in regard to ourselves and to make an abstraction of ourselves, it permits us to transform and make ourselves. Perhaps we are never better ourselves in all our humanity than at this high point of abstraction and freedom where we express ourselves and where we already escape ourselves, in our work or in our speech.

By transposing the sensed world onto a world of signification and symbols, into a universe of discourse, speech frees from the immediate environment or from its hold. It substitutes for sets of powers and for mechanical determinations, not only systems of signs and of comprehensible motivations, but even sets of symbols which cannot be reduced to simple relations of significations.[17] Beyond signs attached to their objects by immediate relations, symbolic thought invents expressions which are adaptable, available, open and universal. Every language, and even conceptual language, frees us from the natural and immediate world and allows us to construct, from more or less implicit conventions and in the interaction of discourse, a human order in which speech can be sufficient cause and in which it is sufficient to command in order to give order. The verb, the symbol of creation, is freedom itself.

Speech, for every man, represents the power to make his freedom manifest to others, to try to make it understood and recognized by them. (Hegel had said that the being for itself does not reach full consciousness of itself unless it is acknowledged by another, and all the more so inasmuch as this other is itself the more a being for itself.) Speech represents and expresses that which, in freedom, is for others. It is freedom for others. It is consequently the proof that everyone exists only by and for others. Freedom is freedom full of meaning only when it is freedom for others. The intelligible order to which freedom is obligated is necessarily an order for others, for others are the major obstacles encountered by the effort to be free and they are the major constraints to which freedom is subjected. The individual himself is only an individual inasmuch as he expresses himself to others and his freedom is only freedom if it is comprehensible to them. As the Ancients liked to observe, speech implies the essential sociability of man. What is true for speech is true for freedom, which is the symbol of speech: man is only free because he is social.

---

[17] Ernst Cassirer, *Essay on Man*, pp. 54-57.

The human species is a species whose distinguishing characteristic, said Bergson, is to be composed of individuals who constitute each in himself a species composed of a unique individual. If the model for a truly human value were proposed to a human individual who was isolated from all other men and abstracted from all of the sociability which is inherent in him, no single solution would be more probable or more reasonable than another. For an individual who had no other obligations than those imposed upon him by a solipsistic freedom, all value, all meanings would be equally plausible and possible. If he were only interested in his projects, the individual would close himself up alone, like a sort of madman of nature in an uncommunicable world. The radically solitary individual, cut off from all men, would be inhuman and like a stranger, an alien among them; his freedom without rules or reasons would obviate his very use of speech, which would henceforth go unused, and everything would take place as if he had no reason. The presence of others, necessary to the existence of every man, brings the individual back to humanity. The more he shows signs of a personality, of an originality, which means that he is himself, unique, incomparable, and through another, the more he develops his humanity and his signification for others. It should be recognized that, not only is sociability essential to man, but, as Auguste Comte proclaimed, it belongs, in its greatest sense, only to him.

The question of man's essential sociability was often decided, of old, by resorting to the voice of reason, making of sociability a natural law revealed by reason. In truth, this was a simple tautology; the essential presence of others, inherent in every man, implies a necessary research for the common, and soon for the universal, the obligation to reason. The presence of others, like the obligation to intelligibility, implies the institution of an order which we tend to make, step by step, universal. Freedom is obligated to reason because it is freedom in view of the universal, which is its work.

As Locke wrote, we are capable of freedom as we are capable of reason. To be capable of reason, to be obligated to reason, means that we are obligated to the research of the universal, obligated to a comprehension shared with others of an order which we have constructed with them and with this intention. Reason is not behind us, nor even within us, but ahead of us. And the reasonable order which we hope and want to construct, which we try to institute effectively, has its principle of universality in the intention which makes us research it and construct it: to institute an order such that it can be justified by its meaning and raised to the level of universality. This intention of order corresponds to a desire and to an obligation, but also to a necessity, as we cannot do anything freely, without obstacle or constraint, unless we make ourselves universal. To be fully recognized in our universal freedom, in our reasonable freedom — this is the condition of our fulfillment as man, of our satisfaction, of our peace.

A perfectly human value should be concentrated around a theory of man which can serve as a universal principle of intelligibility; a human existence will find its most human meaning when, by virtue of original culture, it rises to that zone of intelligibility where men and, at best, all men, can succeed in understanding and acknowledging their differences under the unity of a reasonable theory, in free consent to the theory and to the others.

III

We would hope to have preserved in the definition of man the most general patterns of tradition. If it does not accord with the most commonplace accepted definitions, how can we hope that it will suit future definitions? How can we hope to obtain an easy consent to a practical theory, a consent which is essential to its efficacity, if it disturbs and divides by its newness and its paradoxes?

By determining the fundamental intention of human values without fixing a unique value to which all men would be obligated, we hope to preserve the open, so to speak, character of the definition of man. There are no limits to the creative freedom of the values of man. From man as a value there can be achievements and determinations of infinite number. The distinguishing characteristic of man is not that he is indefinable, but indefinitely definable. Humanity is the species to which there is always a new definition to be given. Man must always remain open.

If a definition of man exceeds the historical bearing of a value to be accomplished, in so doing it exposes its own insufficiency; hence the weakness of a humanism which strives to erect in absolutes a possible definition of man. In presenting it as eternal, it blocks it in a position which is necessarily inadequate to the human in general. And every humanism is inclined to present itself dogmatically as the unique and exclusive doctrine of man and to shut itself up in a moralizing sermon. But neither should we, by calling Heraclitus and Parmenides to the rescue, as has sometimes been done, fall into an anti-humanism which has as its dogma the primacy of the being over the human. The Heideggerian attempt to constitute an ontological humanism results in making man reside in the being; it reduces him to being no more than the revelation of the destiny of the being, the discovery of the truth of the being. It is not man, he says, but the being which makes man exist. The substance of man is to remain within the truth of the being, his native land, or, more exactly, it is *das ekstatische Innestehens der Wahrheit des Seins*.[18] By condemning the traditional humanisms, Heidegger wants to refuse man, the citizen and shepherd of the being, any subjective and practical signification. Here is a paradox as intolerable as it is brilliant. It is the history of man, and not the history of the being which is important to the practical, which is a theory of freedom and, consequently, a theory of the individual-subject. Freedom is inseparable from its ethical and subjective signification. By identifying the being with destiny, necessity, truth and thought itself, does not Heidegger shut himself up, and man along with him, in a theory without a practice? Does he not turn his back on action, which makes up the whole of man?

The classic "Become what you are" would be inhuman because it would exclude man from his obligation to creative freedom; in any case, it is empty and vain, because it is completely indeterminate. Every time we invoke man as man, man as such, man in his humanity, we are appealing to an empty form which, deprived of any intrinsic sense, can apply to any merchandise. Man is not defined by a formal tautology which repeats his essential attributes — which are purely formal and functional and which make him merely available for something else — but by the position and the research for another than himself; that is, by the realization of ends exterior to his essence, to which he is obligated and which give his function a sense. Man is not born human; he is born potentially human; he is educated, matures and becomes human through invention and the conquest of other than himself. He is transformed into man by mastering the other, which he considers as other, by integrating him with himself, by humanizing him, but by humanizing himself, by reciprocal action, in this test. In this educational training, man has come out of himself and is made by projecting himself outside of and beyond himself.

In other terms, man is only made by becoming, by transforming himself, and, consequently, by alienating himself. But, as Hegel affirmed, and despite Marx, all alienation does not necessarily lead to a loss of freedom and subservience; it merely entails the risk of that eventuality. On the contrary, it is even fundamentally the exercise of freedom in its gradual development. To be free is never to develop and become what one is in a simple explication of oneself; one is never free, one frees oneself.

---

[18] M. Heidegger, *Über den Humanismus* (Frankfurt, Klostermann, 1947), p. 19.

This freeing of oneself is not merely a simple exteriorization of oneself, nor even of an "objectification," after the manner of Hegel; this is a liberation going beyond in regard to oneself and to one's conditions, a transformation. One is freed from what one was, one becomes different, other, new, foreign. Every work accomplished implies an alienation. The work which one completes oneself temporarily and from which one has always to be freed risks, certainly, falling into the grasp and the mastery of others; but this is a second, redoubled alienation; it is the bad alienation justly denounced by Marx. But the bad alienation is never but a contingent accident of the good one, which is the alienation necessary to every liberation. Moreover, it always remains possible, if need be, to escape the accident of a bad alienation: one can always be freed of one's own works, no longer to reside within them. One can always escape them as it is their essence to escape us. Does not freedom, by essence, and in everyone, carry the obligation never to rest on one's accomplished works, on one's dead works, and to go beyond, indefinitely?

Far from becoming what he is, man expresses himself in his accomplishment, pushes and projects outside of himself the man which he makes of himself. His vocation, his obligation, consists of expressing himself, himself and all things, in an intelligible, that is, comprehensive and comprehensible manner. To exist is to express oneself in a significant manner and for values. Man, who is the indeterminate being, but the capacity and the means to all senses, has as his sense to give sense, to give a sense. Everyone is, in his way, the artist and the artisan of himself: in a language which he forges for himself and which — this is what is sometimes called his style — belongs to him in his own right, whether it is a question of words, poems, forms, colors, sounds, gestures, affective effusions, acts, or works, he expresses himself. By dint of expressing himself for others, man becomes more and more human.

All of these values put down by man, which form his ends and his duties, are only defined by signs exterior to him; they appear to him in the form of goods which are located exterior to him. Man's ends are always outside of man and, so to speak, inhuman, as long as they have not been integrated into an intelligible order and humanized. Consider the ideals which so often serve him as landmarks: eternal salvation, charity, mastery of nature, happiness, strength, glory, security, peace, fortune, culture, absolute knowledge, or, simply, preservation of life and health. Each one taken apart can be sufficient to make another or all of the others unjustifiable and arbitrary. The affirmation of a certain value of man is the result, not of a necessary analytical liason between the essence of man and his meaning, but of a creative and, in a way, arbitrary synthesis, as long as it has not been set up as the principle of a reasonable order and thus made justifiable.

Every humanism is inclined to go beyond the aspects of accessibility and openness, which are characteristic of the function of man, to become immobile and fixed in a limiting and, finally, inhuman definition of the human. The insufficience of a humanism comes from its necessarily closed attitude towards that which makes up its essence, and this closing can never be essential to man. This is why a humanism always risks degenerating into an anti-humanism.

Christian humanism runs this risk when it defines the human creature by its anguished finitude and by the fragility of a freedom caught between original corruption and hope for eternal salvation, and it runs this risk no less when it maintains the existence of a truly divine charity. This is the risk to which succumbs Nietzsche's superhumanism, which claims to be opposed to all humanisms which are merely human, but which only succeeds, as soon as it takes a positive turn, in immobilizing man for eternity, beyond himself, in the use of force for the sake of force — unless it flies away on the wings of myth and mystique, towards a poetic and purely symbolic dream of an eternal return of every instant. Marxist humanism would escape more easily a risk of this order, inasmuch as Marx does not give it a positive definition, even in his youthful works. He does say that man is to accomplish his function as man in the same way that the eye is to accomplish its function, that is, to see. But although the accomplishment of man who is truly man gives history its meaning, for Marx, the concept of man is indeterminable from within history. Marxist humanism takes on a positive meaning only in relation to a political tactic and by means of concrete condemnations of that which dehumanizes man and alienates the human in him. Just as the Christian God was the object of a negative theology, Marxist man is the object of a negative anthropology.

As every humanism is an art of expression, expression for the other than oneself, expression through the mediation of the nonhuman, every humanism can only be viable and supportable if it has will to be, as well as an art of making understood, an art of comprehension.

The human vocation of expression is deformed and corrupted when it strives for the unreciprocal triumph of one system of expression over others. The obligation to express oneself implies the obligation to understand or, in other words, man has the right to express himself only if he imposes upon himself the obligation to understand. There is no admissible humanism which is not an open and accessible humanism, a humanism of call and openness, and not a humanism of refusal and of combat. This is the only way to give man's essential freedom its double signification of liberation through negotiation and also liberation through the creation of intelligibility.

Every humanism, as every man, should be available for other than himself, ready to transcend himself. There is no ultimate humanism; there is no supreme form of the human, of man perfectly man, after which the art of being man would be no more than an art of imitation and of repetition. There is no model of perfect man, no necessary archetype. There is no end to the history of men, either by the completion of a perfect man, or by the appearance of a superman or of a superhumanity. If we hope to preserve for freedom a human sense and a permanent sense, we must even refuse to enclose the formation of the human in a unique history which develops progressively and necessarily immanent potentialities, or which moves towards a necessary end and perfection. There is no single history of man, but an infinity of histories of men, and only the most general among them are established, in proportion to the values of man which have blossomed or which will blossom in momentarily triumphant civilizations.

The paths taken by the human are infinite in number, as men compensate their finitude with the infinitude and the plurality of their history. But these are always paths of expression and comprehension of men among themselves; by silence or by speech, these paths go from the most mystical to the most conceptual, from the most perceptible and the most existential to the most reflective and the most philosophical. What matters is the type, the degree, and the universality of intelligibility that they make possible. This is because the universality of man lies only abstractly and potentially in his essential attributes: freedom, consciousness, speech, reason; and thus is always potentially contradicted by the diversity and the particularity of its individual realizations. But the concrete universality of men lies, at the end of their efforts, at the highest summits of their civilizations, in the communion of those who have risen to the most perfect forms of culture.

As far as we can see, the only humanism which remains perfectly open and accessible is that which proposes a reasonable theory of man and of the world; reasonable in that it can, in principle, be intelligible to, and agreed upon by all those who want freely to submit to the obligation of universality. The most human man, the man who has arrived at the most advanced humanity, will be he who will "act in such a way that there can be an intelligible theory of his work." That man will have submitted, in complete freedom, to the obligation to be man.

In this perspective, there will be many ways and many degrees in the realization of a man's humanity. The formation of a man, the realization of his most human accomplishment, is a question of talent, chance and

education. The educational formation of every individual does not constitute a homogenous progress; it is composed of variations of factors
which are very independent of one another. Everything depends, first of
all, on biological growth, and on the maturation, so to speak, of every
individual. The adult state can be defined as the state man reaches when
he can effectively use the ordinary powers of the human race, which
means at the very least the ability to preserve oneself and those one
engenders, by means of an autonomous conduct: consciousness of oneself and of one's speech, a sense of one's responsibilities in regard to
others and in regard to the future, the ability to regulate one's conduct
by virtue of a rational calculation. In this regard, men come very unequally to realize this model, as it were, of the human being, and some,
despite their age, never reach a finished adult state.

Onto this first growth curve is superimposed the development of the
culture we acquire through the assimilation and use of the knowledge,
arts and techniques which are characteristic of the civilization to which
we belong, and which in turn gives place to very varied achievements.
Belonging to a civilization actually means belonging to a multiplicity of
groups which are more or less consistent and compatible, more or less
opposed and irreducible. By participating in a number of them, each
person acquires morals, values, opinions, certain ways of acting and
thinking which form for him the given conditions of his existence — an
acquired formation, a formation which is all the more difficult to transcend and to dominate the more deeply integrated it has been right from
childhood. And yet, to live these conditions humanly is to transcend
them and to make oneself master of them. However, they often finally
determine lives which are poorly human and which, dominated by their
childhood, their "archeology," become the exclusive prey of their past
and submit to their destiny. Truly human lives, while succeeding in
transcending their conditions and in existing in regard to their future,
never cease to remain relative to the conditions of their history.

Without pretending to settle the problems of knowing what part education and experience which are lived can play in the development of
virtue, we must also give special emphasis to the progress of moral
qualities, to the evolution in each man of his virtues and vices. And
finally, there is the manifestation of the extraordinary powers of certain
men and the intellectual and moral achievement by which a man participates effectively in the creation of a civilizations, makes himself recognized as the author and the principle of an order which he has made
intelligible and, so doing, has reached that high point of veritable origi-

nality and uniqueness which can be made perceptible and comprehensible to all.

We must nevertheless not forget that human value of a man does not depend merely upon himself and on the art with which he puts his talents to work. Hegel said once that every man is the son of his people or of his time. Of course we must devote a place to those individuals who can truly be called historical, to those creatures who spring out of the margins of civilizations or who, almost alone, succeed in founding one, giving it its values, its meaning and its laws. But, except when the truly exceptional bearing of a creation transcends the limits of civilizations, the degree of human accomplishment to which we see men rising can hardly be separated from the value of their civilization. One is rarely more a man than are the best of those with whom one lives. One can hardly rise to a degree of humanity which is different from that to which belong the institutions upon which one depends.

Under these conditions, it is entirely probable that all of the individuals belonging to the human species will realize very different forms and degrees of human value. Certainly, in principle, and that is sufficient to assure the unity of the human species, it is possible for everyone to obey the obligation to be man and to participate in the organization of an intelligible order, since all men are capable of freedom, speech and reason and since these are the sufficient instruments of their humanity. But with the potential equality among men correspond, according to the hazards of aptitudes, the successes of educational formation and the chance of events, profound and real inequalities among them. The equality of men among themselves has become a common bond and we have made of egalitarian ideas the mark of our time. [19] Egalitarian ideology, which sometimes takes on the form of a myth, masks the abstract quality of all equality among men, whether we make of it the consequence of a universal metaphysical definition of the human species, or the judicial condition of the existence of a political community. For lack of a natural equality in fact, philosophers, like Hobbes or Rousseau, have sought out very subtle means of determining the equality which they consider necessary to the realization of a social contract. And, within the framework of equality of civil and political rights, we witness around us, in numerous modern regimes, an equality which Aristotle would have called proportional (as opposed to an arithmetical equality),[20]

---

[19] C. Bouglé, *Essai sur les idées inégalitaires* (Paris, Alcan, 1905).

[20] Aristotle, *Nichomachean Ethics*, ed. W. D. Ross (London, Oxford University Press), Vol. IX, Book V, 6, 1134a.

which applies the law to the actual inequality of powers, merits, accomplishments and situations.

As for the value of man, this is not a specific given which we bring with us at birth, but a value we create ourselves, which we realize more or less completely, and the merit of which we acquire. The spiritual, moral and social completion, by which a man freely binds himself to contributing to the most intelligible order and accomplishes in the most harmonious fashion his function of reasonable creation, is profoundly unequal among men. Although they are all recognizable by essential structures, the members of the human race will all deserve unequally the name and a value of men, for they will be, according to their accomplishments and in history, more or less human. We cannot be kept, at the very least, from distinguishing among those who, by a sort of breach of duty, have excluded themselves from humanity and have forfeited their rights as man; those, innumerable, who, due to their age or their inaptitude, have not been capable of fulfilling their obligations as man, nevertheless maintaining hope and rights; and those finally who, by their works and their merits, have given proof of a value of man and can fully claim qualification as human. Whether they are at fault or not, all men are not by a long stretch effectively and equally human.

It must be said: men are born neither free nor equal. They are born capable of freedom and capable of reason. Reason advises that we make equality, which is not a natural power, an artificial right wherever freedom is fulfilled by obedience to a law. In a reasonable political community, the citizens are obliged to obey the egalitarian systems of the law. They must be kept, by laws, from the excess of wealth and power and led to remain so by morals.

But where freedom is creative it becomes incompatible with actual equality. To maintain, eyes closed, the contrary, whether by charity, naiveté or hypocrisy, is to discredit the abstract equality in civil rights and by the law, which are nevertheless indispensable to the effective protection of the creative freedom which is potentially in everyone. It is, at the same time, to destroy the effort of those who, recognizing that inequality is essential to social structure, to the essentially hierarchical structures of the collective enterprises of men, fear the mortal dangers of its excess and abuse, and try to contain it within moderate and reasonable bounds. Beyond this, and even in spite of what he has not yet done or what he has already done, what counts above all to a man is his irreducible potential for freedom, and what he can still do with it. It is the power to make oneself human which should always, by convention, be equally protected in all.

All men deserve equally protection and assistance, protection and education for all that there is in them of possible human value, for everything of which they are virtually capable. For everything that they are potentially, which is sufficient to define a human species and to distinguish them from all other beings and things, they have a dignity which deserves equal respect in all.

For truly human men who participate in a truly creative humanity, systems of simply egalitarian distribution, which are concerned merely with the distribution of consumption, and not production and creation, are not suitable. For those men, who appeal to one another and encounter one another throughout ages and civilizations, is reserved that generous esteem Descartes spoke of and which they should accord one another to the highest degree to which it is reasonable to do so.*

LA SORBONNE, PARIS.

---

* Translated by Edouard Morot-Sir and Barbara Reid.

ESSENCE REVISITED

JACK KAMINSKY

In his interesting paper, the distinguished visitor from the Sorbonne, Professor Raymond Polin, seeks to bring back a degree of philosophical respectability to the concept of essence. Polin argues that it is no longer intellectually tenable to think of essence in the traditional sense of a nature that is implicit in all men and which, under the proper conditions, can and ought to come to fruition. Traditionally, an analogy was drawn between the physical and the moral maturation of human beings. Men developed physically and, ideally, were expected to develop morally, which meant that they were to strive to behave in accordance with a given set of a priori moral concepts. But the analogy has ceased to be influential in the contemporary period and, as Polin points out, men no longer feel compelled to acknowledge the inherent validity of any a priori set of moral views. Man is indeed free in the existentialist sense that he can make his own tomorrow. And here we have, according to Polin, what truly characterizes the human essence. Human beings can act freely; they can recast the present into a more desirable future without any prior commitments. Nothing in the past or the present or the future determines what men ought to become or even what they will become. They might be compelled by others and thus be destroyed or incarcerated; they might be forced against their will to fight for causes they take to be unjust, but the compulsion is always by men against men. There is no metaphysical *moira* forcing human beings to move inevitably in certain prescribed paths. Nor are there any prescribed ends which, like Platonic forms, stand as the eternal ideals that men ought to strive to attain. At any moment men can legitimately say "no" to all beliefs and to all theories, and thus negate whatever may be expected of them.

This sort of indeterminism has, of course, its own problems. There is clearly some question whether the fact that men can *say* "no" means that they can indeed act contrary to the ways that they do act; that they are really free to make choices undetermined by any prior social or psychological considerations. But Polin is not concerned with freedom in this fundamental sense whereby the whole enterprise of inquiry into actions and endeavors could be seriously compromised. For if, as Spinoza and other determinists have argued, men are not really free to make choices, then all questions about goals to be pursued and hopes to be realized become futile. What Polin does is to attempt to define freedom in the Hegelian sense of a process inherent in certain kinds of human actions. But unlike Hegel who, paradoxically enough, ascribed a dialectic necessity to the growth of freedom in human beings, Polin does not conjoin freedom with necessity. No man is born free, but he is not determined either; he becomes free insofar as he strives to attain goals and to be creative. But he can be uncreative and he might decide not to strive to attain goals.

Now there is a subtle but significant shifting of grounds in Polin's argument. It is one thing to say that some — perhaps all — men are constantly seeking to attain various ends. But it is quite another thing to say that what men ought to strive for is to be creative. First of all, there is the important question of what it means to be creative. When is a man creative? Are we to take this term in its artistic sense so that all men ought to strive to become artists or writers? Or are we to take it in some wider sense in which every man, artist or otherwise, has the capacity to be creative? John Dewey made the point in his *Art as Experience* that creativity is not reserved strictly for artistic and literary activity. Every man can make his very experiencing of the world an enriching experience, and thus for Dewey every man, from the storekeeper to the aesthete, can enjoy the rare fulfillment that comes from being creative. I think that Polin does want his notion of creativity to be of the more inclusive kind so that any man who endeavors to refashion or even reinterpret his conditions of existence, either by physical or intellectual means, is involved in being creative and thus in making himself free. But this broadened definition has the disadvantage of being too broad for we must now ask who is *not* creative. Every Hitler and every Stalin suddenly become creative and free in the very highest sense since they surely seek to refashion their conditions of existence. Every man who fights against totalitarianism or fights for it must be taken to be equally creative and equally free. In fact, since every man must sooner or later make some change in the conditions under which he lives, the mere act of existing is sufficient to make him creative. In other words, there is an ambiguity — in Dewey's analysis and now in Polin's — about what exactly distinguishes the creative free man from the uncreative free man. Can we point to an uncreative man? And assuming that we can make such a selection, can we tell him what to do in order to become creative?

Secondly, as Polin is aware, it is always philosophically unsafe to move from a position which defines what man is to a position which defines what he ought to be. It is undoubtedly a fact — perhaps a very trivial one — that men strive to attain ends. Perhaps it is even trivially true to assert that some men strive to create great works of art or significant scientific theories and hypotheses, or simply to make the world a better place to live in. But it clearly does not follow that men *ought* to strive to accomplish these goals. Why should men try to attain such goals? Polin apparently seeks to avoid any metaphysical entanglements. He does not want his *ought* to be based on some underlying metaphysics that makes it an inherent fact in the universe that creation and production are better than non-creation and non-production. But then on what grounds can he speak of creativity as being in some way more significant than non-creation? Is the "hippie philosophy" — if I may be permitted this phrase — of merely enjoying existence without attempting to change it automatically to be rejected? Are we sure that Omar Khayyan's fatalism would not be preferable to the frustrating and despairing experience that usually accompanies the attempt to create? We ought to remember that philosophers have frequently associated true freedom with inward serenity and peaceful meditation. Must freedom be equated with creation rather than the lack of it?

It should be clear that I am not arguing for a fatalistic philosophy. Polin may indeed be correct in arguing for creation and invention as goals for which human beings ought to strive. But I am saying that he has not shown us in what sense we are to understand creation and why its attainment is more preferable than the pursuit of other kinds of goals. Is Camus' stranger — the man who wishes no more than to be left alone and live his life in tranquillity — automatically living a less consequential life than the political activist?

Polin, however, does endeavor to give answers to both of these objections. First of all, he does seek to make clear what he means by creative activity. He tells us that the man who is most free, and thereby most creative, is one who will "act in such a way that there can be an intelligent theory of his work." Also he tells us that whatever is created must be characterized by an order that is intelligible, that will be understood by the world. But this reference to what is intelligible, to what is understood or understandable, is itself not very understandable. How is a distinction to be drawn between what is and what is not intelligible? In a strictly formal language, or a mathematical calculus, we can construct rules whereby certain sentential or mathematical units are taken to be ill-formed or semantically deviant. But we are not here dealing with formal systems of this sort. Intelligibility is in some way to be attributed to some series of actions or productions but not to others. Yet how is this distinction to be drawn? In art — and especially in politics — we can easily see how what is intelligible to one man is unintelligible to another. Were Hitler's actions intelligible or unintelligible? Polin sometimes argues that the degree of universality makes one action intelligible but not another. We can say of some series of actions that they are universally acceptable or at least recognizable as the kind of behavior which people can be expected to perform. But if we take this kind of universality in its strictest form then only the most minimal behavior, e.g. the nod of a head in agreement or the smile of satisfaction, can ever be intelligible since most human behavior is more complicated and can be interpreted as intelligible or unintelligible in accordance with what one approves or disapproves. Thus the notion of "intelligibility" requires a more elaborate definition than the one supplied by Polin. Similar remarks can be directed against the notion of order as a way of evaluating a creation. Polin states "a creation is not recognized as such except when it is the creation of an order." But here also we must ask first of all what is meant by an "order." Is order the same as organization or are we speaking of order in the sense of some rational scheme of things? Neither one of these definitions will do since both "organization" and "rational scheme" themselves require definition. Only in a very formalistic system can "disorganization" be sensibly distinguished from "organization" and "irrational scheme" from "rational scheme." Secondly, as in the case of "intelligibility" so here we must ask how a distinction is to be drawn between "order and "disorder." Is communism more orderly than democracy? Is Dali's *Premonition of Civil War* orderly or disorderly?

Furthermore the entire reference to order may very well be gratuitous. Men frequently fight against an established order of things and this in itself has value even though they may have nothing to take its place. Isn't the man who fights selflessly to destroy a tyrant or a tyrannical system involved in a great task? He is destroying an order and yet, apparently, on Polin's analysis, there would seem to be something wrong with such action. Order is being destroyed and this would seem to mean a loss of freedom. Of course the reply can be made that such destruction involves an implicit attempt to substitute one order for another. But then the whole notion of order becomes tautological. No matter what actions a man takes he is always involved in creating order. Disorder cannot exist. But then who is it that does *not* create?

At one point Polin seeks to give "order" a more cogent analysis by relating it to "meaning." He tells us that "An order without meaning would not be received as an order." But now how are we to think of meaning here? On one analysis every order has a meaning since an order must be recognized as such and this very fact of recognition is an attribution of meaning. If I recognize something as an apple, then clearly I have attributed some meaning to what I see. Perhaps what Polin wishes to say is that the order attached to creation must be meaning*ful* in the sense that it must have some significance for human affairs. Thus I might criticize the surrealist painting on the grounds that its order and symmetry lack that quality of human significance that is expressed in the order and symmetry of the truly great painting. The patterns of lines and colors depicted in a painting by Mondrian are admirable, but surely they do not have the same significance as the patterns of lines and colors found in Picasso's *Guernica*. But if Polin wishes us to understand order and meaning in this way then more investigation will be required for neither in art nor in other fields is there any clear understanding of how meaningful orders are to be distinguished from unmeaningful ones.

Polin's stress on the social context in which all creative endeavors must occur also gives him a possible answer to the question of why men ought to attempt to be creative. Men are born into a society and their existence, their happiness, is dependent upon a society that can satisfy needs which no single man can ever satisfy for himself. Thus when men attempt to recreate their present conditions, to realize more consummate ends, they are in effect seeking to produce a society that could more successfully satisfy their demands. No man is an island unto himself. He is born into a social context just as he is born into an environment containing air and sunshine. And he is just as easily damaged when he refuses to acknowledge his social existence as he would be damaged if he were to refuse to partake of air and sunshine. Thus men can refuse to be productive, but they damage themselves by so doing. It is important to remember that there can be both physical and intellectual suicides.

I am not sure of how strongly Polin wishes to insist upon the need to regard man as essentially a social animal, although he does assert, "not only is sociability essential to man, but ... it belongs, in its greatest sense, only to him." And elsewhere he insists, "man is only free because he is social." But let us ask now how man's freedom, his ability to create, is related to the fact that he is a social animal.

We might take Polin to mean that man cannot be isolated from his fellow creatures and, therefore, he must, at least to some extent, live among them. But this is trivially true. Some isolation is important, but men undoubtedly require some human contact — even if it consists merely of paying a grocery bill — if they are to exist at more than a subsistence level. But what I do take Polin's view to be — one that is of great significance — is that those who are creative or inventive ought to create or invent objects that have social import, that have some "social message." But now what are we to say to this? Should art that does not reflect great social ideals be derogated or rejected as insignificant or trivial? Artists would categorically deny this view not merely because they wish to support an "art for art's sake" theory but because they interpret it as a restriction rather than an expansion of their freedom. Art, to be free, ought to be able to move in whatever direction it wishes, from the realistic art of a Rembrandt to the surrealism of a Kandinsky. But aside from these objections it is not at all clear why an artist or a scientist or any one engaged in doing creative or inventive work ought to be involved solely in subject matters that have social implications. Are we to reject or discourage those "pure" mathematicians, scientists, and scholars who are concerned strictly with the problems of their own work, regardless of their social value? I am not at all sure whether a concern with the foundations of set theory or with the construction of formal uninterpreted calculi ever will have any social or perhaps even philosophical consequences of a serious sort. Yet it would seem to be the epitome of presumption to rule out such work as inconsequential. Polin might claim that such work *might* have social consequences and to that extent it is important. But when we define social consequences in terms of what *might* be, then nothing is ever rejectable since every work can be analyzed so that it might at some time have some social significance.

In conclusion, I should like to add that while I have criticized some of Polin's views I have not rejected the main thesis of his paper. Rightfully he points out that men are primarily responsible for the ways in which they exist. There is no implicit law in the universe that indicates what men ought to strive to become. Man is indeed manmade. Rightfully, it would seem to me, Polin stresses the need to foster inventiveness and an interest in novelty in human beings so that they are more inclined to think about the reshaping of their social, political and economic conditions rather than to accept fatalistically the status quo. But I have tried to indicate why it is difficult to give a cogent defense of this thesis. As the well known song puts it, "To dream the impossible dream" is one thing; to argue for it logically and analytically is another.

STATE UNIVERSITY OF NEW YORK AT BINGHAMTON.

REJOINDER TO KAMINSKY

Raymond Polin

I shall reply very briefly to the interesting remarks Professor Kaminsky made after reading my paper. The opposition between two types of philosophy seems to me here very obvious: Professor Kaminsky is aiming at the establishment of an analytic philosophy, which pretends to impose itself as the only legitimate method for philosophizing, and, in the long run, as the only true philosophy.

On the contrary, I do not believe in the possibility of achieving a scientifically demonstrated philosophy. My starting point has to be considered as a presupposition, as the affirmation of an irreducible difference of each man as such, in his irrepressible freedom to make himself different, different from what he is, from what the already given is and from what the others are.

I believe that a philosophy as such is, first of all, a conceptual effort to make one's own existence intelligible to others and justifiable to them, not even perhaps to convince them of one's own truth, but to enable them to understand the values and the meaning of one's own existence and to obtain their "acknowledgement," in the Hegelian meaning of that word. Philosophy is the inexhaustible dialogue between men claiming that a universal intelligibility is attainable through the forever open affirmation of their difference, of their originality. The more different they are, the better they can philosophically understand each other.

And, secondly, as action is the way to create, in the real world as well as in the universe of thoughts, an order intelligible according to one's own values, philosophy has to be a theory of practice, a practical philosophy, beyond any science, even beyond any scientific philosophy, and depending upon the realm of ends, values and norms.

With this perspective in mind, it will be easier to reply to some of Professor Kaminsky's questions.

1) About creative freedom, I am accustomed to distinguish between two very general types of theories concerning freedom. The classical one describes freedom as the achievement of one's own existence according to one's own essence, as a becoming in conformity with one's own essence, with one's own being. The very motto of this freedom would be:

119

become what you are. On the contrary, the modern conception of freedom stresses the power to become different from what you are, to transcend your situation and your past existence, to create yourself beyond what you are, to achieve a historical newness, to be, in your own freedom, a first beginning. In such a perspective, to be free is to be able to choose, not between several possibilities already given, but to be free by creating new possibilities. (May I refer to the phenomenological analysis of creation that I proposed in my book *La Création des Valeurs* to answer some of Professor Kaminsky's objections?)

2) Such a creation does not consist in a mere activity of negation, in a destruction of what is already given for the sake of destruction only. It is not even an arbitrary operation, or a gratuitous caprice. There is no creation where there is no creation of an order susceptible of justification and comprehension. This order is proposed as a project, a project of existing in common, of thinking in common. It is given, through its law, as a possible work in progress. That is the reason why any human freedom is unseparable from its law, which is a law of creation imposed by the creator on himself or consented to by himself. We rediscover, here, as Kant once did, the fundamental relation between freedom and obligation, freedom being the power to oblige oneself to exist, to act beyond what one is, to create, according to a law invented or consented and imposed by oneself to oneself. There is neither contradiction nor sophistical transfer between "to be" and "ought to be," between *Sein* and *Sollen*: we are already beyond that distinction, in the realm of action, of practice (think of the Marxist *praxis*).

3) The order I am thinking of is essentially an anthropological and a practical one: it is, in its broadest appearance, the cultural order of ideas, of values, of manners in which a group of men are living; in its strictest sense, it represents the practical order and especially, the political order which imposes its frame on the existence of a political community.

Is that just "a dream?" Perhaps indeed philosophy is just a dream, a coherent dream, but it is a wide awake dream, an active and efficient dream, expressing the permanent opposition between the present situation of a group of men, in their given world and the ever-transcending order of values and meanings along which they try to use their powers of freedom, of self-consciousness, and of reason to transform their old world and to create a new world. Is the relation of the new world to the old one just a dream, or, as error is for Hegel, the necessary condition for action?

LA SORBONNE, PARIS.

HUMAN NATURE AND VALUE: COMMENTS ON POLIN

Paul Kurtz

Professor Polin's paper touches on issues that are not often discussed in contemporary Anglo-American philosophy. He is concerned with "the sense of the human;" that is, with a basic philosophical theory of man and a generalized account of the mode of human existence.

He correctly points out, I believe, that any ethical theory presupposes a theory of man. Accordingly, if we are to treat adequately questions of ethics, we must have a clear notion of what it means to be human. Thus he attempts to provide an ontological account of the distinctive and essential attributes of man. Although such an inquiry may be quite alien to the contemporary fashions in Anglo-American thought, in a way a theory of human nature may lurk hidden as an unexamined assumption; and it would be well for philosophers to be clear as to whether or not a conception of human nature is implicit in what they say. There is, I suspect, in most theories of language an underlying set of presuppositions about the nature of the human being, the way humans use language, and how language functions in behavior and life. Similarly, there are embedded in our analyses of normative language different views of the nature and function of moral language and experience, and rooted in our normative values different models of man.

Thus I think that we should welcome efforts to clarify our "philosophical anthropology;" in its minimal sense at least, in so far as basic categories about man are involved in one's attempt to understand and interpret various aspects of human existence. Indeed, recent analytic philosophy (for example, in the philosophy of mind, or the philosophy of action) does begin to approach Professor Polin's task and suggests the need for this kind of analysis; though this kind of inquiry is pursued under a different heading and name—"philosophical psychology" rather than "philosophical anthropology"—and it is far less ambitious.

Professor Polin's paper, being within the spirit of continental philosophy, nevertheless raises serious problems for one not within that tradition, even for one predisposed to follow his lead and to begin "to investigate the nature of the human being." The most puzzling questions no doubt have their source in different methodological principles, as Professor Polin himself recognizes, when in his response to Professor Kaminsky he says that he does not believe in the possibility of achieving a scientifically demonstrated philosophy.

There are at least two key doubts that many Anglo-American philosophers might have with his paper. The first is analytic and the second empirical. First, one might quibble about the often vague use of general terminology that one encounters in his paper. In comparison with the typical Heideggerian analysis, Professor Polin's language is a model of clarity. Yet without being unnecessarily captious, one should point out that his general language often resists precise or rigorous interpretation. Thus any effort to understand "the sense of the human" would have to carefully disentangle a whole cluster of concepts, theories, terms and sentences that we apply to man. Professor Polin does this. He talks about "freedom," "consciousness," "reason," "value" and other root concepts applicable to man. But we must not merely state such concepts, but unravel the vagaries of their employment and try as far as possible to reach clear definitions. One doesn't often find this in Professor Polin's paper.

A second likely question to be raised about his approach concerns his criticisms of the modern scientific approach to man. He says that "modern scientists are . . . more hindered than helped by the huge gap which separates the characteristics recognized in the human being and the characteristics peculiar to a particular animal." And he is not at all sanguine about the success of the scientific program. Accordingly, he does not think it necessary or useful to draw upon the body of data from the behavioral and social sciences in his theory of man, and he bypasses any attempt to generalize from the empirical sciences of man. Here, Professor Polin might find considerable support from much contemporary analytic philosophy, where "action" is distinguished from "behavior" and analyses of human action are followed with little reference to or benefit from the behavioral sciences. The view seems to be that one's general philosophical categories can be arrived at independently of scientific inquiry, or without taking it into account. My own view, consonant with the tradition of pragmatic naturalism in American philosophy, is that the philosophy of man should, at some point at least, take into account the behavioral and social sciences, and try to interpret the key concepts and methods of the sciences of man. Any philosophy which claims to be a philosophy of man and which does not do so is, in my view, simply incomplete.

This latter point is not simply methodological, for it comes into conflict with Professor Polin's own basic theory of man. What is at issue is the dimension of freedom that Professor Polin attributes to man. If this were a symposium in Anglo-American philosophy we would most likely discuss "hard determinism" versus "weak determinism" and seek to resolve our differences by comparative analyses of the meaning and uses of terms such as "cause," "condition," "constraint," "decision," "freedom," or "liberty."

Be that as it may. Although I think Professor Polin says much that is significant—and that I could accept—there is a basic difference in emphasis; for he would give freedom a greater role than I would. The real question concerns the relationship of human freedom to human nature. Unlike Sartre, Polin is not denying a nature to man, but merely insisting that his nature is unstructured and free. Like Sartre, he claims that there is no fixed model of human nature that we may impose upon man *a priori,* but rather man's nature is forever being remade in a process of becoming. I should agree that man is malleable and plastic, that what he is depends upon social and environmental conditions, and that his creativity may modify conditions, invent new possibilities and redirect his future. Yet I do not see how we can deny a more fundamental "nature" to man, i.e., a set of limiting conditions or causal structures on various levels of behavior. The human species has a genetic endowment, a bio-chemical structure; he has distinctive psychological characteristics; and there are socio-historical conditions that to some extent determine his decisions and actions. Perhaps this is what Polin means when he alludes to "an intelligible order," though I would prefer to relate these structures to the large body of concepts, hypotheses and explanations that we have in the sciences of man. Perhaps this is a mere American cultural prejudice; for there is in the United States in the twentieth century a vast amount of energy that has gone into the behavioral sciences, whereas the typical French approach to man is humanistic and literary.

In any case, freedom, I should insist, is always within and in terms of this causal structure, not separate or distinct from it. Man, like other forms of animal life, is capable of choice and decision. His mode of causality is teleonomic and cybernetic; that is, goal directive, preferential, motivational and intentional; it involves selections from an open field of alternative possibilities. I would defend a form of weak determinism. Decision makes sense and is free and responsible only if it follows from a stable personality or character structure and if it can count on an ordered environment in which choices have predictable consequences and effects.

In other words, radical freedom is not freedom but chaos and any meaningful sense of human freedom presupposes some order within the personality and the enviroment. The apparent character of organic life is that it is both determined and free: choice is selective, adaptive and adjustive, and it involves a creative response. Man is not unique in this capacity, which he shares with other forms of life, only in the degree of his creativity, and in his ability to employ symbolic systems as instruments for functional behavior.

Let me conclude with a last comment concerning the ethical values that are intrinsic to Professor Polin's philosophy of man. I suppose that the typical Anglo-American reaction would be that he has committed "the naturalistic fallacy," for he seems at times to derive his normative judgments from his theory of man. Polin has correctly seen that normative ethics presuppose a theory of man, and he faces it head on. In my view the behavioral and social sciences may again provide some clues; for there are, I submit, a discoverable set of common human values and needs. Men live in a common world, they face similar problems, and they have similar basic needs. Interestingly, Professor Polin has to some degree reversed the usual classical procedure in his appeal to ethical value. For his value judgements are not simply derived from his theory of human nature; but on the contrary, his sense of the human is derived from his value judgements. He shows in his theory a commitment to the values of creativity and freedom, values which are open, pluralistic, and are sensitive to the diversity and variety of human life. Clearly, value and human nature are intimately intertwined in his theory. He moves from a theory of value to a conception of man; and his theory of man is based upon and is a reflection of his values. Has he committed the naturalistic fallacy? Yes and no. On the one hand, one may say yes, value and nature are related. But in another sense, no. For Polin seems to be saying that one cannot define value nor find a fixed scale of values which serves as an authoritarian standard. Rather, values are open-ended and creative, continually being remade and reworked; they have individuality and uniqueness. The chief values that he has are those of freedom and reason. But these are highly general. How they work out is apparently situational and contextual and depends upon the originative and seminal character of human creativity.

Whether this commits Professor Polin to subjectivism in value, in spite of his commitment to reason, and to what extent, is an important further question that should be raised. Although I would, like him, s⁺are the values of creativity, freedom and individuality, I fear that if pushed too far, Polin's theory cannot account for the kinds of objectivity that we often find in morality and value. But this is a question for another paper. Suffice it to say that Professor Polin has provided us an interesting and stimulating paper.

State University of New York at Buffalo.

COMMENTS ON POLIN

Raymond Polin's essay on the advantages of defining "human" not in terms of human nature but in terms of what it actually means to be human seems to me timely and reasonable. I also agree with his criticism of some of the current conceptions of "human freedom," of "man's openness to Being," and of "alienation." Where I have difficulty in following him and agreeing with him is in his exposition of the thesis that man must have a "universal, intelligible order" if his life is to have any meaning.

On the face of it, this seems to be too rationalistic, if it is to be understood as the meaning of man's creative work. What Polin seems to intend is that the formulation of such an order is the ideal for a reasonable humanistic philosophy, or for a philosophy of the "ground" of human civilization. For example, this seems to me to be the "sense" of the following paragraph:

> Reste enfin la manifestation des pouvoirs extraordinaires de certains hommes et cet achèvement intellectuel et moral par lequel un homme participe effectivement à la création d'une civilisation, se fait reconnâître come l'auteur et le principe d'un ordre qu'il a rendu intelligible et, ce faisant, parvient à ce haut point d'originalité véritable et d'unicité qui peut être rendue sensible et préhensible à tous.

This is truly a "highpoint of originality" and of "extraordinary" philosophical reflection. Though the theory of such an order may be made intelligible to all, I do not understand why it is a definition of what any man really is, or of what he means to be and do. Perhaps I do not understand what is meant by "order." It seems not to be a system of work, or a political and moral order, but rather an "order of intelligibility" and of "universal liberty." Such an order resembles the philosophical foundations which a Kant or a Hegel tried to provide for mankind. On the other hand, passages like the following indicate that it is supposed to have a concrete human content, and not to be merely formal:

126

La liberté se fonde sur l'intelligibilité et la compréhension
effective de l'oeuvre qu'elle cherche à accomplir. . . . L'impératif
. . . "Agis de telle sorte qu'il puisse y avoir de ton oeuvre une
théorie intelligible" est bien l'obligation essentielle et caracté-
ristique de l'homme en tant qu'homme.

L'universalité concrète des hommes réside, au terme de leurs
efforts, aux plus hauts sommets de leurs civilisations, dans la
communion de ceux qui se sont élevés aux formes de culture les
plus achevées. L'homme le plus humain, l'homme arrivé a
l'humanité la plus elaborée, sera celui qui "agira" de telle sorte
qu'il puisse y avoir une théorie universellement intelligible de
son oeuvre.

If this theory is applicable primarily to the man who has arrived at
"humanity," whose work has aspects of universality in it, it seems to be
intended primarily for philosophical workers. But the implication seems
to be that no man is truly human unless a good humanist can understand
him as an example of universality. This puts a rather heavy obligation
on workers generally. There is an emphasis throughout the paper that
interprets really human work as an expression of the three universals,
"liberty, language, and reason." Human work must be "expressive;" and
Polin goes so far as to say:

Peut-être ne sommes nous jamais mieux nous-mêmes dans toute
notre humanité, qu'à ce haut point d'abstraction et de liberté où
nous exprimons et où nous échappons déjà à nous-mêmes, dans
notre oeuvre ou dans notre parole.

Here I should like to emphasize the "peut-être," for this kind of
abstraction and "liberté" seems too close to the romantic doctrine that
man is most human when he transcends himself. These vestiges of tran-
scendentalism in Polin are unexpected, in view of his critique in the
early pages of the essay. I agree that man should be understood in terms
of what he is continually becoming, not in terms of what he "essentially
is," and that therefore:

L'humanité est l'espèce dont il y a toujours une nouvelle défini-
tion à donner. L'homme doit demeurer toujours disponible.

But I do not understand why such a continual creativeness in man
must be interpreted as a series of transcendences, and why this
"disponibilité" must be regarded as a form of transcendental liberty à
la Sartre.

If we are to look for the meaning in men in terms of their creative
works, why must men have this obligation of projecting their meanings

in an order of the intelligibility of mankind as a whole? Why, especially, if mankind is always on the move? It would appear to be easier to make sense out of men than out of humanity. If, for the sake of the argument, we should admit that the many meanings of varied lives and works can all be included in an intelligible order, would the nature of this order throw much light on the particular integrations of values and interests that constitute a particular person and that constitute what his life means to him? Is there no meaning unless humanity as a whole makes sense as an intelligible order? Is it not possible to live meaningfully and reasonably without this universal blessing?

My own hypothesis is that this order of "liberty, language, and reason" may well constitute the necessary general conditions for human creative work. It may be the "grounding" of civilization. But this does not imply that such a necessary condition for human advance is also an obligation for working. It does not also constitute the meaningfulness of creative human lives. It may define the possibilities that must be present for working conditions, without defining the "sense" of human lives or even the sense that humanity as a whole may be making.

CLAREMONT GRADUATE SCHOOL
CLAREMONT, CALIFORNIA.

COMMENTS ON POLIN

V. J. McGill

A definition of man is invoked at every historical epoch, as a means of safeguarding accepted human values already achieved, or to be achieved, or for the critical purpose of instituting new values while transcending the old. But if it is important to define the human, to understand the scope of human nature and potentials, the philosophical difficulties involved, as Professor Polin's "The Sense of the Human" shows, are considerable. Two of the dilemmas he encounters might be put as follows:

1) If a universal essence of the human is accepted, limits are set to human freedom which this freedom can always transcend.

If a human essence is rejected, out of consideration of man's ability to transcend himself and to negate old and create new values *ad infinitum,* it becomes impossible to define or even delimit the human (or else this ability itself becomes a kind of essence). Thus if we attempt to define or delimit human nature, we are obliged to deny human freedom, or else to confess that human nature is incomprehensible.

2) If *a priori* moral principles determine what is essentially human, then again human freedom is limited: the moral principles cease to be moral principles insofar as they are not freely chosen, and human beings may transcend or explicitly reject them. On the other hand, if *a priori* moral principles do not determine what is essentially human, the idea is all-inclusive in a moral case, and any human trait or conduct, no matter how shocking it may be to us, could become essentially human. Thus in neither case can an acceptable definition of man be framed.

Professor Polin agrees with Sartre that "existence precedes essence;" man is not to be defined as a thing or substance is defined. But "a philosophy of freedom," he says, does not at all exclude "a functional definition of human nature." Man's essence can be "the function of freedom, the ability to become, the power to create." Such a definition of man as freedom does not delimit or restrict human nature since it does not specify how this freedom will be used, but merely states a necessary condition of human existence. The present definition leaves everything open. Must we not therefore conclude that, according to Polin, human nature is so indeterminate as to be incomprehensible, and that it includes essentially what we should call the worst as well as the best of human performance? The answer appears to be yes, so long as Polin sticks to Sartre's understanding of freedom as pure unlimited freedom of choice.

Polin, however, goes on to state that freedom is necessarily freedom for an order, and that freedom which is not creation of an order is not freedom (or not fully so). Moreover, the order created must embody meaning, and be of such a nature that there can be an "intelligible theory" of it. In men in whom the defining freedom is fully developed, it appears, there is "a sense of . . . responsibility in regard to others," and their creative works are on a universal scale the value of which is comprehensible to all. Indeed, "a definition of man is fundamentally a moral definition, as it is affirmed as a value and imposed as a duty," and the definition of man as freedom is clearly a moral one. To adopt freedom in this sense, unfortunately, is to be caught on the other horn of the above dilemma. In the unforeseeable future, or even in the next few years, men may override or reject the particular creativity, lucidity, reasonableness, etc., which we have insisted is their essence; or if they cannot, then they are not completely free, i.e., cannot always say no.

The impression is that Polin unintentionally slips from the unlimited freedom of choice, which can say no to the most utter reasonableness and advantage, to a moral conception of freedom, according to which we are really free *only* when we choose what is reasonable and good, from Sartre's freedom to Hegel's. Polin in fact complains that Sartre's freedom cannot, like Hegel's, develop from and beyond "preservation, negation, and creation." Arising in neantization and being "total," it is unable to serve "as a means to action and as a motor to history." Yet, as if he saw a reconciliation of the two freedoms, he also argues that "freedom for an order, freedom creating order, preserves its pure character of integral freedom, since it itself gives the principles of this order, which is an order to come and to be made." Man's freedom is not limited by its being a freedom for order, since he chooses the principles of the order. But the question is whether he could freely choose other principles, and disorder. The two freedoms remain distinct. It is not clear which, in a showdown, Polin would prefer.

Polin does take promising steps toward resolving what I have called dilemmas, as when he says: "By determining the fundamental intention of human values without fixing a unique value to which all men would be obligated, we hope to preserve the open . . . character of the definition of man. There are no limits to the creative freedom of the values of man." We cannot foresee the values which history will make available, and thus humanism errs in erecting its definition of man into "an absolute." This is the beginning of a judicious settlement of the question, but unfortunately Polin elsewhere insists on values which are to be binding on all men in perpetuity, as when he says: "The order which free creation is obliged to project and to accomplish is . . . an order of which there could be an intelligible theory." The danger here is that if we state explicitly what we mean by an intelligible theory and give examples, we are in danger of saddling the whole human race, as long as it may survive, with our own 20th century conception, or perhaps a conception derived from selected patterns of our Western tradition. And if we leave the meaning of "intelligible theory" vague, we say next to nothing about man.

This last proposal of an "open" definition, nevertheless, is attractive and approaches the suggestion I should like to make. It seems to be important to frame definitions of man in his recent and proximate future circumstances, to assess his powers, values, and developmental trends, on the basis of facts and forecasts, and of experiments, formal and informal, going on all the time. Human nature in the distant future, as in the distant past, is best approximated by extrapolation. Philosophical definitions of man are not likely to count unless they are empirically based, and they should be regarded as hypotheses to be tested against new knowledge at every turn. To be a useful guide to humanist goals such an hypothesis cannot separate man from the concrete environment which invites and supports his activities, nor from the influence of out-moded institutions and appropriative organizations which can give the lie to his reputed creativity, reasonableness and intelligence, The image of man becomes an image of his world with all its dangers and promises, which enjoin study and testing of what man can be in special environments. More important than the framing of an over-all definition of man, it seems to me, would be the bequeathing to the next generation of a readiness to put ideas on trial by the evidence, including the idea of man.

Though this point of view departs from Polin's intention, there are passages in his penetrating, many-sided essay which point in this direction.

San Francisco State College.

COMMENTS ON POLIN

Joseph Margolis

Raymond Polin, I take it, prefers a kind of Hegelian (or Bergsonian) view of man to that of either a Sartrian existentialism or an attenuated Heideggerian essentialism. I find his account a sort of paean to human freedom, not without philosophical difficulties. In particular, I should like to grasp the conceptual features of the dialectic he sketches between freedom and what he himself calls "the essence of the human." But his thesis strikes me as, ultimately, self-contradictory, however gymnastic it may be.

Had he confined his account to the formulation of his Kantian-like principle of human values, namely, that one ought "act in such a way that there can be an intelligible theory of his work," I should have agreed in large measure with the prepared remarks of his commentator, Jack Kaminsky, that Polin's categorical imperative would have excluded absolutely nothing. It is, of course, clear that Polin *does* have *some* substantive views of what constitutes, at any given phase of human history (*à la* Hegel), the supreme value he terms creativity of freedom. Thus, even though he insists that "there is no single history of man, but an infinity of histories of men," he is prepared to grade particular historical developments in terms of the mysterious concept of "intelligibility" that he posits. Not only does he insist, therefore, that every humanism fails insofar as it pretends to have discovered the "eternal" nature of man ("The distinguishing characteristic of man is not that he is indefinable, but indefinitely definable."), but, though not a Marxist, he is entirely willing to agree, *on his own grounds,* with what Marx condemns as "bad alienation." I think one finds here precisely the same difficulties that confront Kantian formalism; or, alternatively put, the very difficulties produced by Hegelian historicizing, in the very effort to resolve such difficulties. At any rate, there is *no* formulated connection between whatever values Polin prefers—call them the values of creativity, if you like—and his account of the essence of man. Even the conservation of older values (whatever they may be) might, for instance, be construed

132

"creatively," since such an effort might constitute a conservation into a new (that is, any) future. What, then, may be rationally excluded?

But, probing more deeply, I cannot see how Polin means to support his denunciation of "a substantialistic definition of human nature." For my own part, I have no intention of defending such a definition, but Polin seems to me to move in clearly incompatible directions. In some mysterious sense—for he offers no clarification—he means to provide "a *functional* definition of human nature," which is somehow about man's "essence and his nature" but not about essential attributes of man. Thus he says, paradoxically, that man "is always free with a total freedom, which continually excludes all nature." Now, I think I *sense* what Polin has in mind in insisting that the exercise of human freedom "surpasses" whatever might be supposed essential or given by "the substantialistic elements of a human nature." The essence of human nature—freedom, consciousness, speech, reason—Polin says, "is not sufficient to determine, or to make determinable, either his value or his sense." Men, he says, "are born neither free nor equal. They are born capable of freedom and capable of reason." Freedom, I take it, is not an *attribute* of man; yet how are we to understand the *capacity* for freedom? And *what* "capacity," on this view, does man not have? Polin actually speaks of the capacity for freedom as "of a given which is merely potential;" but, extrapolating from other familiar contexts, the potentialities that anything possesses—man included—are the potentialities of systems that have determinate structures. He lists alternative formulas for the essential human potencies: "powers, aptitudes, functions, factors, qualities, traits;" but the intelligibility of the very notion itself is rather doubtful.

Thus, to press directly the self-contradictory strain of Polin's proposal, let me say that he declares: "Man is not free; he frees himself . . ." But this (rightly) suggests a structured organism of some sort who has capacities for further development. Polin gauges the *freedom* of men in terms of the intelligibility of the historical future they "invent." But he never speaks directly of the *metaphysical* relevance of the past and, only grudgingly, of the meaning of human finitude. In fact, he wishes to deny that man is "divine" (which he thinks is purely indeterminate), but he never explains what he means by conceding to man "a finite and limited power" to create. It looks very much as if the concession of finitude is, on his own grounds, an admission of essential attributes (however historicized their manifestation may be); and it looks very much as if his own brand of essentialism (as clarified above) is incompatible with his thesis that freedom is "a veritable first beginning."

The only possibility is that Polin is juggling his terms. The freedom he is speaking of must be a purely valuational notion; but then, he says nothing about how to appraise human history in terms of comparative creativity. On the other hand, if, though a man's freedom must begin "from a set of given conditions," "certain ways of acting and thinking which form for him [in a given civilization] the given conditions of his existence," then Polin seems forced to admit that man has *some* antecedent attributes that *condition* his freedom, that constitute (against his explicit view) some sort of "necessary determination." I think this is all captured and obscured, at one and the same time, in Polin's remark that "the future counts indefinitely more than the past." The proper question is whether the past counts metaphysically at all—and, if not, in what sense the future does; or, if the past provides a determinate setting within which human freedom functions, in what sense is the future, however strenuous and inventive human freedom may be, not also conditioned by this past. As far as I can see, Polin does not and cannot (consistently) say.

TEMPLE UNIVERSITY
PHILADELPHIA.

ON THE BASIS OF MORAL OBLIGATION:
COMMENTS ON POLIN

Joseph J. Kockelmans

In his paper "The Sense of the Human" Raymond Polin has sketched with remarkable lucidity the problem philosophy faces the moment it conceives of man in terms of freedom and, nevertheless, wishes to develop an ethics as "a practical theory of man." For Polin it is obvious that there can be no ethics without a certain conception of man. Many philosophers have first developed a philosophical conception of man and have founded their views on ethics upon that basis. For Polin ethical philosophy *is* a philosophy of man and its principles should determine the meaning of the human.

In determining his own position in regard to the problem mentioned Polin rightly takes his course between the Scylla of an essentialist conception of man and the Charybdis of Sartre's conception of man as total freedom. In Polin's view one cannot attribute to man once and for all an invariable structure which determines his essence. But on the other hand, man is not totally free; in man's freedom the given is somehow preserved and transcended at the same time; man's freedom essentially comprises both nothingness and creativity. That is why in Polin's view a philosophy of freedom does not necessarily exclude a *functional* definition of man's nature in which what is given and what is universally definable in man is the function of freedom, the ability to become, the power to create.

In harmony with these basic insights Polin argues that to determine the meaning of man is to assign each time to his function as man a specific end and to treat him as a value around which the world of men should be ordered in relation to him. That is why for every definition of man there is a corresponding conception of the world and an effort to make it come·true. Man is, thus, defined by vocation; his function as man takes on a meaning in relation to the value he proposes to realize and to which he feels bound by an obligation. In other words, a definition of man is essentially a moral definition because it is affirmed as a value and imposed as a duty.

In the further elaboration of this view Polin makes it convincingly clear that every attempt to specify man's "nature" by means of the characteristics: freedom, consciousness of self, consciousness of the future, speech, and reason (which are quite generally recognized traits of man's being), remains inadequate, that is merely formal and negative, *as long as* one does not take into consideration the elements 'value' and 'meaning.' For the characteristics mentioned *as such* have only the value of a means; and among them freedom is the universal means of all means.

Freedom now takes on meaning only in relation to a given which is defined by its order. Every freedom takes on meaning according to the meaning of the order *from which* it is freed. Many philosophers who have tried to think along similar lines have made the mistake of taking the given order as something unquestionable which is already there, either in the form of a divine presence, or in the form of an essential order inscribed in the nature of things and men, or in the form of a historical determination. And they have done so because they felt that there is no other way of justifying the obligatory character of moral 'standards,' whatever they concretely may be.

In Polin's view, however, there is no danger in conceiving of man's freedom as a genuine creative freedom which is capable of being freed from all previous given order which it transforms and surpasses, provided one maintains that freedom is not freedom of a nothing and for a nothing, but freedom for an order to be established from a set of given conditions.

It is of importance to realize here that what is essential for order is not a given basic structure, but the presence of a meaning. Order *is* meaning, because it consists essentially in a system of comprehensible relations. In this way freedom becomes founded on the intelligibility and the effective understanding of the order, not of the order which is already there, but of that which it itself seeks to accomplish. Of such an order one can develop an intelligible theory. From this then one can also derive the moral imperative: "Act in such a way that there can be an intelligible theory of your work." The intelligibility of the order, as well as of the theory which can describe it, is obviously and necessarily intelligibility for all of us, just as the intelligible order itself is necessarily an order for all. The essential presence of others implies a necessary research of the common and, soon, of the universal. The presence of others and the obligation to intelligibility imply the institution of an order which we tend to make, step by step, universal. Polin concludes that man will find his most human meaning when, by virtue of his original culture, he rises to that realm of intelligibility in which man, and ideally, all men can succeed in recognizing their differences under the unity of a reasonable theory, in free consent to the theory and to the others.

The strong aspects of this approach to the bases of ethics are, in my view, that it is able to determine the fundamental intention of human values without fixing in advance one unique value and, thus, that it is able to preserve the open character of the definition of man. In this way it surpasses all forms of classical humanism as well as those of modern anti-humanism.

We must now ask ourselves whether Polin's conception indeed succeeds in what it wants to accomplish. I wish to limit myself to some reflections which are not meant as criticism but rather as an invitation to further dialogue. Let me therefore take my point of departure by expressing my being in sympathy with the way Polin approaches the age-old problem concerning the bases of ethics and his serious attempt to transcend humanism as well as anti-humanism. I am particularly impressed by the way he re-thinks some basic continental European ideas from Kantian and Hegelian motives too often neglected by contemporary thought which, nevertheless, claims Kant as well as Hegel as its major historical sources.

However, there are in my view three points which ask for further reflection. My first theme of reflection is the question of whether within the tradition the possibilities of radically founding the obligatory character of moral 'standards' have not been exhausted which means that Polin's view rather than being radically new only opens up a new approach to a previously developed conception. The obligatory character of moral 'standards' can 'easily' be justified by appealing to an absolute being, to an absolute realm of intelligible ideas, to an unquestionable a priori, to a set of unquestionable postulates, to a goal which historical mankind has unquestionably to achieve, all possibilities referred to in philosophy's long history between Plato and Marx. I do not immediately see that an appeal to values on the basis of an intelligible order to be created opens a radically new perspective. For does the intelligibility of the order not necessarily presuppose an unquestionable 'ideal' of order and intelligibility? And do these two basic ideas of Polin's conception, in turn, not again refer to an unquestionable absolute or a priori, or, on the other hand, lead us back to the conceptions of order and intelligibility of the past (a certain culture, a certain civilization, a certain political order, etc.)? This would mean again a return to relativism.

A second point, closely connected with the first is the question of whether Polin really overcomes Sartre's ethics of ambiguity as briefly outlined by Simone de Beauvoir. To be more specific, is Polin's conception of the root of moral obligation really substantially different from Sartre's view? There is no doubt about the fact that there is indeed a great difference between the ways in which both philosophers conceive of man's freedom, and I am convinced that Polin's conception is by far the preferable one. But if we limit ourselves to the way Polin introduces the concepts of value and obligation he still seems to be very close to Sartre's interpretation of Kant. This becomes clear immediately when one compares the following formulations of the moral imperative: "Act as if the maxim of your action were to become through your will a universal law of nature" (Kant); "Act in such a way that you not only choose what you will be but are at the same time a legislature deciding for the whole of mankind" (Sartre); "Act in such a way that there can be an intelligible theory of your work which is valid for all men" (Polin). The main difference in these imperatives is that whereas Polin refers to an intelligible order to be produced, Kant and Sartre *immediately* appeal to the 'humanity of man' which is to be brought about for all men. I am asking myself, however, what could be the meaning of creating an intelligible theory valid for all men, if it is not because in this way one wants to bring about the 'humanity of man' for all of us?

Speaking about order, Polin explicitly admits that order can only be and be understood within a certain context of meaning (a certain civilization for instance), and that this order consists in a system of comprehensible relations, relations full of the meaning of the elements of order in relation to one another and to the whole. Elsewhere he says that the sum of all the radical inventions brought to light by freedom constitutes an entirely human *world* which serves as a mediation between man and the given. On the other hand, Polin argues that man is not freed toward Being, and that for him it is unacceptable to conceive of man as residing in Being and to reduce him to being no more than a discovery of Being's truth. There seems to be a latent contradiction in these two sets of statements. Does Polin not deny on the one hand what he precisely wishes to establish on the other? For in contemporary European philosophy Being is without a doubt the totality of all meaning, the total meaningfulness, the matrix of all possible comprehensible relations. But is that which is called Being here not precisely that which Polin refers to under the heading 'intelligible order'? The totality of meaning obviously is not identical with the world in which we actually happen to find ourselves in this period of time in our Western civilization, but rather that toward which we can transcend in that it, as the horizon of all possible horizons of meaning, is already predelineated and 'pre-understood' in the given world which our 'freedom' encounters. There is obviously a great difference between 'existential phenomenology' and Polin's practical philosophy. But if we limit ourselves to the conception of Being as found in existential phenomenology and Polin's view on the intelligible order, then I see no longer any danger in ascribing to man as his basic and essentially human task "the discovery of the truth of Being."

The Pennsylvania State University.

Section 4

ON THE OBSERVABILITY OF THE SELF

RODERICK M. CHISHOLM

I.

> "A traveller of good judgment may mistake his way, and
> be unawares led into a wrong track; and while the road is
> fair before him, he may go on without suspicion and be
> followed by others; but when it ends in a coal-pit, it requires
> no great judgment to know that he hath gone wrong, nor
> perhaps to find out what misled him." Thomas Reid, *In-
> quiry into the Human Mind.*[1]

The two great traditions of contemporary western philosophy — "phenomenology" and "logical analysis" — seem to meet, unfortunately, at
the extremes. The point of contact is the thesis according to which one
is never aware of a *subject* of experience. The thesis in question does
not pertain to the perception of one's *body*. If we are identical with our
bodies and if, as all but skeptics hold, we do perceive our bodies, then,
whether we realize it or not, we also perceive ourselves. The thesis has
to do, rather, with what we find when we consult the data of our immediate experience, or when, as Hume puts it, we enter most intimately
into what we call ourselves. Thus Sartre seems to say that, although we
may apprehend things that are *pour-soi,* things that are manifested or
presented to the self, we cannot apprehend the self to which, or to whom,
they are manifested — we cannot apprehend the self as it is in itself, as
it is *en-soi.*[2] And Russell has frequently said that the self or subject is
not "empirically discoverable"; Carnap expressed what I take to be the
same view by saying that "the given is subjectless." [3] I say it is unfortu-
nate that the members of the two great philosophical traditions happen
to meet at this particular point, of all places. For at this particular point,
if I am not mistaken, both groups have lost their way.

---

[1] Chapter I, Section VIII.

[2] Jean-Paul Sartre, *L'Être et le Néant* (Paris, Librairie Gallimard, 1943), pp. 134,
145, 652-3.

[3] Bertrand Russell, *Logic and Knowledge* (London, George Allen & Unwin, Ltd.),
1956, p. 305; Rudolf Carnap. *Der logische Aufbau der Welt* (Berlin, Weltkreis-
Verlag, 1928), pp. 87-90.

Both traditions trace their origins, in part, to Hume.[4] I suggest that, if we are to find out what went wrong, we should turn back to the doctrines of Hume, where we will find a number of obvious, but disastrous mistakes.

II.

The first mistake was a very simple one. Consider the following remark which may be found in Hume's "Abstract of a Treatise of Human Nature." Hume wrote: "As our idea of any body, a peach, for instance, is only that of a particular taste, color, figure, size, consistency, etc., so our idea of any mind is only that of particular perceptions without the notion of anything we call substance, either simple or compound." [5] This seems to me to be very obviously false, but many philosophers, I am afraid, tend all too easily and unthinkingly to assume that it is true.

Is it true that our idea of a peach is an idea only of a particular taste, color, figure, size, consistency, and the like, and analogously that our ideas of such things as ships, trees, dogs, and houses are ideas only of the particular qualities or attributes that these things are commonly said to have? One is tempted to say instead that our idea of a peach is an idea of *something that has* a particular taste, color, figure, size, and consistency; and analogously for the other familiar physical things. But even this is not quite right. Our idea of a peach is not an idea of something that *has* the particular qualities, say, of sweetness, roundness, and fuzziness. It is an idea of something that *is* sweet and round and fuzzy.

More pedantically, our idea of a peach is an idea of an individual x' such that x is sweet and x is round and x is fuzzy. By thus using variables and adjectives, we express the fact that the object of our idea is not the set of qualities, sweetness, roundness, and fuzziness, but the concrete thing that *is* sweet and round and fuzzy. We also make clear, what is essential to our idea of a peach, that the thing that is round is the *same* thing as the thing that is sweet and also the *same* thing as the thing that is fuzzy.

---

[4] Husserl wrote of Hume: "Dessen genialer *Treatise* hat bereits die Gestalt einer auf strenge Konsequenz bedachten strukturellen Durchforschung der reinen Erlebnissphäre, [ist] in gewisser Weise also der erste Anhieb einer 'Phänomenologie'." E. Husserl, *Phänomenologische Psychologie* (The Hague, Martinus Nijhoff, 1962), p. 264. The members of the Vienna Circle traced the "scientific world-outlook" to the same source; see *Wissenschaftliche Weltauffassung* (Vienna, Artur Wolf Verlag, 1929), p. 12.

[5] The passage may be found on page 194 of Charles W. Hendel's edition of Hume's *An Enquiry concerning Human Understanding* (New York, The Liberal Arts Press, 1955).

Leibniz saw the point very clearly when he criticized Locke's *Essay concerning Human Understanding*. When we consider any person or thing, he said, what comes before the mind is always a *concretum* and not a set of abstract things or qualities; we may consider something as knowing, or something as warm, or something as shining, but we do not thereby consider knowledge or warmth, or light. The abstract things, he noted, are far more difficult to grasp than are the corresponding *concreta*.[6]

I cannot help but think that the point is a simple-minded one. "Our idea of a peach is not an idea of sweetness, roundness, and fuzziness . . . ; it is an idea of something that is sweet and also round and also fuzzy . . ." One would not have even thought of mentioning it, had not philosophers denied it and constructed fantastic systems on the basis of its negation. A small mistake at the outset, as the Philosopher said, turns out to be a great one in the end.

If the first part of Hume's observation is wrong, then so is the second. Our idea of "a mind" (if by "a mind" we mean, as Hume usually does, a person, or a self) is not an idea only of "particular perceptions." It is not the idea of the perception of love or hate and the perception of cold or warmth, much less an idea of love or hate and of heat or cold. It is an idea of that which loves or hates, and of that which feels cold or warm (and, of course, of much more besides). That is to say, it is an idea of an x such that x loves or x hates and such that x feels cold and x feels warm, and so forth.

III.

I would say that a second error we find in Hume's writings, and in the writings of those who follow him with respect to the observability of the self, has to do with the interpretation of certain data or evidence. Hume argued, it will be recalled, that he and most of the rest of mankind are "nothing but a bundle or collection of different perceptions." And in support of this "bundle theory," he cites a kind of *negative* evidence. He tells us, with respect to a certain proposition, that he *has* certain evidence for saying that he has *no* evidence for that proposition.

---

[6] *New Essays concerning Human Understanding*, Book II, Ch. xxiii, sec. 1. ". . . c'est plutôt le *concretum* comme savant, chaud, luisant, qui nous vient dans l'esprit, que les *abstractions* ou qualités (car se sont elles, qui sont dans l'object substantiel et non pas les Idées) comme savoir, chaleur, lumière, etc. qui sont bien plus difficiles à comprendre." Erdmann's edition of Leibniz' *Opera Philosophica*, p. 272.

But when he cites the evidence he *has* for saying that he has *no* evidence for the proposition, he seems to presuppose, after all, that he *does* have evidence for the proposition.

What Hume said was this: "For my part, when I enter most intimately into what I call *myself,* I always stumble on some particular perception or other, of heat or cold, light or shade, love or hatred, pain or pleasure. I never can catch *myself* at any time without a perception, and never can observe anything but the perception." [7] As Professor Price once observed, it looks very much as though the self that Hume professed to be unable to find is the one that he finds to be stumbling — to be stumbling onto different perceptions. [8] How can he say that he doesn't find himself — if he is correct in saying that he finds himself to be stumbling and, more fully, that he finds himself to be stumbling on certain things and not to be stumbling on certain other things?

We must take care not to misinterpret the difficulty. The difficulty is *not* that, in formulating his evidence for the "bundle theory" of the self, Hume presupposes that there *is* a self. For this presupposition, that there is a self, is not contrary to what Hume wishes to say. The "bundle theory," after all, is not intended to *deny* that there is a self. It is intended merely to say *what* the self is and what it is not. There is a self, or there are selves, according to Hume, and what selves are are "bundles of perceptions."

The difficulty is that Hume appeals to certain evidence to show that there are only perceptions, and that when he tells us what this evidence is, he implies not only (i) that there is, as he puts it in his example, heat or cold, light or shade, love or hatred, but also (ii) that there is *someone* who finds heat or cold, light or shade, love or hatred, and moreover (iii) that the one who finds heat or cold is *the same as* the one who finds love or hatred and *the same as* the one who finds light or shade, and finally (iv) that this one does not in fact stumble upon anything but perceptions. It is not unreasonable to ask, therefore, whether Hume's report of his fourth finding is consistent with his report of the second and the third. If Hume finds what he says he finds, that is to say, if he finds not only perceptions, but also that *he* finds them and hence that there is *someone* who finds them, how can his premises be

---

[7] *A Treatise of Human Nature,* Book I, Part IV, Section vi ("Of Personal Identity").

[8] H. H. Price, *Hume's Theory of the External World* (Oxford, The Clarendon Press, 1940), pp. 5-6. Compare P. F. Strawson, *Individuals* (London, Methuen & Co. Ltd., 1959), pp. 96-7.

used to establish the conclusion that he never observes anything but perceptions?

One may protest: "But this is not fair to Hume. It is true that, in reporting his data, he used such sentences as 'I stumble on heat or cold' and 'I never observe anything but perceptions.' He didn't need to express himself in this way. Instead of saying 'I stumble on heat or cold' or 'I find heat or cold,' he could have said, more simply, 'Heat or cold is found.' And instead of saying 'I never observe anything but perceptions,' he could have said, more simply, 'Nothing but perceptions are found.' He could have reported his data in this way; and had he done so, he would not have presupposed that there exists an x such that x succeeds in finding certain things and such that x fails to find certain others."

But *could* Hume have reported his data in this selfless way? Let us recall that his findings are both positive and negative and let us consider just the negative ones. It is one thing to say, modestly and empirically, "I find nothing but impressions or perceptions." It is quite another thing to say, rashly and nonempirically, "Nothing but perceptions or impressions are found." The point will be clearer, perhaps, if we consider another type of example. I may look around the room and, from where I stand, fail to see any cats or dogs in the room. If I express this negative finding modestly and empirically, I will simply say "I do not see any cats or dogs." But if I say, solely on the basis of my negative observation, "No cats or dogs are seen," then I will be speaking rashly and nonempirically and going far beyond what my data warrant. How do I know what other people or God may find? And how can I be sure that there are no unseen dogs or cats? Clearly Hume would not have been justified in saying, "Nothing but impressions are to be found." And in fact he made no such subjectless report. He said, referring to himself, that *he* found nothing but impressions.

The difficulty may be put briefly. It is essential to Hume's argument that he report not only what it is that he finds but also what it is that he fails to find. But the two types of report are quite different. The fact that a man finds a certain proposition p to be true does warrant a subjectless report to the effect that p is true. For finding that p is true entails that p is true. But the fact that he fails to find a certain proposition q to be true does not similarly warrant any subjectless report about q. For one's failure to find that q is true entails nothing about the truth of q. The fact that a man fails to find that q is true entitles him to say only that *he,* at least, does not find that q is true. And this would not be a subjectless report.

What Hume found, then, was not merely the particular perceptions, but also the fact that *he* found those perceptions as well as the fact that *he* failed to find certain other things. And these are findings with respect to himself.

Referring to the view that the self is a substance persisting through time, Hume said that we have no "idea of self, after the manner it is here explain'd. For from what impression cou'd this idea be derived?" Given our first two general points, could the proper reply be this — that one may derive the idea of such a self from any impression whatever? [9]

IV.

Why, then, is it so tempting to agree with Hume in his report of his negative findings?

I think we tend to reason as follows. We suppose — mistakenly, it seems to me — that if we do perceive or apprehend ourselves in our immediate experience, then such perception or apprehension must resemble in essential respects the way in which we perceive or apprehend the familiar external things around us. And then we find, in fact, that we do *not* perceive or apprehend ourselves in our immediate experience in the way in which we apprehend or perceive the familiar external things around us.

Thus whenever we perceive — say, whenever we *see* — a spatial object, then the object that we perceive has certain proper parts that we perceive and certain proper parts that we do not perceive. Suppose, for example, that I see a cat. Then we may say of that side of the cat that faces me that I see certain parts of *it*. But I do not see *all* the parts of the side that faces me (I do not see those parts I would see if I took a closer look or used a microscope) and I do not see *any* of the parts of the insides or any of the parts of the sides that face away. One of the results in changes of spatial perspective is that certain parts become seen that had not been seen before and certain parts cease to be seen that

---

[9] Compare Brentano's remark about the concept of substance: "Those who say that this concept is not included in any perception are very much mistaken. Rather it is given in every perception, as Aristotle had said . . ."; Franz Brentano, *Versuch über die Erkenntnis* (Leipzig, Felix Meiner, 1925), p. 30. Referring to the thesis according to which we know only "phenomena" and not "things in themselves," he wrote: "But what does it mean to say that one apprehends something as a *phenomenon?* Simply that one apprehends it as a phenomenon to the one for whom it is a phenomenon. This means, in other words, that one apprehends that one is presented with or intuits the phenomenon in question and hence that one apprehends the one to whom it is presented, the one who intuits. But this a thing that one apprehends in itself." *Die Vier Phasen der Philosophie* (Leipzig, Felix Meiner, 1926), p. 92; my italics. But Brentano also held, unfortunately, that so-called external perception is "blind."

had been seen before. And so if the distance between our body and the perceived object is not too great, we may now look over this part and now look over that. We may look more closely and scrutinize — and this means that we may now see smaller parts that we had not seen before. And analogously for the nonvisual senses. But whatever our perspective upon the perceived object may be, there will always be certain parts of the perceived object that we do perceive and certain other parts of the perceived object that we do not perceive. Moreoever, and this is the important point about external perception, if we know that we are perceiving a certain physical thing, then we are also capable of knowing that we are perceiving something that is just a proper part of that thing. But the situation is different when we perceive ourselves to be thinking.

I may perceive myself to be thinking and know that I am doing so and yet be unable to know whether I am perceiving any proper part of anything that I am perceiving. It may be, for all anyone knows, that whenever I perceive myself to be thinking, I *do* perceive some part of myself. This would be the case, for example, if I could not perceive myself to be thinking without perceiving some part of my body, and if, moreover, I were identical with my body or with that part of my body. But it is not true that, whenever I perceive myself to be thinking I thereby perceive what I can *know* to be a part of myself. (Whether or not I am identical with my body or with some part of my body, I do not *know* that I am.) In short, to know that I perceive the cat to be standing, I must know that I perceive a proper part of the cat, or of the cat's body; but to know that I perceive myself to be thinking I need *not* know that I perceive what is a proper part of myself. Sartre said that the ego is "opaque"; I would think it better to say that the ego is "transparent." [10]

Ordinarily if a man can be said to perceive *that* the cat is standing, then he may also be said, more simply, to perceive *the cat*. But the locution "S perceives that *a* is F" does not entail the simpler locution, "S perceives *a*." [11] Compare "Jones perceives that Smith is no longer in the room" and "Jones perceives that the lights are on next door." Could it be, then, that a man might be aware of himself as experiencing *without* thereby being aware of himself? Let us approach this question somewhat

---

[10] Jean-Paul Sartre, *The Transcendence of the Ego,* trans. Forrest Williams and Robert Kirkpatrick (New York, Farrar, Strauss and Cudahy, 1957), p. 51.

[11] I am indebted to Keith Lehrer for this point. I am also indebted to him and to Charles Caton for criticisms enabling me to correct an earlier version of this paper.

obliquely, by recalling still another familiar source of philosophical perplexity.

During the first third of this century, British and American philosophers were perplexed about the status of what they called "sense-data" or "appearances." They thought, for example, that if a man were to walk around a table, while focusing upon the white tablecloth on the top, he could experience a great variety of sense-data or appearances. Some of these entities would be rectangular like the table-top itself; they would be the ones he would sense if he were able to get his head directly above the table and then look down. Most of them, however, would be rhomboids of various sorts. If the lighting conditions were good and the man's eyes in proper order, most of the appearances would be white, like the table-cloth. But if the man were wearing rose-colored glasses, he might sense appearances that were pink, or if he were a victim of jaundice, he might sense appearances that were yellow. The other senses, as well as imagination, were thought to bring us into relation with still other types of appearances or sense-datum.

The nature and location of these strange entities, as we all know, caused considerable puzzlement, and imposing metaphysical systems were constructed to bring them together with the rest of the world. I am sure that it is not necessary now to unravel all the confusions that were involved in this kind of talk, for the sense-datum theory has been ridiculed about as thoroughly as any philosophical theory can be ridiculed. But we should remind ourselves of one of these confusions — another very simple mistake. It was the mistake that H. A. Prichard had in mind, I think, when he used the expression, "the sense-datum fallacy." [12]

It was assumed that, if a physical thing appears white or rhomboidal or bitter to a man, then the man may be said to sense or to be aware of an appearance that *is* white, or an appearance that *is* rhomboidal, or an appearance that *is* bitter. It was assumed that if a dog presents a canine appearance, then the dog presents an appearance that *is* canine. (Thus Professor Lovejoy wrote: "No man doubts that when he brings to mind the look of a dog he owned when a boy, there is something of a canine sort immediately present to and therefore compresent with his consciousness, but that it is quite certainly not that dog in the flesh." [13])

---

[12] See H. A. Prichard, *Knowledge and Perception* (Oxford, the Clarendon Press, 1950), p. 213. Compare his much earlier *Kant's Theory of Knowledge* (Oxford, The Clarendon Press, 1909) and his "Appearances and Reality," first published in *Mind* in 1906 and republished in Roderick M. Chisholm, ed., *Realism and the Background of Phenomenology* (Glencoe, Ill., The Free Press, 1960), pp. 143-150.
[13] A. O. Lovejoy, *The Revolt against Dualism* (New York, W. W. Norton & Company, Inc., 1930), p. 305.

And then it was assumed, more generally, that whenever we have a true statement of the form "Such-and-such a physical thing appears, or looks, or seems - - - to Mr. Jones," we can derive a true statement of the form "Mr. Jones is aware of an appearance which is in fact - - -." But this assumption is quite obviously false.[14] Consider the following reasoning, which would be quite sound if the assumption were true: "I know that Mr. Simione is an Italian and that he is also old and sick. I saw him this morning and I can assure you that he also appeared Italian, and he appeared old and sick as well. Therefore Mr. Simione presents an appearance which, like himself, really is Italian, and he also presents an appearance which, like himself once again, is old and sick." It is absurd to suppose that an appearance, like a man, may be Italian or old or sick; it is absurd to suppose that an appearance may be a dog; and, I think, it is equally absurd to suppose that an appearance, like a table-cloth, may be rectangular, or pink, or white.

When the philosophers thus talked about sense-data or appearances, they were, however inadequately, reporting *something* that is very familiar to us all, and we should not let their philosophical theories blind us to the fact that there is such a going-on as sensation and that the experiences we have when we observe the familiar things around us may be varied merely by varying the conditions of observation. Suppose now we were considering this fact on its own, and without any thoughts about Hume's theory or about Hume on the observability of the self. How would we describe it if we are to avoid the absurdities of the sense-datum fallacy?

I think we would do well to compare the "grammar" of our talk about appearances with that of our talk about feelings. Consider the sentence "I feel depressed." It does not imply that there is a relation between me and some other entity; it simply tells one *how* I feel. The adjective "depressed," in other words, does not describe the *object* of my feeling; rather, if I may put the matter so, it describes the *way* in which I feel. It could be misleading, therefore, to use the longer sentence "I have a depressed feeling" in place of the shorter "I feel depressed." For the longer sentence, "I have a depressed feeling," has a syntactical structure very much like that of "I have a red book." Hence one might be led to suppose, mistakenly, that it implies the existence of *two* entities, one

---

[14] "The general rule which one may derive from these examples is that the propositions we ordinarily express by saying that a person A is perceiving a material thing M, which appears to him to have the quality x, may be expressed in the sense-datum terminology by saying that A is sensing a sense-datum s, which really has the quality x, and which belongs to M." A. J. Ayer, *The Foundations of Empirical Knowledge* (New York, The Macmillan Company, 1940), p. 58.

of them *had* by the other. And taking "a depressed feeling" as one would ordinarily take "a red book," one might also be led to suppose, again mistakenly, that the feeling which the person is said to have resembles the person in being *itself* depressed. I say one *might* be misled in these ways by the sentence "I have a depressed feeling," though I don't know of anyone who ever *has* been misled by it.

It is quite obvious, I think, that in such sentences as "I feel depressed," the verb is used to refer to a certain type of *undergoing*. This undergoing is what traditionally has been called being in a conscious state, or being in a sentient state. And the adjective, in such sentences as "I feel depressed," is used to qualify the verb and thus to specify further the type of undergoing to which the verb refers. The adjective could be said to function, therefore, as an adverb. Thus the sentences "I feel depressed" and "I feel exuberant" are related in the way in which "He runs slowly" and "He runs swiftly" are related, and not in the way in which "He has a red book" and "He has a brown book" are related. In short, *being depressed* is not a predicate of the feeling; rather, *feeling depressed* is a predicate of the man.

I suggest that the sentences "I am aware of a red appearance" and "I am experiencing a red sensation" are to be interpreted in the way in which we interpreted "I have a depressed feeling" and "I feel a wave of exuberance." Despite their grammatical or syntactical structure, neither sentence tells us that there are *two* entities which are related in a certain way. They, too, ascribe a certain type of undergoing to the person. The adjective "red," in "I am aware of a red appearance" and "I am experiencing a red sensation," is used adverbially to qualify this undergoing.[15] It would be useful, at least for the purposes of philosophy, if there were a verb — say, the verb "to sense" — which we could use to refer to this type of undergoing. Then we could say that such a sentence as "I am aware of a red appearance" tells us *how* the subject is sensing. Or, better perhaps, it tells us in what *way* he is sensing. For to be aware of "a red appearance," presumably, is to sense in one of the ways that people do, when under favorable conditions, they look at objects that are red.[16] (If we may say that a man "senses redly," may

---

[15] Compare Thomas Reid: "When I am pained, I cannot say that the pain I feel is one thing, and that my feeling of it is another thing. They are one and the same thing and cannot be disjoined even in the imagination." *Essays on the Intellectual Powers'*, Essay I, Chapter 1.

[16] But there are still two alternative interpretations of such expressions as "sensing red." or "sensing redly." (i) We might define "sensing redly" in such a way that our definiens makes explicit reference to things that are red. Using the expression in this way, we may say that no one can *know* that he is sensing redly unless

we also say that he "senses rhomboidally," or "senses rectangularly?" There is no reason why we may not — especially if we can identify one's sensing rhomboidally, or one's sensing rectangularly, with one of the ways in which a person might be expected to sense if, under favorable conditions, he were to observe objects that are rhomboidal, or rectangular.)

We may summarize this way of looking at the matter by saying that so-called appearances or sense-data are "affections" or "modifications" of the person who is said to experience them.[17] And this is simply to say that those sentences in which we seem to predicate properties of appearances can be paraphrased into other sentences in which we predicate properties only of the self or person who is said to sense those appearances. If this is correct, then appearances would be paradigm cases of what the scholastics called *"entia entis"* or *"entia per accidens."* These things are not entities in their own right; they are "accidents" of other things. And what they are accidents *of* are persons or selves.

It is interesting to note, in passing, that Hume himself criticizes the view that appearances are modifications of persons or selves — and that, in doing so, he provides us with an excellent example of the sense-datum fallacy. First he notes the absurdity of Spinoza's view, according to which such things as the sun, moon, and stars, and the earth, seas, plants, animals, men, ships, and houses are in fact only "modifications" of a

---

he *also* knows something about red things and the ways in which they appear. Or, more empirically, (ii) we might take "sensing redly" as undefined, in which case we may say that a man who knows nothing about red things may yet know that he is sensing redly. For in this second case, the proposition connecting his sensing redly with one of the ways in which people are appeared to by things that are red would be a proposition that is synthetic.

[17] And so are "thoughts." Consider a man who is thinking about a unicorn. We may say, if we choose, that he has a thought and that his thought is about a unicorn. Whether or not we say, as Meinong did, that the situation involves a relation between, an existent man and a nonexistent unicorn, we should not say that the situation involves a relation between a man and a certain independent entity which is his thought. There is not *one* relation between a man and a thought, and then a *second* relation between the thought and a nonexistent unicorn. Though we say, quite naturally, that the unicorn is the object of the man's thought, it would be less misleading to say that the unicorn is the object of the man to the extent that he is thinking. For thinking, like feeling and like what we may call "sensing," is an affection, modification, or state of the man. Compare Leibniz's assertion that ideas are "affections or modifications of the mind," in his "Thoughts on Knowledge, Truth. and Ideas" in Erdmann's edition of Leibniz's *Opera Philosophica*, p. 81. Sartre, too, has said that the appearance is "the manner in which the subject is affected [la manière dont le sujet est affecté]," but he adds, unfortunately, that "consciousness has nothing of the substantial [la conscience n'a rien de substantiel]"; *L'Être et le Néant,* pp. 13, 23.

single divine substance. And then he argues that, if this Spinozistic view is absurd, then so, too, is the view that "impressions" or "ideas" are only modifications of the self. But the reason he cites for this seems clearly to be based upon the sense-datum fallacy. For, he says, when I consider "the universe of thought, or my impressions and ideas," I then "observe *another* sun, moon, and stars an earth, and seas, covered and inhabited by plants and animals; towns, houses, mountains, rivers . . ." [18] In other words, if a real dog cannot be a modification of God, then an appearance of a dog cannot be a modification of me!

Why this way of interpreting appearances? For one thing, it seems to me, we multiply entities beyond necessity if we suppose that, in addition to the person who is in a state of undergoing or sensing, there is a certain *further* entity, a sense-datum or an appearance, which is the object of that undergoing or sensing. And for another thing, when we do thus multiply entities beyond necessity, we entangle ourselves in philosophical puzzles we might otherwise have avoided. ("Does the red sense-datum or appearance have a back side as well as a front side? Where is it located? Does it have any weight? What is it made of?")

And now we may return to the question that brought us to this consideration of appearances: "Could it be that a man might be aware of himself as experiencing without thereby being aware of himself?" If what I have suggested is true, then the answer should be negative. For in being aware of ourselves as experiencing, we are, *ipso facto,* aware of the self or person — of the self or person as being affected in a certain way.

This is not to say, of course, that we do not *also* perceive or observe external physical things. It is in virtue of the ways in which we are "appeared to" by the familiar things around us, of the ways in which we are affected or modified by them, that we perceive them to be what they are. If, under the right conditions, the fields should appear green to me, then I would *see* the fields to be green.[19] And at the same time I could become directly aware of — immediately acquainted with — the fact that I myself am modified or affected in a certain way.

If what I have been saying is true, then there are two rather different senses in which we may be said to apprehend ourselves.

The first type of apprehension was what Hume himself reported —

---

[18] *Treatise of Human Nature,* Book I, Part IV, Section 5; my italics.

[19] I have tried to say what these conditions are in *Theory of Knowledge* (Englewood Cliffs, Prentice-Hall Inc., 1966), Chapter Three, and in *Perceiving: A Philosophical Study* (Ithaca, Cornell University Press, 1957). An excellent summary of this view of perception may be found in Keith Lehrer, "Scottish Influences on Contemporary American Philosophy," *The Philosophical Journal,* Vol. V (1968), pp. 34-42.

that *he* found heat or cold, that *he* found light or shade, and that *he* did not find himself, at least in the sense in which he found heat or cold and light or shade. He found, to repeat, that there was *someone* who found heat or cold, that this same someone found light or shade, and that this same someone did not in the same sense find himself. That we apprehend ourselves in this first sense would seem to be clear whatever view we may take about the nature of appearances, or of being appeared to.

And if the particular view of appearances that I have proposed is true, then we apprehend ourselves in still another sense. For if appearances, as I have said, are "accidents" or "modifications" of the one who is appeared to, then *what* one apprehends when one apprehends heat or cold, light or shade, love or hatred, is simply oneself. Whether one knows it or not, one apprehends *oneself* as being affected or modified.

The two points may be summarized by returning to the figure of the bundle theory. One may ask, with respect to any bundle of things, what is the nature of the bundle and what is the nature of the bundled. What is it that holds the particular items together, and what are the particular items that are thus held together? Now, according to the second of the two points that I have just made, the items within the bundle are nothing but states of the person. And according to the first point, as we may now put it, what ties these items together is the fact that that same self or person apprehends then all. Hence, if these two points are both correct, the existence of particular bundles of perceptions presupposes in two rather different ways the existence of selves of persons that are not mere bundles of perceptions.

VI.

And there is one more simple mistake that we may note briefly.

One may grant everything that I have said ("Yes, there are those senses in which one may be said to observe the self") and yet insist, at the same time, that we really know nothing about the self which we do thus observe ("Knowing what states the self is in doesn't entitle you to say that you know anything about the self"). What kind of reasoning is this?

Let us recall what Kant says about the subject of experiences — about the I which, as he puts it, we "attach to our thoughts." Whenever we find ourselves thinking or judging, he said, we attach this I to the thinking or judging, and then we say to ourselves, or think to ourselves, "I think" and "I judge." Yet, although we manage somehow to "attach" the I to the thinking or judging, we do so "without knowing anything of it, either by direct acquaintance or otherwise." The I is known, he says, "only through the thoughts which are its predicates, and of it, apart from them, we cannot have any concept whatever." [20]

Kant seems to be telling us this: even if there is a subject that thinks, we have no acquaintance with it at all and we can never know what it is. And his *reason* for saying we have no acquaintance with it all and can never hope to know what it is, would seem to be this: the most we can ever hope to know about the subject is to know what predicates it has — to know what properties it exemplifies; and apart from this — apart from knowing what predicates it has or what properties it exemplifies — we can never know anything of it at all.

During the latter part of the nineteenth century and the early part of the twentieth century, there were philosophers in the idealistic tradition who reasoned in a similar way. They seemed to say that we can never hope to have any genuine knowledge of reality. The most we can hope to know about any particular thing is to know what some of its properties or attributes are. But, they said, we can never know what the thing is that has those properties or attributes.[21] In the present century, Jean-Paul Sartre has despaired because we seem to have no access to the *en-soi* — to the self as it is in itself. What ever we find is at best only *pour-soi* — the self as it manifests itself to itself.[22]

Despite the impressive tradition, shouldn't we say that this is simply a muddle? The reasoning seems to be as follows.

---

[20] "Durch dieses Ich oder Er oder Es (das Ding), welches denkt, wird nun nichts weiter als ein transcendentales Subject der Gedanken vorgestellt = X, welches nur durch die Gedanken, die seine Prädicate sind, erkannt wird, und wovon wir abgesondert niemals den mindesten Begriff haben können ... Es ist aber offenbar, dass das Subject der Inhärenz durch das dem Gedanken angehängte Ich nur transcendental bezeichnet werde, ohne die mindeste Eigenschaft desselben zu bemerken, oder überhaupt etwas von ihm zu kennen oder zu wissen." *Kritik der reinen Vernunft,* A346, A355; see N. Kemp Smith's edition, pp. 331, 337.

[21] Compare A. E. Taylor: "What we call one *thing* is said, in spite of its unity, to have many *qualities*. It is, *e.g.,* at once round, white, shiny, and hard, or at once green, soft, and rough. Now, what do we understand by the *it* to which these numerous attributes are alike ascribed, and how does it possess them? To use the traditional technical names, what is the substance to which the several qualities belong or in which they inhere, and what is the manner of their *inherence?* ... The notion *that* things have a that or substance prior to their *what* or quality ... is thus unmeaning as well as superfluous." *Elements of Metaphysics,* Fifth Edition (London, Methuen & Co., Ltd., 1920), pp. 128, 133.

[22] "Ainsi le Pour-soi en tant qu'il n'est pas *soi* est une présence à soi qui manque d'une certaine présence à soi et c'est en tant que manque de cette présence qu'il est présence à soi." *L'Être et le Néant* (Paris, Librairie Gallimard, 1948), p. 145.

It is noted (i) that a person can be acquainted with the subject of experience to the extent that the subject manifests itself as having certain properties. (And this we can readily accept — provided we take care not to commit at this point the first of the errors on our list above. What we should say is not merely that the subject manifests certain qualities; it is rather that the subject manifests *itself as having* certain qualities.)

Then one adds an "only" to what has just been said. One now says (ii) that a person can be acquainted with the subject of experience *only* to the extent that the subject manifests itself as having certain qualities. The "only" is thought to express a limitation. (But consider the limitation expressed by the "only" in "One can see what is only an object of sight" and "Trees are capable of growing only below the timberline.")

From these two premises one then deduces (iii) that no one has acquaintance with the self as it is in itself.

But it is not difficult to see, it seems to me, that (ii) does not add anything to (i), and that (iii), moreover, does not follow from (i) and (ii). Indeed I would say, not only that (iii) does *not* follow from (i) and (ii), but also that the *negation* of (iii) *does* follow from (i) and (ii). From the fact that we are acquainted with the self as it manifests itself as having certain qualities, it follows that we are acquainted with the self as it is in itself. Manifestation, after all, is the converse of acquaintance: x manifests itself to y, if and only if, y is acquainted with x. How can a man be acquainted with *anything* unless the thing manifests or presents itself to him? And how can the thing manifest or present itself unless it manifests or presents itself as having certain qualities or attributes? [23]

The muddle was neatly put by Wittgenstein. We are all naked, he said, underneath our clothes.

Brown University
Providence, Rhode Island.

---

[23] Compare Leibniz again: "En distinguant deux choses dans la substance, les attributs ou prédicats et le sujet commun de ces prédicats, ce n'est pas merveille, qu'on no peut rien concevoir de particulier dans ce sujet. Il le faut bien, puisqu'on déjà séparé tous les attributs, où l'on pourroit concevoir quelque détail. Ainsi demander quelque chose de plus dans ce pur *sujet en général,* que ce qu'il faut pour concevoir que c'est la même chose (p. e. qui entend et qui veut, qui imagine et qui raisonne) c'est demander l'impossible et contrevenir à sa propre supposition, qu'on a faite en faisant abstraction et concevant separément le sujet et ses qualités ou accidens." *New Essays concerning Human Understanding,* Book II, Chapter 23, Section 2; Erdmann, *Opera Philosophica,* p. 272.

REPLY TO PROFESSOR RODERICK CHISHOLM AND COMMENTS

Henri Lefebvre

Looking from a different viewpoint from that of Professor Roderick Chisholm, we can connect the problems of the Subject with the philosophy of Descartes as well as with a long line of thought whose chief exponents are Kant, Hegel, Marx and Nietzsche.

1. Starting-point of the comparison: the Cartesian Subject, the *Cogito*. In the light of European rationalism, the "Cogito ergo sum" appears as existence inseparable from an essence, as unity of being and thought, of ontology and the theory of knowledge, of substance and act. Thus is defined the constituent thesis of modern philosophy: the I and the Me, indistinguishable, are situated in the perfect transparency of an initial and final intuition.

This is an untenable position. Indeed it is a commonplace of critical analyses of Cartesianism that this thesis or hypothesis of the absolute Subject binds existence to essence and substance to the act of the subject only by dissociating it from the object. The "res extensa" and the "res cogitans" can come together by the mediation of the infinite, be it will or thought.

2. It follows that those who try three centuries later to maintain this Cartesian conception of the Subject are depriving it of the power of mediation which it had in Descartes' thought. In the philosophical part of Jean-Paul Sartre's work, for instance, the subject is defined by anguish rather than by knowledge; it has existence without any power except that of "projecting" an essence; reduced as it is to this static existential activity, it is negative rather than positive; essence is inaccessible or hypothetical. In spite of these precautions, the separation of the Subject and the Object presents difficulties and the object becomes no more than the elusive Other. Consequently, the Subject as act loses all actual transparency. The Subject can be maintained (in philosophical reflection) only at this price.

3. Critique of the Cartesian Subject begins with Kant; it is hardly necessary to insist on this point. Kant asserts the inverse principle: no

155

subject without an object, no object without a subject. While remaining on the same ground, he thus profoundly modifies the thesis. No consciousness without the formation and functioning of categories, without the "matter" and the "contents" of these categories, the phenomenal world. Moreover, empirical consciousness, unable to grasp the whole of its conditions and pre-suppositions, refers itself to the Noumenal, to the transcendency of the intelligible. When relativized, the subject has only an ethical and practical link, if one may say so, with the absolute, through the mediation of the will, whereas it becomes active as knowing. The rift between the subject and the object disappears as such, but reappears in the interior of the subject as a separation between the immanent and the transcendent.

4. If it is possible to say in a certain sense that the critique of the Subject starts with Kant, the *crisis of the Subject* dates back to Hegel. Indeed, Hegel is not content simply to relativize the subject, to thematize the relation of the subject with the object, to render the relation of the subject with himself problematical. By "historicizing" these relations, he tries to overcome the antinomy: knowledge and/or ontology.

For him, there is first of all, that is, at the beginning, at the moment of any emergence and any appearance, the *hic et nunc,* immediacy in its purest state: perceiving (this or that), feeling and wanting (this or that, but here and now). This immediacy is necessary but not sufficient: there is this or that, this and that, only by and for the subject. But he cannot stop at this or that: he conceives them and conceives this only in relation to that and *vice versa.* Everything is in a *hic et nunc,* except the concepts of space and time. The necessity of the *hic* and of the *nunc* falls into a contingency, that of sensing and feeling, while the contingency of representation is elevated to the degree of a superior necessity, that of conceptual thought. The subject cannot avoid the *hic* and the *nunc.* He is always linked to a present which is not self and makes him present for himself, but he can exist for himself only by rising to a higher plane, that of reflection. He thinks the *hic* and the *nunc* by situating them in time and space by the mediation of the concept being born and reborn, always reflecting. Then the *hic* and the *nunc* transcend themselves, have a meaning or rather acquire and receive it; they have "value" for the subject, or rather for a subject which apprehends himself as such only in the objectivity of the concept and the development of reason. The *hic* and the *nunc* then become part of coherent speech and language, and never disappear nor allow their irreducibility to dissolve.

It is hardly necessary to add that the lines above translate Hegelian thought into modern language. The idea of coherent speech giving perceptible data to language and concepts, establishing itself at a higher degree in relation to the degree called first or neutral (zero), cannot be, strictly speaking, found in Hegel. Yet it is there insofar as Hegel has shaped contemporary thought and as "pure" philosophical speech remains Hegelian to this very day.

What becomes of the subject in Hegel's dialectical rationalism? Tearing objects away from themselves, being torn away from himself by objects, the subject is developed in front of and by thought which reflects and constitutes at the same time. *The Phenomenology of Mind* and *the Science of Logic* formulate this development. Each "layer," each degree of philosophical speech envelops the lower degree: perceptible naturality (the *hic* and the *nunc*), the figures of consciousness, the moments of the concept and the Idea.

But what becomes of the Subject at the end of this development? For Hegel indeed there is an end. The *hic* and the *nunc* being the "terminus a quo," the development aims at a "terminus ad quem." It bears a name, it has an existence (perceptible, practical). It rests in a "hic et nunc," although it is the supreme end of the Subject which has passed through figures and moments. It is the *State*. It envelops, it raises to its own level, that of philosophico-political speech, it builds together all the subjects and all the objects: individuals, groups and social bodies, partial states (families, corporations, cities, etc.), objective sub-systems, needs, juridical rules and the law, ethical rules, etc. The supreme Subject, transcendent and immanent, is not God. It is the State, deified, deputizing for the absolute Lord. It is not individual consciousness, but the historical and social, collective and generic, Individual, composed of parts inseparable in their distinctions and differences. The supreme Subject, superior to all subjects, incarnates the Idea by giving it its earthly seat.

5. Now let us examine Marx's thought. He accepts the principle resulting from the philosophical reflection taken in its integrality: "no subject without an object, no object without a subject"; but such are the consequences that he draws from it, that the formula and its constituent elements (the philosophical concepts of the subject and the object) split up. *No subject without an object:* man is a being with needs and desires. Considered in his biological, practical, historical and social context, man as individual cannot be separated from generic man (the human species always given by and in particularities and singularities). The individual needs the group. He cannot survive an instant without *the other:* the other human being, the other natural or social being, the object of his lack of or his capacity for action, the object of need, the instrument, etc. Inversely, there can be no determined object without a subject (individual and social). Any determined object has been made, that is, it is a product or creation; it is the result of an activity composed of many

elements: language, concepts (outlined or detailed), work (divided up and organized), different and usually unequal social functions.

The existence of the object outside the subject (before him, without him) and the mode of existence of qualities and properties, are no longer a problem. It is here that we meet an illusory "problematics," that of "materialism," a philosophical illusion kept alive by the partisans and adversaries of Marxist thought. That the hardness or the smoothness of this stone "is" or "is not" within me or outside me is an interesting but speculative question from Marx's point of view. What is important is that this stone is no longer a shapeless block, a part of nature — that it has been extracted by social work, carried here, cut or polished, that it is thus a product or creation, intended for a house or a monument, and therefore already inscribed in a social context. Immersed in nature, in the heart of the quarry and the earth from which it was extracted, it existed before men and without them, no doubt. But it was not an object. It had no outline, no name. It dwelt and stagnated in the unnameable and the unnamed: "pure" nature, or, if one prefers, the in-itself. Such a discourse has no importance.

It follows that philosophical concepts properly speaking, such as "subject" and "object," when necessary at the outset, are not however sufficient to analyze activities and their products (or their creations, a creation being unique and the product repetitive). Even more, these concepts in their speculative usage turn into representations and ideologies. They stop the analysis of social practice; they bar the way to it; they limit the view. If they subsist in thought, it is only through their transcendence and as transcended. They are not thereby abolished. Knowledge (political, historical, economic, etc.) and more generally the analysis of social practice and the account of the connections between its elements, gave a content to these concepts of philosophical origin. They are now transformed and become concrete instead of abstract. If knowledge demands the use of those concepts and thus revives them or finds in them its birthplace, thought also develops, springing from this fertile ground. One might say, to translate Marx's thought into "modern," that is contemporary, language, that from his point of view, knowledge is developed in a specific time or temporality, which is neither the time of history in general, nor that of philosophy and its history in particular. In and through knowledge, philosophy and its concepts continue to exist as references. But practical knowledge and action (especially revolutionary action) acquire existence and meaning only by rising *above* this ground, by discovering a horizon which is no longer that of philosophy and which philosophers as such cannot discover. Philosophy (and its concepts) do not disappear but become absorbed and resorbed on one hand in the analysis of "real" social practice and on the other hand in revolutionary practice, which discovers the horizon because it *makes* it (thus going beyond and transcending at the same time the product and the creation).

The philosopher loses the privilege of being the Subject *par excellence,* hidden beneath the System or the State whose servant and apologist he becomes. What Subject? In the Marxist orientation, there is a multiplicity of "subjects" which are born, appear, and disappear: *society* (that is, a mode of production, always implying particularities and singularities, for instance the capitalist mode of production with French or American particularities and the singularities of the events of the year 1968!), the social class or classes, the State, etc. The State is a Subject, but with no privilege. On the contrary, as supreme Subject, the State is doomed to disappear. Revolutionary practice in Marx's sense stands up against it. It threatens it; it breaks it up and leads it to decay and death. If there is a "Subject" at a higher level, he will be found in society. Social practice, language and concepts, is a degree higher than philosophico-political speech of which it carries the truth while outclassing it, fighting it and aiming to eliminate it. Between these degrees there is hierarchy, insertion or integration, envelopment and development. The relation is found to be *conflictual.* The reference to philosophy on one hand, to social practice on the other hand, and still more the introduction of revolutionary practice are the foundations of dialectics. It is at this level, that of the State and of philosophico-political discourse, that we must place the separation between Hegel and Marx. This separation is far from being simply an epistemological or philosophical separation, but goes much further, for it concerns practice, the relation between existing practice and the perspective of revolutionary practice. Is it necessary to add that Marx's thought does not refer to such and such a State, or such and such political formation, but to the State in general and the fetishism of the State and the political thought permeated by this ideology? Is it necessary to say that this political critique is quite different from anarchising nihilistic negation, and that it is even a political theory, that of the decline of the State and of politics? If we have to insist on this point, it is because this essential aspect of Marxist thought has been hidden, kept in the background. Not even disputed, forgotten! Marx's socialism has been confused with the socialism of the State, for which the State remains the supreme and absolute Subject, depository of philosophico-political rationality and totality. The Stalin era completed this confusion and we are undergoing its consequences today.

6. Still speaking of Marx and Marxist thought, can "man" consider himself as a *subject?* That is the position of Feuerbach's anthropology

which is a stage and a moment in Marxist thought. For Feuerbach "human nature" is defined on an almost biological plane, as the general or generic essence of the species: perception, desire, enjoyment. In relation to this essence lost in the course of history, alienation is defined.

It is easy to show that Marx used Feuerbach against Hegel and Hegelian dialectics against Feuerbach's anthropology. There is no generic human essence lost in the course of history, since the "human being" comes into existence thanks to his productive and creative activity; but this production of the human being by himself in the course of history does not re-produce the phases and moments of the Idea.

Although it is superseded, put back in its place, the anthropology of Feuerbach does not become ideology pure and simple with Marx, after the period when he confronts the teachings of his predecessors and inspirers. It still has a meaning. It implies a political *project,* that of liberalism and advanced democracy. Without going as far as the idea of total revolution, originated by the working-class, with it, by it and for it, this anthropology stands out as a landmark: humanism, that is, concern with "the human being," sensitive, sensorial, sensual.

Consequently, the human is not a subject. It does not disappear for all that. The "human world" is defined:

a) by the totality of social relations, with their contradictions, and the conflicts between partial "subjects": society and social groups, classes, etc.;

b) by the totality of the objects, products and creations, thanks to which they become a human "world";

c) by the totality of the possibilities of social practice, including those of revolutionary action.

7. This theory of the "subject," and of the modifications and transformations of this concept, cannot be found in the often-quoted *Manuscripts of 1844,* nor in *Capital* which is often contrasted to the *Manuscripts* in the way that a product of science might be contrasted to a philosophical work. One must consult the *Grundrisse der Kritik des politischen Ekonomie (Foundations of the Critique of Political Economy)* (1857-58).

In *Capital,* a work in which economic theory implies and presupposes the critique of economic science as fragmentary knowledge in the service of a policy and a State, the notion of the subject becomes two-fold. It is the *subject of knowledge,* which comprises:

a) the social support of knowledge, that is to say revolutionary practice, the activity of the working-class;

b) the theoretical support of knowledge, that is to say the logical form taken by the exposition and especially by the theory of exchange-value, considered as a form linked to logical form. On this point, the literal reading of the first chapter of *Capital* is still to be recommended, this initial and fundamental chapter never having been really understood!

8. In what concerns the individual "subject," *private* conscience outside social conscience, class conscience and the other degrees, modalities and possibilities of conscience (political conscience, for instance) belongs to a critique implied in the term. Far from being considered as an essence or a model, this subjectivity reveals itself on analysis as *private:* outside social relations and especially relations of production, and yet linked to property and the representations accompanying it. In other words, *individualism* does not give rise to a philosophy of subjectivity or intersubjectivity. It is considered:

a) as a certain social practice in bourgeois (capitalist) society;
b) as an ideology;
c) as an element which dissolves social relations in bourgeois society

itself.

This critical appreciation does not do away with the problem of the individual and his social status. Far from eliminating it, dialectical critique sets the problem of the "subject" in its entirety. In a bourgeois society the individual falls a victim to the powers of repression from the very moment that he does not conform to the norms and constraints by which this society produces "individualistic individuals," which are isolated, separate and alike if not identical because they accept the same values. For the concrete individual in this society where individualism is the dominant ideology, his own accomplishment and development appear to him like a fleeting mirage, a promise never to be kept: *a possible-impossible.*

9. Here of course we have left the texts of Marx and their 19th Century context to describe and analyze in the same orientation (radically critical) the situation of the individual as a concrete subject. The dialectical category of the *possible-impossible* answers the questions relating to the reality, that is to say, the realizations of the individual subject. Everyone knows and feels himself to be entangled in a series of possibilities and impossibilities' in which are intermingled presences and absences, the far and the near, the strange (which stimulates) and the alien (which puts an end to the adventure and blocks any possible opening).

In this adventure (ever repressed and ever recommenced) of the individual seeking for self-realization outside the norms and constraints of individualism, the substantiality of the "subject" finally dissolves. What becomes of him? What is he? A set of substitutions. "I" am an "other?" No. Several others. Those whom I can understand, excluding those whom I refuse and reject, those whom I love and with whom I identify myself, those whom I love without identification or imitation, those whom I understand and hate, etc. A certain dissolution of the meaning of "me," a marked conflict between the "I" and the "me" and between the self and the other, and consequently an extension of the subjective conscience which accompanies this dissolution; thus can the situation be defined.

10. Non-Marxist critics of Hegelianism and of traditional philosophy such as Kierkegaard and Schopenhauer, Nietzsche, Freud, or Heidegger foreshadow the crisis of the subject and of subjectivity. The "end of man" which has recently become fashionable again in France was foretold by Nietzsche as well as the death of God. Nietzsche accompanies this thesis by a profound and radical critique of the "subject," which stresses its crisis. What is the "subject"? Sometimes the moving surface, meeting-place of the depths and the light, Dionysos and Apollo, sometimes the deceptive flowering of the will, of hidden powers and of the will to power: their mask and the scene of their wily manifestations. The unthought and perhaps unthinkable relations which hide under the subjective surface are relations of power rather than rational relations (or irrational ones in the affective sense).

It is not our intention here to show in detail how certain psychoanalysts, certain linguists and especially some philosophers inspired by linguistics and psychoanalysis, have brought the "crisis of the subject" to its culminating point. For them the subject evaporates and the illusions of subjectivity are reduced to seemingly actual experiences dispelled by knowledge. Thus language is a system whose coherence has no need of that accidental support, speech.

11. In our view the problem is no longer to criticize the subject and the object of philosophers. This critique has been accomplished and terminated. The problem is to *reconstruct the subject,* practically and theoretically. It must be a multiple and multiform reconstruction answering multiple questions: "Who? For and by whom? How and why?" We have to reconstruct the *historical subject* which is not or is no longer the State, the class, the people or the nation. This reconstruction of the historical subject might coincide with that of the *political subject* which can no longer be the party but would consist essentially of a new "avant-garde," comprised of workers, students and intellectuals. We shall also probably have to construct or reconstruct the *subject of knowledge* (epistemological or logical) and even the *psychological subject* (which might be the task of those psychoanalysts who are freest from psychoanalytical dogmatism and ideology).

Thus can be defined an aspect of the "problematics" which we have elsewhere called "meta-philosophy." It cannot avoid a risk, that of passing from the old *philosophism* (which has split up under the pressure of the fragmentary sciences) to an economism, a historicism, sociologism, that is to say, to a privilege granted, implicitly or explicitly, to a particular fragmentary science.*

UNIVERSITY OF PARIS, NANTERRE.

---

* Translated by Gérard Deledalle.

COMMENTS ON CHISHOLM AND LEFEBVRE

Chaim Perelman

The paper by Professor Chisholm "On the Observability of the Self" is a good sample of the use of the analytical method in philosophy, such as has been fashionable in Anglo-American philosophy. I am surprised that Professor Chisholm's criticisms have also been addressed to phenomenologists, and especially to existentialists. If there exists a philosophy which accords a reality to the "self," it is certainly phenomenology, and in fact it is fundamental to its method; the same thing is true of existentialism. In effect, if of the objects which are given to us, we only perceive the appearances, the being in itself may be conceived as the infinite series of these appearances; but this is never the case with the "self," of which the existence transcends its manifestations. It is for these reasons, and without examining in detail the diverse attitudes of the phenomenologists, that I prefer to limit myself to Professor Chisholm's criticism of Hume, which is really the center of his paper.

The paper is prefaced by an extract from Thomas Reid, which assures us that:

> A traveller of good judgment may mistake his way, and be unawares led into a wrong track; and while the road is fair before him, he may go on without suspicion and be followed by others; but when it ends in a coal-pit, it requires no great judgment to know that he hath gone wrong, nor perhaps to find out what misled him.

Professor Chisholm applies this to Hume, in the doctrines of whom he claims we find "a number of obvious, but disastrous mistakes."

I believe enough in the intelligence of Hume to be convinced that if he had made such an obvious mistake, then he obviously would have seen it. And if he had seen it, and nevertheless had maintained his point of view, this would mean that he believed that he had sufficiently valid reasons not to be limited by common sense in this case. May I allude to the useful distinction made by Strawson between "descriptive"

164

and "revisionary" metaphysics.[1] It is necessary to point out that what seems to be an error because it is opposed to common sense in descriptive metaphysics, may be lucidly opposed to common sense in revisionary metaphysics, if there are sufficient reasons to do so. Accordingly, the analysis presented by Professor Chisholm and which conforms to common sense (e.g., "that our idea of a peach is an idea of something that has a particular taste, color, figure, size, and consistency"), may be in contradiction with what the empiricist methodology of Hume obliges him to assert (i.e., that all of our knowledge is derived from impressions). Hume is very conscious of the paradoxical conclusions to which he is led, but he maintains them to remain faithful to his method, and he professes to oppose the habitual manner of speaking (instead of speaking of the "self" he speaks of "what I call myself"). The systematic construction of a philosopher doesn't present itself—and the example of Hume shows this clearly—as a simple analysis of what seems *obvious* to common sense, but very often is a choice consciously made by the philosopher between incompatible possibilities. If, personally, I accept the conclusions of Professor Chisholm rather than those of Hume, it is because finding myself with the same option as Hume, I do not choose as Hume did, because I do not have the same confidence in the empiricist thesis.

By limiting himself to the method of linguistic analysis, Professor Chisholm treats at the same time three different problems which have received different solutions in the systems of Berkeley, Hume and Kant. These problems concern, besides the problem of the *self,* those of the *substance* opposed to its *predicates,* and of the *subject* opposed to the *object* of knowledge. If Berkeley, before Hume, had negated the existence of material substances, he had maintained the existence of spiritual substances, which manifest themselves by the will. For Kant substance is a category which we impose on the given to structure it. Kant does not deny that we observe the self as a phenomenon, but he denies the possibility of observing the "transcendental ego," which conditions all of our knowledge but cannot be, as such, an object of knowledge. I believe that if Professor Çhisholm had taken into account the different analyses of the above three concepts, he perhaps would be obliged to introduce some further distinctions in his approach—which I am sympathetic to, because I do not believe that impressions exist without a subject.

---

[1] P. F. Strawson, *Individuals* (London, Methuen, 1959), pp. 9-10.

Professor Lefebvre has entitled his paper "An Answer to Professor Chisholm;" yet it is odd that he says almost nothing about Professor Chisholm's paper directly. He is apparently simply content to affirm that since Hegel the epistemological problem of the relationship between subject and object has been superceded. The actual problem for him is to reconstruct the subject of history, i.e., the political subject, which he doesn't consider to be the state, as for Hegel, nor the party, as for Marxism-Leninism, but the new *avant-garde* composed of workers, students and intellectuals. The problem of knowledge is, in his eyes, an expression of the philosophy of individualism that he considers to be an outworn ideology of the bourgeoisie. Perhaps he is right. But it seems to me that the classical Marxist distinction between materialism and idealism is more relevant to the theory of knowledge than it is to the philosophy of history. Should he not demonstrate how and why in a revolutionary ideology epistemology has lost all of its meaning? This claim indeed would be a radical critique of epistemology; but I do not believe that useful philosophical dialogue can be carried on by simply ignoring the thesis and the analyses of the philosopher against whom one is invited to take a critical stand.*

UNIVERSITY OF BRUSSELS.

---

*Translated by Paul Kurtz

REJOINDER TO PERELMAN

RODERICK CHISHOLM

Professor Perelman has understood what I have tried to say and his observations seem to me to be entirely to the point.

He notes that the mistakes I have attributed to Hume would not be mistakes if Hume's empiricism were true. The question, therefore, is whether we should accept Hume's empiricism or whether we should accept what I have called the obvious. The choice, it seems to me, is between Hume's empiricism and the view, that we all tend to accept, according to which I can perceive various physical things around me, I can be immediately aware of myself, and I can remember having perceived such things and having been thus aware of myself in the past. What is the reasonable man to do when confronted with such an alternative?

I think that the reasonable man would be what Peirce called a "critical commonsensist." He would regard the natural beliefs of common sense as being epistemically innocent until there is positive reason to think them guilty. In other words, he would say that such beliefs are *prima facie* credible and are worthy of retention until they have been shown to be inconsistent with something that is more credible than they are. If this point of view is correct, then inconsistency with Hume's philosophical theory is, in itself, no objection to our natural beliefs. But if there is some good reason to accept the philosophical theory, then it may be that the theory is preferable, epistemically, to the beliefs in question. What reason is there, then, for accepting the theory?

Consider once again the observation quoted from Hume's "Abstract," an observation that could be said to be basic to Hume's empiricism: "As our idea of any body, a peach, for instance, is only that of a particular taste, color, figure, size, consistency, etc., so our idea of any mind is only that of particular perceptions without the notion of anything we call substance, either simple or compound." What reason does Hume give us for this remarkable doctrine? So far as I have been able to find out, he doesn't give us any reason at all.

167

Professor Perelman also notes, again quite correctly, that my paper is concerned with *three* fundamental philosophical concepts—with the concept of *substance*, with the concept of a *subject* of experience, and with the concept of a *self* or *person*. (Perhaps the particular term "substance" might be avoided because of some of its Aristotelian connotations. In such a case, we could use Leibniz's *"concretum,"* or Brentano's *"ens reale,"* or Strawson's "individual.") Among the theses I have taken to be at least *prima facie* credible and thus worthy of acceptance until discredited, is the thesis according to which *some* substances (*concreta, entia realia,* or individuals) are persons or selves. Moreover, I have suggested, as many other philosophers have held, that the concept of substance is one that we derive, in part, from the notion that we have of ourselves. I have also defended and tried to explicate the sense in which that substance which is the self or person is also the *subject* of experience. I agree, therefore, that there are these three fundamental philosophical concepts—that of a substance, that of a subject of experience, and that of a person or self. But couldn't we say, with respect to the third of these concepts, that the first is its genus and the second its specific difference? (Compare Boethius: "A person is an individual substance of rational nature.")

I quite agree that what I have said about the subject of experience is not consistent with what Kant said about it. But I wonder whether such *reasons* as Kant had for what he said may not presuppose some of the errors I have attributed to Hume.

BROWN UNIVERSITY
PROVIDENCE, RHODE ISLAND.

SARTRE ON THE OBSERVABILITY OF THE SELF

GILBERT VARET

This short notice doesn't claim to handle the full topic suggested by the title. I am by no means an official interpreter of Sartre (I never have been his pupil, nor his "disciple"). Actually, there have been some uses made of Sartre during this conference, by way of either direct or allusive quotations, which are not always completely pertinent. Perhaps some clarification may be suitable here. After all, Sartre remains, amongst French living philosophers, the most characteristic.

Professor Chisholm's subtle and substantial paper, offered us under the same title, belongs in its entirety to the dominant tradition of Hume: the best of which lies in its critical spirit, the spirit of "philosophical inquiry." This small note of mine is only a footnote, a marginal, parenthetical clause, when compared to the general framework of the paper it refers to. Professor Chisholm takes a non-Humean position, though he is part of the genuine tradition of Hume; and Sartre remains a faithful "non-Cartesian," though he is in the historical lineage of Descartes.

Of course, it is phenomenology which is generally assumed among historians and critics to be, first of all, the point of departure of Sartre as a philosopher. As a matter of fact, I think that at the outset, in the 1930's, Sartre only knew of Husserl the French text of his *Cartesian Meditations* and *Phenomenology of Internal Time-Consciousness* edited by Heidegger; then, after 1935, Heidegger's *Being and Time,* at least through the pages of the book which has been just translated into French by Henry Corbin; and finally the *Descartes* of Jaspers, translated in 1937, in the epoch of the "Descartes Congress" in Paris. This small set of books doesn't allow us to point out an exclusive German influence to the detriment of the other sources, chiefly the domestic ones. On the other hand, there is no evidence of an early, personal knowledge of Hume, or even of Berkeley.[1]

---

[1] In the first pages of *Being and Nothingness,* trans. Hazel E. Barnes, (New York, Washington Square Press, 1966), p. lix, his "esse est percipi" is only quoted as a *locus,* a commonplace of a scholastic philosophical literature. Cf. John Passmore, *A Hundred Years of Philosophy,* third edition, (New York, Basic Books, 1966), p. 477 and footnote 1.

Anyway, at this moment, the phenomenological school was tortured by the internal quarrel between Husserl and his pupils (Scheler, Heidegger, and others) about *solipsism*. Wasn't it the inevitable, necessary consequence of any philosophical undertaking that first granted the Cartesian privilege of the *Cogito?* Vainly Husserl tried to reduce the difficulty, when from the start, in the second *Cartesian Meditation,* he denounced the confusion made by Descartes between the *Cogito* and the *res cogitans.* For at the same time that he was reducing this Empirical *Ego*—i.e., the Soul or the "Psyche"—he reduplicated it in affirming its fundamental reality again and again as a pure, transcendental one. Was actually this so-called "solipsism" of Husserl the effective, direct consequence of his "idealistic" avowal? I am not sure personally, and so far I don't see that this discussion had been even definitively resolved by any evidence. For, almost at the same moment, Wittgenstein[2] was forcibly driven back to the same "dead-end" of "solipsism," though surely it was not because of a Cartesian, idealistic persupposition. So, I am inclined to think that, in all likelihood, this quarrel about solipsism was not dependent upon a basic philosophical point of view; for it was a topic of the epoch, perhaps a mere polemical one, rather than a logical, necessary consequence of such and such set of premises. Anyway, and whatever one should think about this final point, the first philosophical paper of Sartre was written in 1935[3] as a piece in this discussion and as an attempt to avoid in a more radical way than Scheler or Heidegger the "solipsistic" consequence of the affirmation of a transcendental Ego by Husserl. But in this regard, the idea of Sartre is that my own "me" is an exactly observable by myself as the "me" of every other man. There is no privileged Ego, no privileged object in the phenomenological field. The whole phenomenological field is a field of *absolute observability.* In other words, even my own "me" as a subject is not transcendental: it is only a factual, factitious, a "transcendent" one.[4] What is transcendental is only Consciousness, a *pure* Consciousness without any Ego as its metaphysical "owner." That is to say, Consciousness is neither the *locus,* nor the private property of a certain, determined "Being" like an "Ego."

---

[2] Wittgenstein was totally unknown to Sartre.

[3] "La Transcendance de l'Ego" ("The Transcendence of the Ego") was first published in the 1936-37 issue of the annual series *Recherches philosophiques.* But the paper was written during the years 1934-1935; we have here the early stage of Sartre's thought.

[4] In the vocabulary of Sartre, "transcendent" means the kind of presence of the *object;* in opposition to consciousness which only is "transcenden*tal,*" transcendent is every object which the consciousness can "intend" in the world.

As pure consciousness, it is only a public field of "absolute existence."

Here, we have another indication of Sartre's philosophical, and extra-philosophical, motives. For, on the other hand, this new theory of the Ego is obviously directed against French contemporary *personalism*—for instance, the personalism of Emmanuel Mounier and his review *Esprit*. In other words, the criticism of every metaphysical Ego is a radical criticism of the French "Bourgeois." *He* is the Landlord, the proprietor, the "owner" of Consciousness. He affirms that his "right" is a meta-physical, almost a divine one; but as a matter of fact, historically, he is the owner only by way of privilege and extortion, as a buyer of common goods. Consciousness is for every man. Even the proletarian has the right to be conscious—the proletarian who is not an "Ego," not a person—who is only his own existence as such, a mere "nothingness."[5]

At least, such was the initial stage of Sartre. Unquestionably, in his following works, little by little, Sartre modified his first notion. Rather than Cartesian, it seems that it might be qualified as *Spinozistic*. Without any personal Ego, the absolute consciousness of 1935 was something like a tremendous, cosmic principle; and it was difficult to justify its first, radical, finitude. So, by successive correction, the egoistic function became more and more complicated, from Saint-Genet to the "Ego" of Sartre's autobiography, *The Words*. Nevertheless, a point remains abso-lutely constant throughout all these variations: the Ego is eminently observable and explainable. How is it possible?

First, the Ego, Sartre says, must be strictly compared with the world. They are at the same level; they are contemporary; both are "totalities." The world is a totality of *external* relationships, the Ego is a totality of *internal* relationships. In this regard, they are strictly parallel, perhaps one and the same thing.[6] That is, neither the world nor the Ego are *observable* as such, as *totalities*. We only preceive them "part by part," by means of externally existing things in the case of the world; by means of internal stages of consciousness and historical events of my own "history" in the case of the Ego. They are only observable as "detotalized totalities," but they are not totalized in the same way. And more precisely, the world is this very *totality* which the Ego only knows and lives as "detotalized." Both are "human;" finally, that is the only horizon of every human event. Under such conditions and limitations, neverthe-less, there is no Ego which could not be observed and understood. Every human reality is explainable exactly as any object of the world, by means of continuous successive approaches and approximations.

---

[5] Cf. The end of the paper "La Transcendance de l'Ego."

[6] The source here is obviously Kant.

By the "internal" relationship—an expression which he borrowed from the "idealistic" vocabulary of Léon Brunschvicg, perhaps unconsciously—Sartre only means the relationship of *time,* and he interprets it from his own, existentialistic point of view. Time is an "objective" relationship; but as such, the moments of time are only connected "from within." This "from within" is all the same the "from within" of the world. Insofar as the world too has a "from within," an interiority, this "from within" is time, and living existence. But a time lived within the world, that is exactly what we called an existing *me,* a human Ego.

On the other side, the pure consciousness, the transcendental "for-itself" is also a "finite" being. But, Sartre says, this finitude has immediately nothing to do with the possession of an Ego: rather it is the Ego whose finitude and limitation appear as the result of the first, radical finitude of Consciousness. This first finitude is impossible to explain. It is a first fact, an initial choice, because it is the ontological condition of every transcendence; that is, of every distinct consciousness. And if this finitude of the pure Consciousness is not the fact of an Ego, what is it? Something like a first ontological principle of individuation, if I have rightly understood. As a "for-itself," existence is individuated from the outset.

On this basis Sartre has unceasingly attempted to unify his composite inspiration. This is not the place to study the details of this story. First Sartre had to reduce the dualism of his two premises—the empirical me, on the one hand, and the transcendentally open existence on the other. The dialectic of *time* answers the problem. For its three dimensions are heterogeneous, though unified in the *present.* But the *future* is the open dimension of my free being, and thus it is really the trenscendental pole of existence. On the reverse side, the *past* is the constantly remaining consequence of my project: it is a "practico-inert" pole, and also a constantly confirmed ground for every new surpassing. So the Ego is knowable through and through, that is forwards and backwards, but not in the same way here and there. More precisely, both sides are only known through their constant mutual *contrast,* what is the present moment of my own awareness. On the other hand, this awarenes of the present instant is unceasingly duplicated, but also strengthened by the constant attendance of the others in the environment of my own being. The Ego lives amidst the world. As its inhabitant, it is always the contemporary of other beings. So "I see myself because somebody sees me." The person is presented as a subjective object to its own awareness insofar as it is an objective subject observable in the world for the other to look at. And to look at my own "me" doesn't require another mode of "look" than the look of the other—or conversely, my own look at the other.

I shall not here evaluate the adequacy of Sartre's views. What I have wished to point out is somewhat different. I have attempted to explain why, in my opinion, there is no ground for a right comparison between the "existentialist" version of phenomenology as illustrated by Sartre, and the contemporary philosophical trend which locates his position within the lineage of Hume. The paper of Professor Chisholm rightly illuminates the fact and the reasons why the Humean theory entails the unknowability of the Ego, insofar as the real Ego was conceived as substantive and hypothetical.

Surprisingly enough, we may notice a more obvious similarity between Sartre and some philosophers who are perhaps more characteristic of American thought— for example, George Herbert Mead and his theory of the social Ego,[7] though as a matter of fact Sartre probably didn't read Mead. But he has been always interested by the philosophical revolution of *behaviorism* and its impact on human sciences. At an early period, he knew the works of the American novelists, who were in vogue in France at the eve of World War II. There lies, in my opinion, a better ground for comparison. For Sartre, finally, the Ego is observable *for himself* because at the same time he acts in the world by means of behavior. I dare say that the idea was original. What remains is that such a notion was rightly chosen for its purpose: it was certainly a fruitful one for a philosopher was has been so constantly concerned with the diverse and multifarious manifestations of human reality.

UNIVERSITE DE BESANCON.

---

[7] Cf. Maurice Natanson, *The Social Dynamics of G. M. Mead,* (Washington, D.C., Public Affairs Press, 1956); Paul E. Pfuetze, *The Social Self,* (New York, Bookman Assoc., 1954); Andrew J. Reck, *Recent American Philosophy* (New York, Pantheon, 1961), Chapter III.

CHISHOLM ON SUBSTANCE

Donald Sievert

Professor Chisholm argues (1) that there are "selves" and (2) that "selves" are "observable." The argument for (1), though expressed in the current linguistic style, leads him to an old ontological view: minds consist, in part, of substances. Chisholm then faces one of the substance tradition's serious issues: do we observe substances? (2) is (part of) his affirmative answer. I believe the arguments for (1) and (2) are unsuccessful. The defense of (1) rests on the view that ordinary language "pictures" an ontology; that of (2) involves incorporating the claim Q, every quality is in a substance, into the notion of "manifestation." The success of the arguments depends, therefore, on serious philosophical issues.

Chisholm argues for the existence and observability of substances in both ordinary objects and minds.[1] He never puts his aim quite this way, so let me justify my doing so. Chisholm denies Hume's claim that ordinary objects consist of qualities *alone*. He claims that they consist of something, in addition to the qualities, which has qualities, something which is, for example, round. He cites A. E. Taylor's characterization of such a view and implies that the characterization is accurate and the view correct. What he objects to is Taylor's apparent denial that substances are observable. When he turns to minds, Chisholm cites, approvingly, Kant and others who claim that minds consist (in part) of substances. (Thus I shall call Chisholm's "selves" substances.) He objects to another claim of these philosophers, namely, their claim that we do not know such substances directly, i.e., by observation.

I shall consider the arguments for the *existence* of substances first. The kind of argument on which Chisholm relies is exemplified by his treatment of an ordinary object, a peach:

> One is tempted to say . . . that our idea of a peach is an idea of *something that has* a particular taste, color, figure, size, and

---

[1] I use 'ordinary objects' for things such as chairs, tables, trees, etc. It is preferable to 'physical object' since the latter is frequently associated with an ontological or scientific view.

consistency; and analogously for the other familiar physical things. But even this is not quite right. Our idea of a peach is not an idea of something that *has* the particular qualities, say, of sweetness, roundness, and fuzziness. It is an idea of something that *is* sweet and round and fuzzy.

He expresses the view again:

> More pedantically, our idea of a peach is an idea of an individual x such that x is sweet and x is round and x is fuzzy. By thus using variable and adjectives, we express the fact that the object of our idea is not the set of qualities . . . but the concrete thing that *is* sweet and round and fuzzy.

Before evaluating the argument, I shall summarize his case for substantial selves.

He claims, correctly, that Hume does not deny that there are selves: specifically, the "bundle" view is not a denial that there are selves. Hume is, again correctly, described as providing a certain explication of 'self.' Yet Chisholm is uneasy. He is bothered by Hume's use of the pronoun in reporting the results of introspection and his use of the *same* pronoun on several occasions. According to Chisholm, the repeated use of 'I' in Hume's reports (of finding only impressions and ideas) shows that Hume ". . . presupposed that there exists an x such that x succeeds in finding certain things and such that x fails to find certain others."

Now we may appraise the arguments. I shall restrict myself to the case of ordinary objects. Since the argument in each case is, as far as I can tell, of the same kind, my criticisms will apply to the case of selves as well. Two features of the argument stand out: the use of italics and the hybrid linguistic items, e.g., 'x is sweet.' (I call the latter hybrids because they are a cross between English sentences and expressions of a more formal language.) I submit that Chisholm construes words such as 'something,' 'is,' 'same,' etc. ontologically and that this is why he italicizes them. What 'something' means would be better expressed by 'some thing,' where 'thing' means an entity, over and above the qualities, in the peach. The hybrid items support my claim. The range of 'x' is, presumably, the substances in ordinary objects; the adjectives express (represent, refer to) qualities of those substances. Since Chisholm denies that the peach is merely a collection of qualities, and claims that it involves something else, something exemplifying those qualities, one may conclude that he believes it is a collection of qualities in a substance.[2]

---

[2] I ignore the issue of whether or not these substances have natures (essences).

The argument is, succinctly, that since we use subject-predicate assertions to characterize ordinary objects, those objects consist of two kinds of entities, and hence do not consist of qualities alone. Clearly, it turns on the premise that if an object is characterized by such an assertion, it consists of two kinds of entities: properties and a substance, the latter exemplifying the former. This premise is false; Chisholm provides no reason to believe it is true. As Leibniz and Berkeley, among others, have argued, there are alternative ways of handling predication.[3] For example, one may hold that subject terms refer to collections of qualities, and that subject-predicate assertions express a quality's being a member of such a collection. If this premise is false, why does Chisholm accept it?

Briefly, his beliefs about *ordinary* languages are encouraged by what can be said about *formal* languages. (In other words, he does not sharply distinguish the two; this is shown by the hybrids he employs.) In formal languages, designed in part to "picture" an ontology, one may conclude, *given certain interpretation rules,* that a given linguistic item say '$f_1(a)$,' represents two entities, different in kind, connected in a certain way. Some want to transcribe ordinary assertions into such a formalism. Many, including Chisholm, are tempted to transcribe a sentence such as 'This is sweet' as '$f_1(a)$,' taking an interpretation of the latter for granted. (While Chisholm doesn't go quite this far, he certainly moves in this direction.)[4] This move is illegitimate. One has to argue *independently* that the ontology represented by the formalism and its interpretation rules is correct. In other words, the interpretation rules presuppose a certain ontology. One may not appeal, as I believe Chisholm tacitly does, to just the fact that a sentence can be transcribed by an expression representing a certain ontological analysis to establish that analysis.[5]

---

[3] See, for example, Leibniz' *Discourse on Metaphysics* (and the correspondence with Arnauld concerning it) and Berkeley's *Principles of Human Knowledge,* section 49.

[4] One might object that I have taken too much liberty with Chisholm's remarks. I do not think that I have. Nevertheless, it is clear that Chisholm argues that the fact that our descriptive language is of a certain sort shows that a certain ontology is correct. Such an argument is illegitimate for the kinds of reasons I mention.

[5] There is an aspect of Chisholm's objection to Hume that I leave unexplored. He cites Leibniz' claim that we must distinguish collections of "abstract" qualities from the set of properties in an ordinary object. The implication is that Hume claims that ordinary objects consist of "abstract" qualities, e.g., warmth, as opposed to particular degrees of qualities, e.g., some particular degree of warmth. Given Hume's discussion in the *Treatise* section "Of Abstract Ideas," Chisholm's claim is untenable.

Chisholm sees a difference between Hume's views about ordinary objects and selves. While Hume is claimed to be simply wrong about the former, he is charged with relying on the existence of selves in arguing that there are no such entities.[6] Chisholm is sensitive to a feature which does distinguish the two cases. While the repeated use of 'I' does not, as I have argued, support the claim that substantial selves exist, it suggests that something other than the "perceptions" Hume finds does exist. One is led to ask: to what does 'I' allude? Without defending it here, I shall propose an answer.[7] Since it provides an alternative way of reading Hume, I shall state it in the context of his views.

Hume believes that there are mental acts, including acts by which we are aware of our own (mental) states.[8] When one introspects, there is an act of awareness (direct acquaintance) with what we introspect. This act, accounting as it does for our being aware of something else, is not itself the object of an act of awareness. Through a "shift in set," one can become aware of it by means of a *second* act which is not itself an object of an act of awareness. The main idea is this: during introspection there is an act accounting for the introspection which is not itself introspected. It is to this act, I submit, that Hume's use of 'I' refers. That he uses 'I' each time indicates that it is the same *kind* of act (direct acquaintance) each time. (That it is a (numerically) different act each time becomes clear in Book I, Part IV of the *Treatise*.) In short, for Hume there is a "self" we cannot "catch": there are acts involved in introspection of which we are not, at the time of the introspection, aware.[9] But since

Note also that Chisholm claims that if Hume's view of ordinary objects is wrong, so is his view of the self. This shows how closely parallel Chisholm believes the problems of selves and ordinary objects to be. Both may be wrong, but they do not stand or fall together. Hume saw the distinction: his attack on substantial selves, while resting on the same ground as that on material substances, is independent of the latter.

[6] For Hume, selves are temporal series of ideas and, probably, impressions. More accurately he says that such series are all we can know about minds.

[7] *Cf.* E. B. Allaire, "The Circle of Ideas and the Circularity of the Meditations," *Dialogue*, V, No. 2, 1966, pp. 131-153. Allaire makes the same suggestion with respect to the *cogito*.

[8] See the end of Book I, Part I, Section 1 of the *Treatise*. There Hume talks of reflecting on our own thinking by means of "secondary" ideas. These ideas are what I would call mental "acts." Hume himself, in Book I, Part IV, Section I, talks of examining our states of understanding or reasonings "by a reflex act of the mind." I submit that the issue of "acts" in Hume's writings centers not on their existence but on his account of their nature. The adequacy of the account is another, important, issue.

[9] This shows that there is a way, other than appealing to a hasty generalization, to eliminate Hume's use of 'I.'

for Hume these are momentary, one may not claim, as Chisholm does,
that the use of 'I' commits Hume to the view that minds have substances
as parts.

As a prelude to his claims about the self's observability, Chisholm
asserts that a large class of so-called sense data are "accidents" of
persons or selves. I am not concerned with the merits of this view. What
interests me is how he employs it to argue that we observe selves. He
leaves no doubt that the accidents in question are properties of substantial selves. Initially, he simply asserts that when we are acquainted
with such properties, we are acquainted with the substances having
them.[10] Many philosophers, including Kant, disagree with him. So he
cites their "argument" for the view that while we do observe properties of
selves, we do not observe the selves.[11] He claims they commit a logical
blunder: they fail to see that the argument shows that we *do* observe
substances.

What they supposedly do not see is that:

> From the fact that we are acquainted with the self as it mani-
> fests itself as having certain qualities, it follows that we are
> acquainted with the self as it is in itself. Manifestation, after all,
> is the converse of acquaintance: x manifests itself to y, if and
> only if, y is acquainted with x. How can a man be acquainted
> with *anything* unless the thing manifests or presents itself to
> him? And how can the thing manifest or present itself unless it
> manifests or presents itself as having certain qualities or attri-
> butes?

Chisholm begs the question. When others spoke of manifestations of
selves, they distinguished the manifestations from the selves and claimed
that we (directly) observe only the former. They deny that "manifestation is the converse of acquaintance;" instead, they maintain that a self
manifests itself to someone if and only if he is acquainted with a manifestation which stands in some relation to the self *and* he knows that
(something of the kind of) the manifestation stands in that relation to
(something of the kind of) the self.[12] In other words, they claim that,

---

[10] Chisholm does not distinguish observing *a* substance, some *particular* substance,
and one and the same substance through time. His claim that we observe substances is, therefore, shallow.

[11] It seems to me that Chisholm's underlying suspicion that the "argument" is
merely a claim is justified.

[12] See footnote 10. I do not mean to suggest that others saw the distinctions.
Most did not.

given Q and acquaintance with some property, one may infer that the property is in a substance.

Chisholm builds Q into the notion of manifestation. A thing can only manifest itself by having certain qualities; if qualities are manifestations of substances and we observe qualities, then we know they are in substances. The grammar of 'manifests' misleads: knowing that something manifests itself is tantamount to knowing it exists. But knowing the manifestation in the sense of observing it does not imply, as Chisholm thinks it does, that we know what is manifested in the same way, *viz.* observationally.

WASHINGTON UNIVERSITY
ST. LOUIS.

THE ENDS OF MAN

Jacques Derrida

"Now, I say this: Man, and in general every reasonable being, *exists* as end in itself, and *not merely as means,* of which such and such a will can make use as it pleases; in all of his actions, in those which concern himself as well as in those which concern other reasonable beings, he should always be considered *at the same time as end."*

Kant, *Foundations of the Metaphysics of Morals*

"Ontology abandons us here: it has simply permitted us to determine the last ends of human reality, its fundamental possibles and the value which haunt it."

Jean-Paul Sartre, *Being and Nothingness*

"Man is an invention whose recent date, and whose nearing end perhaps, are easily shown by the archeology of our thought."

Michel Foucault, *Les mots et les choses*

Every philosophical congress has by necessity a political significance. This is not only due to what has always bound the essence of the philosophical to the essence of the political. Essential and general, this political implication adds weight to it, renders it more serious, and determines its character, especially when the philosophical congress is also an international one.

The possibility of an international philosophical conference can be investigated endlessly, along different lines and on multiple levels of generality. In its most general sense, such a possibility implies that, contrary to the essence of philosophy, philosophical nationalities have been formed. At a given moment in a given historical, political and economic context, these national groups have deemed it necessary to organize international meetings, and to be represented by their national identities, and there to determine or relate their respective differences. Such a meeting of differences can take place only to the extent that national philosophical identities are presupposed that are defined by their doctrinal content or by a certain philosophical "style." But the relating of differences also presupposes a common element: a meeting can take

180

place only through a common image which all the participants share, which in this case would be the so-called universality of philosophical discourse. By these words I designate less a fact than a project which is associated by its essence (indeed by the essence and the idea of Being and of truth) with a certain group of languages and "cultures." For it is evident that something has happened to the diaphanous purity of this element.

How should we understand otherwise the fact that it seems necessary to hold international meetings, which have as their aim to repair, overcome, or relate national philosophical differences? Inversely, how should we interpret the fact that an international philosophical meeting is an extremely rare thing throughout the world? The philosopher knows that this recent occurrence, which was beyond imagination a century ago, is becoming a frequent and easy phenomenon in certain societies, though it is rare, surprisingly and admirably, in most of the world. In regard to philosophical thought, which is adverse to haste and volubility, it seems that what is disquieting about many congresses is the often feverish quality and proliferation of improvised exchanges. The fact remains that there are numerous societies, languages, cultures, political or national organizations in which no exchange in the form of international philosophical conventions are possible. This impossibility should not be hastily interpreted. It is not essentially the result of an intentional political-ideological interdiction. In those instances where such an interdiction exists, it is quite likely that this disagreement has already taken on meaning in Western metaphysics or philosophy, that it has already been formulated in political concepts drawn from metaphysics. Speaking of the nonconventions, I am not alluding to ideologico-political fences or barriers which divide a field which is already philosophical. I am thinking first of those cultural, linguistic, and political areas where the organizing of a philosophical convention would simply make no sense. If I take the liberty of reminding you of this obvious point, it is because I believe that a conference which has chosen "anthropos," philosophical anthropology, as its theme must be feeling at its borders the persistent weight of differences which are of another order than internal or intra-philosophical disputes.

I should like to point to what seems to me to be one of the general political implications of this conference. Taking care not to hastily evaluate this point, I wish to indicate the connection between the possibility of an international philosophical convention and the *form* of *democracy*.

Democracy must be the form of the political organization of the society in which the members of this convention live. This means, at the least, that:

1. The philosophical national identity come to terms with a non-identity, that it does not exclude the existence of a relative diversity and the expression of this diversity, possibly as a minority. It is obvious that the philosophers here present naturally no more identify themselves with one another in their thinking than they are representative of some unanimous national discourse.

2. The philosophers here do not identify with the official political policy of their country. Permit me to speak here in my name. When I had the honor of being invited to this meeting, my hesitation could be overcome only when I was assured that I would be able to bear witness here to my agreement with those in the United States who were struggling against what was then the official policy of their country in certain areas of the world, notably in Vietnam. It is clear that such an action, and the fact that I have been allowed to perform it, signifies that those who hear my speech no more identify with the policy of their country than I do and feel no obligation to uphold it, at least insofar as they participate in this conference.

And yet, there would be a sort of naiveté in letting oneself be reassured by the appearance of such freedom. It would be an illusion to believe that political innocence is restored and collusion stopped as soon as oppositions can be expressed in the country itself, not only through the voices of the citizens but also through those of foreigners, and that from then on diversity or even oppositions can come together freely in discursive relations. That a statement opposing some official policy is authorized by the authorities, indicates that it does not upset the social order; it *does not disturb.* This last expression, "it does not disturb," can be understood in all of its meanings. This is what I wanted to remind you of at the beginning when speaking of the *form of democracy* as being the political milieu of any international philosophical conference. And it is also the reason for which I proposed to emphasize *form* no less than *democracy.* Such is the question which posed itself to me during the preparations for this meeting, from the time of receiving the invitation and deliberating upon it to the writing of this paper, which I date very precisely the month of April 1968 — these were also the weeks when the Vietnam peace talks began and when Martin Luther King was assassinated. A little later, while I was typing this text, for the first time in history, the universities of Paris were invaded at the request of a rector by the forces of social order, then reoccupied by the students in the upheaval. Because of its indetermination or its complexity, this political and historical horizon would call for interminable analysis. It is not to be undertaken here. I simply felt obliged to note and date the incertitude and anxiety in which I prepared this paper. These feelings seem to me to belong by right to the essential domain and the general problematics facing this conference.

I

Where does France stand with regard to man?

This question seemed to me to command our attention for two reasons. For one, a Frenchman participating in an international scholarly conference on philosophical anthropology should, according to a tradition of the three preceeding centuries of philosophical interchange, give the latest views prevalent in his country. Secondly, the question of "man" is currently being raised in France along highly significant lines and in an original historico-philosophical structure. Thus, on the basis of a few indications, what I will call "France" in the course of this paper will be only the non-empirical locus of a movement, a structure, and an articulation of the question of "man." Later it will be possible and probably necessary — but only then — rigorously to relate this position to any other instance defining something such as France. Naturally this cannot be discussed here.

Where, then, does France stand with regard to man?

After the war, under the name of existentialism, either Christian or atheistic, and conjointly with a fundamentally Christian personalism, the dominant school of thought in France professed to be essentially humanistic. Even if one does not wish to summarize Sartre's thought in the slogan "existentialism is a humanism," one has to acknowledge that in *Being and Nothingness, L'esquisse d'une théorie des émotions (Outline of a Theory of Emotions)*, etc., the major concept, the theme in the last analysis, the irreducible horizon and origin, is what is then called "human-reality." This is, as we know, a translation of Heidegger's "Dasein." A terrible translation in many ways, but all the more significant. That this translation which was proposed by Corbin was adopted, that it was dominant through the authority of Sartre, leads one to give much thought to the reading or non-reading of Heidegger at that time and to the interest that existed in reading him or in not reading him in this way.

Certainly, the notion of "human-reality" expressed the project of rethinking at new costs, if I may say so, the humanity of man. If one substituted for the idea of man, with all its metaphysical heritage, with the substantialist motif or temptation that is included with it, the neutral and indeterminate idea of human-reality, it was also in order to suspend all the presuppositions which had always constituted the concept of the unity of man. It was thus as well a reaction against a certain intellectual or spiritual humanism which had dominated French philosophy (Brunschvicg, Alain, Bergson, etc.) And this neutralization of any metaphysical or speculative theses with regard to the unity of the anthropos could be considered in some ways as the faithful heritage of Husserl's transcendental phenomenology and of the fundamental ontology of *Sein und Zeit* (the only Heidegger known at that time, along with *What is Metaphysics?* and *Kant and the Problem of Metaphysics*). And yet, in spite of this supposed neutralizing of metaphysical presuppositions,[1] we have to admit that the unity of man is not in itself called into question. Not only is existentialism a humanism, but the ground and horizon of what Sartre then called his "phenomenological ontology" (this is the subtitle of *Being and Nothingness*) remains the unity of human-reality. In so far as it describes the structures of human-reality, phenomenological ontology is a philosophical anthropology. Whatever decisive breaks from classical anthropologies may be indicated by this Hegelian-Husserlian-Heideggerian anthropology, there is no interruption in a metaphysical familiarity which so naturally relates the *we* of the philosopher to "we-men," to the *we* of the total horizon of humanity. Although the theme of history is present in the discourse of this period, the history of concepts is not studied; and, for example, the history of the concept of man is never questioned. Everything takes place as though the sign "man" had no origin, no historical, cultural, linguistic limit, not even a metaphysical limit. At the end of *Being and Nothingness,* when Sartre poses programmatically the question of the unity of Being (which in this context means the totality of being), when he titles this question "metaphysics" in order to distinguish it from phenomenological ontology, which

---

[1] The humanism which in its depth characterizes the philosophical theses of Sartre is nevertheless most unerringly and ironically dismantled in *Nausea*. In the caricature of the Autodidact, for example, the same figure joins together the theological objective of absolute knowledge and the humanistic ethic, as one and the other is put into practice in the form of an encyclopedic love of knowledge (epistemophily). This causes the Autodidact to undertake the reading of the universal library (actually Western and in the final analysis parochial) in alphabetical order in order to locate the sections in which he can love Man ("There is a goal, sir, there is a goal ... there are men ... we have to love them ..."), through the representation of men, preferably young men. It is in the conversation with the Autodidact that Roquentin attacks humanism most severely. For example, at the moment when nausea is rising slowly within him, he says to himself: "I do not want to be identified with it or to have my good red blood go to fattening this lymphatic creature: I will not commit the stupidity of calling myself 'anti-humanistic.' I am not humanistic, that is all there is to it."

itself described the essential specificity of regions, it is obvious that this metaphysical unity of Being, as a totality in itself and of itself is precisely the unity of the human-reality in its final project. Being in itself and Being for itself were *Being* and this totality of being within which they were put together was linked to itself, referred to itself, became apparent to itself by the essential project of human-reality.[2] That which was thereby named, in a supposedly neutral and indeterminate way, was none other than the metaphysical unity of man and God, the project of becoming God as a final objective constituting human-reality. Atheism changes nothing in this fundamental structure. Sartre's attempt is a remarkable example verifying Heidegger's proposition according to which "all humanism remains metaphysical," metaphysics being the other name for onto-theology.

Defined in this way, humanism or anthropologism was at this time a sort of common ground of existentialisms whether Christian or atheist, of the philosophy of values, whether spiritualistic or not, of personalisms, whether rightist or leftist, and of Marxism in the classical style. And if one's references is on the ground of political ideologies, anthropologism was the unnoticed and uncontested common ground of Marxism, of social-democratic or democratic-Christian discourse. This profound agreement, in its philosophical expression, was based on the authority of anthropologistic readings of Hegel (interest in *The Phenomenology of Mind* as it was read by Kojève), of Marx (special attention to the *Manuscripts of '44*), of Husserl (whose descriptive regional work was

---

[2] "Every human-reality is at once a direct project of metamorphosing its own For-self into In-self-For-self, and the project of appropriating the world as totality being- in-self, in the patterns of a fundamental quality. All human-reality is a passion, in that it projects losing itself in order to found Being and to constitute, at the same time, the In-self which avoids contingency by being its own foundation, the *Ens cause sui* that religions call God. And thus the passion of man is the opposite of that of Christ, for man loses himself as man in order that God be born. But the idea of God is contradictory and we lose ourselves in vain; man is a useless passion" (p. 707-8). The unity of the totality of being is bound up and appears to itself in human-reality as consciousness for-self: "For-self and In-self are joined by a synthetic union which is none other than the For-self itself." (*In-self and For-self: metaphysical glimpses*, p. 711). This synthetic unity is determined as *lack:* lack of totality of being, lack *of* God, which could have easily been transformed into lack *in* God. Human-reality is *missing* God: "The *ens causa sui* then remains as the missing" (p. 714). ". . . The for-self is determined in its Being as *lack*" (p. 720). As for the sense of the Being of this totality of being, as for the history of this concept of negativity as relation with God, as for the sense and the origin of the concept of (human) reality, as for the reality of the real, no question is raised. In this respect, that which is true of *Being and Nothingness* is even more true of *Critique de la raison dialectique*.

emphasized and the transcendental questions neglected), and of Heidegger, in whose work only a project for a philosophical anthropology or an existential analytics was known or retained *(Sein und Zeit)*. Of course, what I am pointing out here are the dominant characteristics of a period. This period is not exhausted in its dominant characteristics. And it is impossible to say, absolutely strictly speaking, that it began after the war; and even less that it has today completed its cycle. I feel, nevertheless, that empirical cuts are justified in this case to the extent that they alone can permit the reading of a dominant motif and that they are backed by fairly incontestable signs for anyone approaching such a period. Furthermore, this cutting is provisional, and in a moment we are going to reinsert this period in the time and space of a larger totality.

To set off in heavy type the opposing characteristics between this period and the following, the one in which we are now and which is probably also undergoing a mutation, we have to remember that during the ten years which followed the war there did not yet reign this all-powerful theme which is now more and more prominent, and given the name of the "so-called sciences of man," indicating by this expression a certain distance, but a still respectful distance. On the contrary, the current questioning of humanism is contemporaneous with the dominating and fascinating extension of the "behavioral sciences" within the philosophical field.

II

As we know, an entire aspect of the anthropological reading of Hegel, Husserl and Heidegger was a misinterpretation, perhaps of the most serious sort. It is this reading which provided French post-war thought with its best conceptual resources.

First of all, *The Phenomenology of Mind,* which had only begun to be read in France, is in no way concerned with something which could be called man. A science of the experience of consciousness, a science of the structures of the phenomenality of the mind in reference to itself, it is strictly distinct from anthropology. In *The Encyclopedia,* the section entitled "Phenomenology of Mind" comes after "Anthropology" and very explicitly exceeds its limits. What is true of *The Phenomenology* is *a fortiori* true of the system of *The Logic.*

Similarly, in the second place, the criticism of anthropologism is one of the inaugural motives of Husserl's transcendental phenomenology. This criticism is explicit and calls anthropologism by its proper name beginning with *The Prolegomena to Pure Logic.*[3] Later it aims not only

---

[3] Ch. 7, "Psychologism as Sceptic Relativism"; 39, "Anthropologism in the Logic of Sigwart"; 40, "Anthropologism in the Logic of B. Erdmann."

at empirical or empiricist anthropologism, but also at transcendental anthropologism.[4] The transcendental structures described after the phenomenological reduction are not those of that intra-mundane being called "man." They are not essentially linked with society, culture or language, or even with man's "soul" or his "psyche." And just as, according to Husserl, a consciousness can be imagined without soul (seelenloses),[5] so can — and a fortiori — a consciousness be imagined without man.

It is therefore surprising and very significant that at the same time that the authority of Husserl's thought was introduced and becoming established in France after the war, and even became a sort of philosophical fashion there, its criticism of anthropologism went completely unnoticed, or in any event was without effect. One of the most paradoxical paths of this misinterpretation passes through an equally distorted reading of Heidegger. It is because the analytics of the Dasein interpreted in strictly anthropological terms that Husserl is sometimes limited or criticized from a Heideggerian viewpoint and everything in phenomenology which is not useful for anthropological description is put aside. I say that this is a very paradoxical path because it follows the same line of reading as Husserl. Indeed, Husserl precipitously interpreted Sein und Zeit [6] as an anthropological deviation of transcendental phenomenology.

Thirdly, directly after the war and after the appearance of Being and Nothingness, Heidegger recalled in his Letter on Humanism to anyone who still was not able to get the point, who had not even been able to take account of the very first paragraphs of Sein und Zeit, that anthropology and humanism were not the milieu of his thought and the horizon of his questions. The "destruction" of metaphysics or classical ontology is, indeed, directed against humanism.[7] After the humanist and anthropological wave which swept over French philosophy, it might have been expected that the anti-humanist and anti-anthropological reflux which was to follow, and in which we now are, would come to rediscover the

---

[4] Ideen 1, cf. 49 and 54.

[5] Ibid.

[6] Cf. Nachwort zur meiner Ideen and marginal notes from the edition of Sein und Zeit at the Husserl Archives in Louvain.

[7] "Every humanism is founded on a metaphysics or makes itself that foundation. Every determination of the essence of man which already presupposes, consciously or not, the interpretation of beings without raising the question concerning the truth of Being, is metaphysical. This is why, if we consider the manner in which the essence of man is determined, the characteristic of every metaphysics is revealed in that it is "humanistic." In the same way, every humanism remains metaphysical, etc. (Letter on Humanism).

heritage of thought which had thus been disfigured, or rather in which the figure of man had been too quickly recognized. Would there not be a return to Hegel, Husserl and Heidegger? Would there not be a more rigorous reading of their texts, removing the interpretation from the humanist and anthropological schemas?

This was not to be the case, and I should like now to question the significance of this phenomenon. The criticism of humanism and anthropologism, which is one of the dominant and guiding motifs of current French thought, far from seeking its sources or its guarantee in Hegel's, Husserl's or Heidegger's criticism of this very humanism and this very anthropologism, seems, on the contrary, in a gesture which is sometimes more implicit than systematically articulated, to *amalgamate* Hegel, Husserl and, in a more diffuse and ambiguous manner, Heidegger, with the old humanist metaphysics. I purposely use the word "amalgam," which joints the alchemic reference, which is primary here, with strategical or tactical reference in the realm of political ideology.

Before trying to interpret this seemingly paradoxical phenomenon, some precautions must be taken. First of all, this amalgamation does not mean that no progress has been made in France in the reading of Hegel, Husserl or Heidegger, nor that this progress has not led to a questioning of the humanist distortion. But this progress and this questioning are not in the forefront, and this should prove significant. Inversely and symetrically, for those who effect this amalgamation the schemas of the anthropological misinterpretation of Sartre's time are still at work, and it is these schemas which sometimes are responsible for Hegel, Husserl and Heidegger being consigned to the shadows of humanist metaphysics. Very often, in fact, those who denounce humanism as well as metaphysics have remained at this "first reading" of Hegel, Husserl and Heidegger, and more than one example of this could be cited from among numerous recent texts. This tends to suggest that, in certain respects and at least in this measure, we have remained in the same camp.

But it is of little matter, for the question I would like to raise, whether a certain author has badly read or simply has not read a certain text, or that he has remained, in regard to thoughts which he believes himself to have surpassed or overturned, in a state of great foolishness. And this is why such and such an author's name or such and such a work will not be cited here. What should concern us, beyond justifications which, de facto, are most often insufficient, is the sort of deep and necessarily subterranean justification which makes apparent the connection between Hegel's, Husserl's and Heidegger's criticism or *delimitations* of metaphysical humanism and precisely the sphere of that which they criticize or delimit. In a word, whether the right has been made explicit or not, whether it has been articulated or not (and I personally believe that it has not), what authorizes us today to consider as essentially anthropic or anthropocentric all that which, in metaphysics or at the limits of metaphysics, has presumed to criticize or to delimit anthropologism? What remains of the "relève," [8] of man in the thought of Hegel, Husserl and Heidegger?

III

First of all let us reconsider, in the order of Hegelian discourse which still holds together by so many threads the language of our time, the relations between anthropology on one hand, and phenomenology and logic [9] on the other. Once the confusion of a merely anthropological reading of the *Phenomenology of Mind* has been rigorously avoided, it must be recognized that the relations between anthropology and phenomenology are not, according to Hegel, relations of mere exteriority. With all that they introduce, the Hegelian concepts of truth, negativity and *Aufhebung* (relève) prevent this from being so. In Part Three of the *Encyclopedia,* which treats of the *Philosophy of Mind,* the first section *(Philosophy of Mind)* places the *Phenomenology of Mind* between *Anthropology* and *Psychology.* The *Phenomenology of Mind* follows *Anthropology* and precedes *Psychology. Anthropology* deals with mind — which is the "truth of nature" — as soul or natural mind (Seele or Naturgeist). The development of the soul, as it is traced by anthropology, passes through natural soul (natürliche Seele), sensitive soul (fühlende Seele), and real and effective soul (wirkliche Seele). This development is carried out, completed, and opens on consciousness. The last paragraph of the *Anthropology* [10] defines the general form of con-

---

8 The word "relève — a tentative translatoin of *Aufhebung* — cannot be translated into English. It means both to elevate, and to replace as in "to relieve one of one's functions."

9 Without neglecting the complexity of the relationship between *Logic* and *The Phenomenology of Mind,* the question we raise authorizes us to consider them *together* at that point of opening where Absolute Knowledge joins them.

10 "The effective soul, in the *habit* of feeling and of its concrete feeling-of-self is in itself the ideality existing for itself of its determinations, interiorized, recalled (erinnert) in itself in its exteriority and in an infinite relation to itself. This Being-for-self of free universality is the superior watch over the I by the soul, abstract

sciousness, precisely that form from which proceeds the *Phenomenology of Mind,* in the first chapter on *Sense-Certitude.* [11] Consciousness, the phenomenological element, is thus the truth of the soul; that is, of that which is precisely the object of anthropology. Consciousness is the truth of man; phenomenology is the truth of anthropology. "Truth" should be understood here in a strictly Hegelian sense. In this Hegelian sense the metaphysical essence of truth — the truth of truth — is arrived at. Truth is here the presence or the presentation of essence as *Gewesenheit,* of *Wesen* as having-been. Consciousness is the truth of man inasmuch as man appears there in his being-past, in his having-been, in his surpassed and preserved, retained, interiorized (erinnert) and taken over (relevé) past. "Aufheben" is to take over, in the sense that "to take over" means at once to displace, to elevate, to replace and to promote in one and the same movement. Consciousness is the *Aufhebung* of the soul or of man; phenomenology is the "relève" of anthropology. Phenomenology is *no longer* but it is *still* a science of man. In this sense all of the structure described in the *Phenomenology of Mind* — just as everything which links them with Logic — are the structures of what has taken over for man. Man remains there in his "relève". His essence lies in the phenomenology. This equivocality of the relation of "relève" undoubtedly marks the end of man, of man past, but at the same time it marks the completion of man, the appropriation of his essence. This is the end of finite man, the end of the finitude of man, the unity of the finite and the infinite, the finite as surpassing of oneself; these essential themes of Hegel are recognized at the end of the Anthropology when consciousness is finally designated as "infinite relation with oneself." The "relève" of man is his *telos* or his *eschaton.* The unity of these two ends of man, the unity of his death, of his termination, of his completion, is enveloped

---

universality, inasmuch as it is for this abstract universality, which is thus *thought* and subject for itself and precisely the subject of its judgment in which it [the I] excludes the natural totality of its determinations as an object, a world *exterior* to it, and refers to it, so that it is reflected in it in itself immediately: this is *consciousness.*

"Die wirkliche Seele in der *Gewohnheit* des Empfindens und ihres *konkreten* Selbstgefühl ist an sich die für sich seiende *Idealität* ihrer Bestimmtheiten, in ihrer Aüsserlichkeit *erinnert* in sich und unendliche Beziehung auf sich. Dies Fürsichsein der freien Allgemeinheit ist das höhere Erwachen der Seele zum *Ich,* der abstrakten Allgemeinheit, insofern sie für die abstrakte Allgemeinheit ist, welche so *Denken* und *Subjekt* für sich und zwar bestimmt Subjekt seines Urteils ist, in welchem es die natürliche Totalität seiner Bestimmungen als ein Objekt, eine ihm *äussere* Welt, von sich ausschlieszt und sich darauf bezieht, so dasz es in derselben unmittelbar in sich reflektiert ist, — das *Bewusstsein*" (412).

[11] That is, objectivity in general; the relationship of an "I" in general with a being-object in general.

in the Greek idea of *telos,* in the discourse on *telos,* which is also discourse on *eidos,* on *ousia* and on *aletheia.* Such a discourse, for Hegel
as in all metaphysics, indissociably coordinates teleology with an escha-
tology, a theology and an ontology. The idea of the end of man is then
always already prescribed in metaphysics, in the thought of the truth of
man. What is difficult to conceive of today is an end of man which is
not organized by a dialectic of truth and of negativity, an end of man
which is not a teleology in the first person plural. The *we* which in the
Phenomenology of Mind joins natural consciousness and philosophical
consciousness and assures the proximity to oneself of that fixed and
central being for which this circular reappropriation is produced. The *we*
is the unity of absolute knowkledge and anthropology, of God and man,
of onto-theo-teleology and humanism. *"Being"* and language — the group
of languages — which it governs or which it opens, such is the name of
that which assures this passage by the *we* between metaphysics and
humanism.[12]

---

[12] The necessity of the schema of this ambiguity or of this "relevance" which
is completed in Hegelian metaphysics and which persists everywhere where metaphysics — that is, our language — maintains its authority, could have been verified
in all of the pre-Hegelian systems, and especially in Kant.
  A) *On the one hand,* it is precisely when Kant wants to conceive of something
as the *end,* the pure *end,* the *end* in itself, that he must criticize anthropologism,
in the *Metaphysics of Morals.* The principles of morality cannot be deduced from
the knowledge of the nature of a particular being called man: "Such a Metaphysics
of morals completely isolated, joined neither with anthropology, theology, physics
or hyperphysics, and even less with occult qualities (which could be called hypo-
physics) is not merely an indispensable substratum of every theoretical knowledge
of duties defined with certitude; it is even a desideratum of the greatest importance
for the effective accomplishment of their stipulations" ... "It is still of the greatest
practical importance that these concepts and laws be derived from the source of
pure reason, that they be presented pure and uncombined and, moreover, that the
breadth of all of this rational, practical, and yet pure knowledge; that is, the entire
strength of pure practical reason, be determined; yet it is important here to abstain,
even though speculative philosophy permits and even sometimes finds it necessary,
from making the principles depend upon the particular nature of human reason,
but rather, since moral laws must be valid for every reasonable being in general,
they should be deduced from the universal concept of a reasonable being in general,
thus laying out all of ethics, which in its *application* to men needs anthropology,
independently of the latter science, as pure philosophy; that is, as metaphysics ...
etc." .... "When carrying out such an undertaking, it is of the greatest importance
to remember that: trying to derive the reality of this principle from the *particular
constitution of human nature* (aus der besondern Eigenschaft der menschlichen
Natur) must never even be considered. For duty must be a practical and unconditioned necessity of action; it must consequently be valid for all reasonable beings
(the only ones to which an imperative can absolutely be applied), and it is *only
as such* that duty is also a law for all human will" (*Foundations of the Metaphysics*

We have just perceived the necessity which links the idea of *phainesthai* with the idea of *telos*. In the same horizon we can read the theory of teleology which commands Husserl's transcendental phenomenology. Despite the criticism of anthropologism, "humanity" is still, here, the name of the being to which transcendental *telos,* determined as Idea (in the Kantian sense), or as Reason, is announced. It is man as *rational animal* which, in its most classical metaphysical determination, designates the place of deployment of teleological reason; that is, history. For Husserl as for Hegel, reason is history and there is no history except that of reason. The latter functions in every man, no matter how primitive he may still be, in that he is "the rational animal" *(Origin of Geometry)*. Every type of humanity and human sociality "has a root in the essential component of the human universal, a root in which a teleological Reason which passes throughout historicity is announced. Thus is indicated an original problematics which relates to the totality of history and to the total sense which, in the last instance, gives it its unity" *(Origin of Geometry)*.13 Transcendental phenomenology would be

of *Morals,* Part Two). In these three passages we see that that which is always of the "greatest importance" (von der hochsten Wichtigkeit ... von der grossten praktischen Wichtigkeit ... von der aussersten Wichtigkeit) is to determine the end in itself (as the unconditioned principle of morality) independently of any anthropological given. The purity of the end cannot be thought on the basis of man.

B) But on the other hand, inversely, the specificity of man, his essence of reasonable being, of rational animal (zôon logon ekon) is only announced to itself on the basis of the thought of the end in itself; it is announced to itself *as* the end in itself; that is, as infinite end as well, since thought of the unconditioned is also thought which rises above experience, or finitude. Thus is explained that despite the criticism of anthropologism of which we have just given some indications, man is the only example, the only case of a reasonable being that can ever be cited at that very point at which the universal concept of reasonable being can justifiably be distinguished from the concept of human being. It is at the point of this fact that anthropology recovers all of its authority which had been contested. It is at this point that the philosopher says "we" and that, in Kant's discourse, "reasonable being" and "humanity" are always associated by the conjunction "and" or "vel." For example: "I say this: man, *and in general* (und uberhaupt) every reasonable being, exists as the end in itself, and not merely as means ... This principle according to which humanity and all reasonable beings in general are considered as ends in themselves" ... etc.

A similar, although essentially distinct ambiguity could be cited in the *Critique of Pure Reason* every time there is a question of defining the finitude of the state of being and the receptivity of the *intuitus derivativus.*

13 "Philosophy in all its aspects is therefore nothing other than rationalism diversifying itself according to the different planes at which intention and accomplishment take place; it is the *Ratio* in its incessant movement towards elucidating itself *(Selbsterhellung)*, beginning with the first eruption of philosophy in humanity, the

the ultimate completion of this teleology of reason which passes through humanity.[14] Thus, under the auspices of the founding concepts of metaphysics, which Husserl revives and restores, assigning them if necessary an index or phenomenological quotation marks, criticism of empirical anthropologism is but the affirmation of a transcendental humanism. And among these metaphysical concepts which form the essential resources of Husserl's discourse, that of *end,* or *telos,* plays a decisive role. It could be shown that, at every stage of phenomenology, and notably every time that recourse to "the Idea in the Kantian sense" is necessary, the infinity of *telos,* the infinity of end, regulates the power of phenomenology. The end of man (as factual anthropological limit) is announced to thought with the end of man. Man is that which is relative to his end, in the fundamentally equivocal sense of the word. This has always been so. The transcendental end can appear to itself and unfold before itself only in the condition of mortality, of relation to finitude as the origin of ideality. The name of man has always been inscribed in metaphysics between these two ends. It has meaning only in this eschato-teleological situation.

IV

From this situation arises the "we" which, in one manner or another, has always had to refer back to itself in the language of metaphysics and in philosophical discourse. Where do we stand with this *we,* finally, in the text which, better than any other, has put before us the essential and historical complicity of metaphysics and humanism in all their forms? Where, then, does this *we* stand in Heidegger's text?

This is the most difficult question and we shall only begin to take it up. There is no question here of sealing off all of Heidegger's text inside an enclosure which he better than anyone delimited. What links humanism and metaphysics as ontotheology has become readable as such since *Sein und Zeit, Letter on Humanism,* and later texts. Referring to this gain, trying to take a faithful account of it, I should like to begin to outline the forms of the hold which the "humanity" of man and the thought of

---

rational of which ... had remained until that time inaccessible to itself, plunged in confusion and night." (*La philosophie comme prise de conscience de l'humanité,* translated by P. Ricoeur.)

[14] In a short 1934 fragment (*Stufen der Geschichtlichkeit. Erste Geschichtlichkeit,* Beilage XXVI in Krisis, pp. 502-3), Husserl distinguishes three levels and three stages of historicity: culture and tradition as human sociality in general; European culture and theoretical scheme (science and philosophy); "conversion of philosophy to phenomenology."

Being, a certain humanism and the truth of Being, have over one another. Naturally there will be no place here for the falsification which, against Heidegger's most explicit warnings, would consist of making of this hold an ontical control or relation in general.

What will concern us here is rather a more subtle, more hidden, more unuprootable privilege which, as in the case of Hegel or Husserl, takes us back to the position of the *we* in the discourse. Once we have given up the idea of placing the *we* in the metaphysical dimension of "we-men," once we have given up investing the *we-men* with metaphysical determination of the property of man (*zôon logon ekon, etc.*), the fact remains that men — and I would even say, in a sense which will be cleared up in a moment, that which is *the property of man,* or the idea of that which is man proper — is inseparable from the question or from the truth of Being. This is so for the paths followed by Heidegger, by what we could call a sort of magnetic attraction.

I can only indicate here the title and some of the effects of this magnetization. In order to unearth it at the continuous depth at which it operates, the distinction between such and such a period of Heidegger's thought, between the texts which are anterior and those which are posterior to the so-called *Kehre,* is less pertinent than ever. On one hand, existential analysis had already gone beyond the horizon of a philosophical anthropology; *Dasein* is not merely the man of metaphysics. And on the other hand, inversely, in the *Letter on Humanism* and beyond, the magnetic attraction of that which is the "property of man" will not cease to direct all of the various paths of Heidegger's thought. This is, at least, what I would like to suggest, and I shall regroup the effects or the indications of this magnetic attraction under the general concept of *proximity*. It is within the enigma of a certain proximity, a proximity to itself and a proximity to Being that we shall see constituting itself against humanism and against metaphysical anthropologism, another instance and another insistence of man, relaying, "relevant," replacing that which it destroys according to the channels in which we are, from which we will no doubt emerge and which remain to be questioned.

Where does this proximity stand? First of all, let us open *Sein und Zeit* to where the question of Being is raised in its "formal structure" (§ 2). Our "vague and common" comprehension of the sense of the word "Being" or "is" is recognized there as a fact *(Faktum):*

> Inquiry as a kind of seeking, must be guided beforehand by what is sought. So the meaning of Being must *already* be available to *us* in some way. As *we* have intimated, *we always* conduct our activities in an understanding of Being. Out of this understanding arise both the explicit question of the meaning of Being and the tendency that leads us towards its conception. We do not *Know*

what 'Being' means. But even if we ask, "What is 'Being' ", we keep within an understanding of the 'is,' though we are unable to fix conceptually what that 'is' signifies. We do not even know the horizon in terms of which that meaning is to be grasped and fixed. *But this vague average understanding of Being is still a Fact.* (*Being and Time,* translated by John Macquarrie and Edward Robinson).

I have underlined *we, always* and *already.* They are, then, in depth determined in correspondence with this understanding of "Being" and of "is." In the absence of every other determination or presupposition, the "we" is at least that which is open to such an understanding, and that which is always accessible to it and that by which such a factum can be recognized as such. It therefore follows that this *we,* as simple, as discreet, and as effaced as it may be, places what is called the formal structure of the question of Being within the horizon of metaphysics and, in a larger sense, within the Indo-European linguistic milieu, the possibility of which is essentially linked with the origin of metaphysics.

It is within these limits that the *factum* can be understood and accredited. It is within these limits, which are determined and therefore material, that it can support the so-called formality of the question.

This "formal structure of the question of Being" having been raised by Heidegger, it is next a matter, as we know, of recognizing the "exemplary being" (exemplarische Seiende) which will constitute the privileged text for a reading of the sense of Being. Let me recall that the formal structure of the question, of any question according to Heidegger, should include three necessary elements: the *Gefragte,* that which is asked, here the sense of Being; the *Erfragte,* which is the asked inasmuch as it is properly aimed at by a question; the sense of Being as questioned; and finally, the *Befragte,* the interrogated, the being which will be interrogated, to which the question of the sense of Being will be posed. It is thus a matter of choosing or of recognizing the paradigm being which is interrogated with a view to the sense of Being: "Into what being should the sense of Being be read (abgelesen) from what being will the opening of Being take its departure? Is this point of departure arbitrary, or has some being privilege (Vorrang) in the elaboration of the question of Being? What is this exemplary being and in what sense has it a privilege?"

By what will the answer to this question be dictated? In what milieu of evidence, certitude, or at least understanding is it to be unfolded? Even before the phenomenological method is appealed to (§ 7), at least in a "provisional concept," as the method of the elaboration of the question of Being, the determination of this exemplary being is "phenomenological" in its principle. It is ordered by the principle of phenomenology, the principle of presence and of the presence within the presence to itself, such as it is manifest to being and in the being which *we* are. It is this presence to itself and this absolute proximity of the questioning being to itself, this proximity to itself of the being which opens itself to the understanding of Being and which intervenes in the determination of the *factum;* it is this proximity to himself of the questioner which motivates the choice of the exemplary state of being, of the text, of the correct text for the hermeneutics of the sense of Being. It is the proximity to itself of the questioning being which results in its being chosen as privileges for being interrogated. The proximity to himself of the questioner authorizes the identity of the questioner and of the interrogator. We, who are near to ourselves, interrogate *ourselves* concerning the sense of Being.

> If the question about Being is to be explicitly formulated and carried through in such a manner as to be completely transparent to itself, then any treatment of it in line with the elucidations we have given requires us to explain how Being is to be looked at, how its meaning is to be understood and conceptually grasped; it requires us to prepare the way for choosing the right entity for our example, and to work out the genuine way of access to it. Looking at something, understanding and conceiving it, choosing, access to it — all these ways of behaving are constitutive for our inquiry, and therefore are modes of Being for those particular entities which we, the enquirers, are ourselves (eines bestimmten Seienden, *des* Seienden, das wir, die Fragenden, je selbst sind). Thus to work out the question of Being adequately, we must make an entity — the enquirer — transparent in his own Being . . . . The very asking of this question (Das Fragen dieser Frage) is an entity's mode of *Being;* and as such it gets its essential character from what is inquired (gefragt) about — namely, Being. This entity which each of us is himself and which includes enquiring as one of the possibilities of its Being, we shall denote by the term "Dasein" (fassen wir terminologisch Dasein). If we are to formulate our question explicitly and transparently, we must first give a proper explication of an entity (Dasein), with regard to its Being. *(Being and Time, § 7).*

This proximity, this identity or this presence to itself of "the being which we are" — of the questioner and of the interrogated — has not the form of subjective consciousness, as in transcendental phenomenology. Doubtless this proximity is also probably even anterior to what the metaphysical predicate "human" could name. Yet the process of extracting or of elaborating the question of Being, as the question of the *sense* of Being, is defined as *explication* or as explicating interpretation. The reading of the text, *Dasein,* is a hermeneutics of unveiling or of development. (cf. § 7). A close examination shows that it is the phenomenological "implicit-explicit" opposition which permits Heidegger to reject the vicious circle objection, which would consist of determining first of all a being in its Being and then raising the question of Being from this ontological pre-determination (§ 7). This style of explicative reading practices a continual elucidation, something which resembles, at least, an act of consciousness (Selbst-Besinnung) without rupture, without movement without change of ground. On the other hand, just as the Dasein — the being which *we* are *ourselves* — serves as the exemplary text, as the good "lesson" for the explicitation of the sense of Being, so the name of man remains the link or the leading thread which joins the analytics of *Dasein* with the totality of the traditional discourse of metaphysics. Hence the strange status of phrases or of parentheses such as these: As different behaviours of man, sciences have the style of Being of this being (man). We assign to this being the term "Dasein" (Dieses Seiende fassen wir terminologisch als *Dasein*)." Again, "The problematics of Greek ontology, just as that of any ontology, should take its leading thread from the Dasein itself. Dasein, that is, the Being of man, is understood (umgrentz) in its vulgar "definition" as well as in its philosophical "definition" as that living whose Being is essentially determined by the power of speech" (of the discourse: *Redenkönnen).* In the same way, a "complete ontology of Dasein" is posited as the prerequisite to a "philosophical anthropology." We see, then, that *Dasein,* if it is *not* man, is *not,* however, *other* than man. It is, as we shall see, a repetition of the essence of man permitting to go back beyond metaphysical concepts of *humanitas.* It is the subtlety and the equivocality of this gesture which have obviously led to all of the anthropological deviations in the reading of *Sein und Zeit,* notably in France.

The value of proximity, that is, of presence in general, therefore determines the essential orientation of this analytics of *Dasein.* This motif of proximity is of course held in opposition which has henceforth constantly ruled Heidegger's discourse. The fifth paragraph of *Sein und Zeit* seems, indeed, not to contradict, but to limit and confine that which was already acquired, that is, that *Dasein* "which we are" constituted the exemplary being for the hermeneutics of the sense of Being due to its proximity to itself, to our proximity to ourselves and to this being which we are. Heidegger thus notes that this proximity is ontic. On the contrary, ontologically, that is, as regards the Being of this being which we are, the distance, is as great as it can be. "The *Dasein* in truth is not merely that which is ontically *(ontisch)* near or even nearest us — we *are* it ourselves. However, in spite of, or rather because of this, it is ontologically *(ontologisch)* the farthest." [15]

---

[15] In demonstrating that Dasein is ontico-ontologically prior, we may have misled the reader into supposing that this entity must also be what is given as ontico-ontologically primary not only in the sense that it can itself be grasped 'immedi-

The analytics of *Dasein* as well as that thought which, beyond the *Kehre,* pursues the question of Being, is situated in the space which separates and which relates to one another such a proximity and such a distance. The *Da* of *Dasein* and the *Da* of the *Sein* signify the near as well as the far. Beyond the enclosure common to humanism and metaphysics, Heideggerian thought is guided by the motif of Being as presence, understood in a more original sense than in the metaphysical and ontic determinations of presence or of presence in the present, and by the motif of the proximity of Being to the essence of man. Everything takes place as if the ontological distance recognized in *Sein und Zeit* had to be reduced and the proximity of Being to the essence of man had to be said.

I should like now to support this last proposition with some indicative references to the *Letter on Humanism.* I shall not dwell on the principle and well-known theme of this text, the unity of metaphysics and humanism. Any questioning of humanism which is not coupled first of all with the archeological radicality of the questions outlined by Heidegger and which does not make use of the indications he gives the genesis of the concept and of the value of "man" (a renewal of the Greek *paideia* in Roman culture, the Christianization of the Latin *humanitas,* a renaissance of Hellenism in the XIVth and the XVIIIth centuries, etc.), any meta-humanist position not within the opening of these questions remains historically regional, periodic and peripheral, juridically secondary and dependent, regardless of its interest and its necessity as such.

The thought of Being, the thought of the truth of Being in whose name Heidegger de-limits humanism and metaphysics nevertheless remains a thought *of* man. In the question of Being as it is raised in metaphysics,

---

ately,' but also in that the kind of Being which it possesses is presented just as 'immediately.' Ontically, of course, Dasein is not only close to us — even that which is closest: we *are* it, each of us, we ourselves. In spite of this, or rather for just this reason, it is ontologically farthest; but pre-ontologically it is surely not a stranger.

I have four remarks to make on this subject: 1. Despite this ambiguity or this opposition it is solely the value of (ontic) proximity which determined the choice of the Dasein as the exemplary state of being. Exemplariness is, then, an ontic motif. 2. This proximity-distance, ontic-ontological opposition will be inseparable from the opposition between the proper and the non-proper (the authentic and the unauthentic: eigentlich/uneigentlich). 3. This same opposition will permit, by distinguishing between proximity and the metaphysical notion of "immediacy," the criticism of a certain style of phenomenology and the primacy of "consciousness," of the "immediate givens of consciousness." 4. The fact remains that there is an essential and explicit bond between this value of proximity — ontically given or ontologically refused, but promised — and phenomenology: the *Dasein* must "be able to show itself in itself and from itself."

man and the name of man are not displaced. And they certainly do not disappear. There is, rather, a sort of re-evaluation or revalorization of the essence and the dignity of man. In Heidegger's eyes, what is threatened in the extension of metaphysics and technique — and we know the great extent to which Heidegger associates the two — is the essence of man, which should here be considered before and beyond its metaphysical determinations: "The devastation of language which is spreading everywhere rapidly is not only a result of the responsibility for esthetic and moral order which we assume in every use we make of speech. It is caused by man's essence being put in danger (Gefährdung des Wesens des Menschen)" . . . "It is only in this way, on the basis of Being, that the absence of native land (die Ueberwindung der Heimatlosikeit), in which not only men but the essence of man are lost (das Wesen des Menschen), begins to be surmounted." It is therefore this essence which must be re-established or restored: "But if man is one day to arrive at the proximity of Being (in die Nähe des Seins), he must first therefore learn to exist within that which has no name (im Namenlosen). He must know how to recognize the temptation of publicity as well as the impotence of private existence. Before speaking (befor er spricht) man must first let himself be appealed to, (demanded anew: wieder Ansprechen) by Being and warned by it of the danger of having little or rarely anything to say in the face of this demand (Anspruch). It is only then that the inestimable wealth is restored to the essence of speech and that man is given shelter (Behausung) to live in the truth of Being. But is there not in this demand (Anspruch) of Being on man, as in the attempt to prepare man for this appeal, an effort which concerns man? What is the orientation of the "concern," if not to re-establish man in his essence (den Menschen wieder in sein Wesen zurückzubringen)? Can this mean other than making man (homo) human (humanus)? *humanitas* remains at the heart of such thought, for humanism consists of this: to reflect and to see that man be human and not inhuman (unmenschlich); that is, outside of his essence. Of what, then, does man's humanity consist? It resides in his essence." [16]

---

[16] Many other passages of the *Letter* could be cited in the same sense, as for example: "But it must be understood that, through it [metaphysics] man is definitively pushed back into the domain of *animalitas,* even though, far from identifying him with animal, he is accorded a specific difference. As a principle, we always think of *homo animalis,* even if the *anima* is posited as *animus sive mens,* and, later, as object, person or mind. Such a position is metaphysical. But, as such, the essence of man is too poorly (zu gering) appreciated. It is not considered in its source, an essential source which, for historic humanity, (geschichtliche Menschentum) remains permanently essential future. Metaphysics considers man on the basis of *animalities,*

Once the notion of essence is removed from the essentia-existentia opposition the proposition according to which "man ek-sists is not a reply to the question as to whether man is real or not; it is a reply to the question regarding the essence of man."

The restoration of essence is also the restoration of a dignity and of a proximity: the corresponding dignity of Being and of man, the proximity of Being and of man. "What still remains to be said today and for the first time could perhaps become the impulsion (Anstoss) which would lead the essence of man to be attentive by thought (denkend) to the dimension, which is omni-reigning over it, of the truth of Being. Such an event could not, furthermore, be produced every time except for the dignity of the being and to the benefit of this being-there which man assumes in ek-sistence (nur dem Sein zur Würde und dem Da-sein zugunsten geschehen, das der Mensch eksistierend aussteht) but not to the advantage of man in order that civilization and culture shine by his action."

The ontological distance from *Dasein* to what it is as eksistence and to the *Da* of *Sein;* this distance which was given as first ontic proximity, must be reduced by the thought of the truth of Being. Hence, the predominance, in Heidegger's discourse, of a whole metaphorics of proximity, simple and immediate presence, associating with the proximity of Being the values of neighborhood, shelter, house, service, guard, voice and listening. Not only is this not insignificant rhetoric, but a whole theory of metaphor in general could even be made explicit on the basis of this metaphorics and of the thought of the ontico-ontological difference. I shall cite but a few examples of this language which is so highly connoted and so clearly inscribed within a certain landscape. "But if man is to arrive one day at the proximity of Being (in die Nähe des Seins), he must first of all learn to exist in that which has no name .... The proposition: 'The substance of man is eksistence' says nothing other than this: The manner in which man in his own essence (in seinen eigenen Wesen) is present to Being (Zum Sein anwest) is the ek-static instance

---

rather than with a view to his *humanitas.* Metaphysics is closed to the simple, essential notion that man is only revealed in his essence (in seinem Wesen west) inasmuch as he is appealed to (angesprochen) by Being. It is only on the basis of this claim that he has found the very dwelling place of his essence. It is only on the basis of this dwelling that he 'has' 'language' as the shelter which assures his essence its ecstatic nature. To stand within the clearing of being is characteristic (eignet) only of man. Ek-sistence thus understood is not only the foundation of the possibility of reason and ratio, it is precisely that in which man's essence retains (wahrt) the source of its determination. Ek-sistence can only be said of the essence of man; that is, of the human manner of 'being,' for only man, as far as we know, is engaged in the destiny of ek-sistence (in das Geschick der Eksistenz)."

in the truth of Being. Humanist interpretations of man as rational animal, as 'person,' as spiritual-being-endowed-with-a-soul-and-a-body, are not held as false by this essential determination of man, nor are they rejected by it. The sole purpose is rather that the highest humanist determinations of the essence of man do not yet experience the dignity characteristic of man (die eigentliche Würde des Menschen). In this sense, the thought expressed in *Sein und Zeit* is against humanism. But this opposition does not mean that such thought is directed in opposition to man, that it pleads for the inhuman, defends barbarism and lowers man's dignity. If we think against humanism it is because humanism does not value highly enough the humanitas of man . . . . 'Being' is not God, nor a foundation of the world. Being is more removed than every being and yet nearer (näher) to man than every being, whether it be a rock, an animal, a work of art, a machine, an angel or God. The being is that which is nearest (Das Sein ist das Nächste). This proximity remains for man, however, that which is farthest. Man holds always, and first, and only, to being . . . . It is because man, as ek-sisting, succeeds in keeping himself within this relation within which Being determines its own destiny, by supporting it ek-statically, that is to say by assuming it within concern, that he fails to recognize the nearest (das Nächste) and is contented by that which is beyond the near (das Uebernächste). He even thinks that this is the nearest. But nearer than the nearest and at the same time farther than the farthest for usual thought is proximity itself: the truth of Being . . . . The unique (das Einzige) which is aimed at by the thought attempting to express itself for the first time in *Sein und Zeit* is something simple (etwas Einfaches). Inasmuch as it is this simple, Being remains mysterious, simple proximity (schlicht) of a non-compelling power. This proximity unfolds its essence (west) as language itself . . . . But man is not only a living being who, in addition to other capacities, possesses language. Language is rather the home of Being in which man lives and thus ek-sists, belonging to the truth of Being, whose custody (hütend gehört) he assumes."

This proximity is not ontic proximity, and the characteristically ontological repetition of this thought of the near and the far [17] must be taken

---

[17] "In the introduction of *Sein und Zeit* (p. 38) this is simply and clearly expressed, and even italicized; 'Being is pure and simple transcendent (das Transcendens schlechthin).' Just as the opening of spatial proximity surpasses all things near or far when considered from the point of view of this thing, so Being is essentially beyond every state of being because it is the clearing (Lichtung) itself. As such, Being is considered on the basis of the state of being, according to a way of looking at things which is at the outset inevitable in the metaphysics which still prevails."

into account. The fact remains that Being which is nothing, which is not a being, cannot be said, cannot say itself, except in the ontic metaphor. And the choice of such and such a metaphorics is necessarily significant. It is in the metaphoric emphasis that the interpretation of the sense of being then appears. And if Heidegger radically deconstructed the authority of the *present* over metaphysics, it was in order to lead us to think the presence of the present. But the thought of this presence only metaphorizes, by a profound necessity which cannot be escaped by a simple decision, the language it deconstructs.[18]

Consequently, the prevalence accorded to the phenomenological metaphor, to all of the varieties of *phainesthai,* of brilliance, of illumination, of clearing, of *Lichtung,* etc., opens on the space of presence and the presence of space, understood in the opposition of the near and the far. In the same way, the privilege accorded not only to language, but to spoken language (voice, listening, etc.) is in harmony with the motif of presence as presence to itself.[19]

---

[18] A few examples of the predominance accorded to the value of ontological proximity: "This destiny appears as the clearing of Being (Lichtung des Seins); it is itself this clearing. It accords proximity-to-Being (Sie gewährt die Nähe zum Sein). In this proximity, in the clearing of the 'there' (Da), man dwells as ek-sisting, even though he is not yet in a position to actually experience and assume this act of dwelling. The discourse on Hölderlin's elegy *Heimkunft* (1943), which is conceived on the basis of *Sein und Zeit,* calls this proximity 'of' Being which is in itself the 'there' of being-there 'the native land'.... The native land of this historical dwelling is the proximity to Being.... In his historico-ontological essence man is that being whose Being as ek-sistence consists in that it dwells within the proximity of Being (in der Nähe des Seins wohnt). Man is the neighbor of Being (Nachbar des Seins).... Therein fundamentally different from every existentia and 'existence,' 'ek-sistence' is the ek-static dwelling within the proximity of Being.... Should thought not attempt, by an open resistence to 'humanism,' to risk an impulse which could finally lead to recognizing the humanitas of homo humanus and its founding principles? Thus a reflection (Besinnung) which would think not only man, but the 'nature' of man, not only the nature, but even more originally, the dimension within which the essence of man, determined from Being itself, feels at home could be aroused, if the present situation of history is not already leading in this direction.... Thought does not surpass metaphysics by surmounting it; that is, by going still higher in order to accomplish it one knows not where, but by re-descending to the nearest proximity (in die Nähe des Nächsten)."

[19] On that which unites the values of presence to oneself and spoken language we take the liberty of referring back to our essays. *De la grammatologie* and *La voix et le phénomène.* Implicitly or explicitly, the valorization of spoken language is constant and massive in Heidegger. We shall study it further on for itself. Having arrived at a certain point in this analysis, such a valorization must be rigorously sized-up. Although it covers the near totality of the Heideggerian text (in that it leads all of the metaphysical determinations of the *present* or of *being* back to the original form of Being as presence (Anwesenheit)), it is effaced at that

If, then, "Being is farther removed than every being and yet nearer to man than every being," if "Being is that which is nearest," we should consequently be able to say that Being is *the near* of man and that man is *the near* of Being. The near is the proper; the proper is the nearest (prope, proprius). Man is that which is proper to Being, which speaks into his ear from very near. Being is that which is proper to man. Such is the truth, such is the proposition which gives the *there* to the truth of Being and the truth of man. This proposition of the proper must certainly not be taken in a metaphysical sense: the proper of man is not here an essential attribute, the predicate of a substance, one feature, as fundamental as it may be, among the others which constitute a being, object or subject, called man. Neither can we talk, in this same sense, of man as the proper of Being. The propriety, the co-propriety of Being and man, is proximity as inseparability. It is as inseparability, further-more, that the relations of being (substance or res) with its essential predicate were conceived in metaphysics. Since this co-propriety of man and Being, such as it is conceived in Heidegger's discourse, is not ontic, it does not relate two "beings" to one another but rather, in language, relates the *sense* of Being with the *sense* of man. The proper of man, his "eigenheit," his authenticity, is to relate himself to the sense of Being, to understand it and to question (Fragen) it within ek-sistence, to stand [20] in the proximity of its own light: "Das Stehen in der Lichtung des Seins nenne ich die Ek-sistenz des Menschen. Nur dem Menschen eignet diese Art zu mein": "To stand within the clearing of Being, that is what I call the ek-sistence of man. Alone, man has properly this manner of being."

Is not that which is perhaps being displaced today this security of the near, this co-belonging and this co-propriety of the name of man and of the name of Being, as it inhabits and installs itself in the language of the Occident, as it is sunk therein, as it is inscribed and forgotten in

---

point where a *Wesen* which would not even be an *Anwesen* is announced, (Cf. our essay, *Ousia et grammè, Note sur une note de Sein und Zeit.*) And thus is ex-plained, in particular, the contempt for literature, as opposed to thought and to *Dichtung,* but also to a craft-like practice of the letter: "In the written word, thought easily loses its mobility . . . . But on the other hand the written word offers the salutary restraint of a vigilant grasp of language . . . . It [the truth of Being] would thus be taken away from pure opinion and conjecture and given back to this craft of writing (Hand-werk der Schrift), which has become rare today . . . . And this is indeed what we need with the present world penury: less philosophy and more attention to thought; less literature and more care given to the letter as such" *(Letter on Humanism).* "The *Dichtung* must be freed from literature" (Text published by the *Revue de Poésie,* Paris, 1967).

[20] I have tried elsewhere *(La parole soufflée, L'ecriture et la différence)* to in-dicate the passage between "proper" and "to-stand-up."

the history of metaphysics, and as it is also being revived in the destruction of ontotheology? But this setting in motion — which can only come from a certain outside — was already required in the very structure it solicits. In the thought and the language of Being, the end of man has always been prescribed, and this prescription has never served except to modulate the equivocality of the *end,* in the interplay of *telos* and death. In the reading of this interplay, the following chain of events can be taken in all of its senses: the end of man is the thought of Being, man is the end of the thought of Being, the end of man is the end of the thought of Being. Man has always been his proper end; that is, the end of what is proper to him. The being has always been its proper end; that is, the end of what is proper to it.

I should like now, to conclude, to assemble under some very general titles the signs which appear, at this anonymous depth which concerns me here, to mark the effects of this total setting in motion of that which, for convenience, with the necessary quotation marks or precautions, I called in the beginning France or French thought.

1. *The reduction of the sense.* The most original and the strongest attention to system and structure; that is, an attention which does not immediately degenerate into cultural or journalistic chatter or, in the best of cases, into the purest "structuralist" tradition of metaphysics. Such an attention, which is rare, does not consist of:

a) restoring the classical motif of the system, of which it could be shown that it is always ordered to telos, aletheia, and ousia, which are the values assembled in the concepts of essence or of *sense;*

b) nor of effacing or destroying the sense. It is a question, rather, of determining the possibility of the *sense* on the basis of a "formal" organization which in itself has no sense, which does not mean that it is nonsense, anguish or absurdity prowling around metaphysical humanism. If we consider that the criticism of anthropologism by recent great metaphysicians (Hegel and Husserl notably) was made in the name of truth and sense, and if we consider that these "phenomenologies" — which were actually metaphysical theories — had as their essential motif a *reduction to the sense* (this is, *literally,* Husserl's claim), then we can see that the reduction *of* the sense (that is, of the signified) takes on the form of a criticism of phenomenology. If we consider, on the other hand, that Heidegger's destruction of metaphysical humanism is first of all the result of a question concerning the *sense* or the *truth* of Being, we see that the reduction of the sense is effected by a sort of rupture with a thought of Being that has all of the traits of a "relève" *(Aufhebung)* of humanism.

2. *The strategic bet*. A radical displacement can only come from the outside. The kind I am speaking about can therefore not be attributed to some spontaneous decision of philosophical thought after some interior maturation of its history. This setting in motion takes place in the violent relationship of *all* of the Occident with its other, whether it is "linguistic" relationships (in which the question of the limits of all that which leads back to the question of the sense of Being is very quickly raised), or ethnological, economic, political, or military, relationships. This does not mean, moreover, that military or economic violence is not structurally bound up with "linguistic" violence. But the "logic" of any relationship with the outside is very complex and surprising. It is precisely the strength and the efficacity of the system which regularly transform transgressions into "false sorties." Considering these effects of system, we now have, from the inside where we are, only two strategies from which to choose:

a) To attempt the sortie and the deconstruction without changing ground, by repeating what is implicit in the founding concepts and in original problematics, by using against the edifice the instruments or the stones available in the house, which means in language as well. The risk here is to constantly confirm, consolidate, or "relever," at a depth which is ever more sure, precisely that which we claim to be deconstructing. A continuous explicitation which proceeds towards the opening risks falling into a closed autism.

b) To decide to change ground, in a discontinuous and eruptive manner, by stepping abruptly outside and by affirming absolute rupture and difference. Not to mention all of the other forms of perspectives in a trompe-l'oeil fashion to which such a displacement (which dwells more naively than ever within the inside it claims to desert) is susceptible, the simple use of language continually relocates the "new" ground on the older one. Numerous and precise examples could be given of the effects of such a relocation or of such a blindness.

It goes without saying that the risks of such effects are not sufficient to obviate the necessity of such a "change of ground." It also goes without saying that the choice between these two forms of deconstruction cannot be a simple and unique one. A new writing must weave and intertwine the two motifs. That is, several languages must be spoken and several texts produced at the same time. I wanted above all to point out that the style of the first deconstruction is more that of Heidegger's questions and that the other is more that which currently dominates France. I purposely speak here in terms of dominant style, because there are also ruptures and changes of ground in Heidegger's type of text, because the "change of ground" is far from upsetting all of the French landscape to which I refer, and because, as Nietzsche said, it is perhaps a change of style that we need.

3. *The difference between the superior man and the superman.* This title stresses both the recourse to Nietzsche, which is more and more prevalent and more and more rigorous in France, and the division which is perhaps being announced between two relèves of man. We know how, at the end of *Zarathoustra,* at the time of the "sign," when *das Zeichen kommt,* Nietzsche distinguishes, in the greatest proximity, in a strange resemblance and an ultimate complicity, on the eve of the last separation of the Great South, between superior man (höherer Mensch) and superman (Ubermensch). The former is abandoned to his distress with a last movement of pity. The latter — which is not the last man — awakes and goes off, without turning back on what he leaves behind him. His laughter will then break out towards a return which will no longer have the form of the metaphysical repetition of humanism any more than it will undoubtedly take the form, "beyond" metaphysics, of the memorial or of the guard of the sense of the being, or the form of the house and the truth of Being. He will dance, outside of the house, this "aktive Vergeszlichkeit," this active forgetfulness ("oubliance") and this cruel (grausam) feast is spoken of in *Genealogy of Morals.* No doubt Nietzsche called upon an active forgetfulness ("oubliance") of Being which would not have had the metaphysical form which Heidegger ascribed to it.

Should we read Nietzsche as the last of the great metaphysicians? Should the question of the truth of Being be understood, rather, as the last drowsy jump of superior man? Should the vigil *(veille)* be understood as the guard mounted around the house or as the awakening *(veille)* to the coming day, which is upon us?

We are perhaps between these two vigils *(veilles)* which are also two ends of man. But who, we?

Ecole Normale Supérieur, Paris.

---

* Translated from the French with the collaboration of Edouard Morot-Sir, Wesley C. Piersol, Hubert L. Dreyfus, and Barbara Reid.

COMMENTS ON PROFESSOR DERRIDA'S PAPER

RICHARD POPKIN

Professor Derrida's paper raises many points that might be commented upon. In the space allotted to me, I shall only touch on a few of these. Before doing so, I feel impelled to preface my remarks with some explanation or apologia.

I am very far from being an expert on the main matter discussed by Professor Derrida, the inner logic or character of recent French humanism and of its German sources in Hegel, Husserl and Heidegger. This is, no doubt, the case of most American philosophers on the current scene. I may have been asked to contribute because I do not particularly share the positivistic or pragmatic or analytic attitudes towards Continental thought, past or present, and do not think that there is much evidence that Anglo-American thought has found better or more fruitful ways of dealing with philosophical concerns than has Continental European thought in this century. In this respect my views are far from representative of something that might be called "American thought." I have grown up intellectually in the changing currents of American thought from 1938 to the present — Marxism, pragmatism, positivism, Oxford analysis, etc., but I have lived on the borders of these movements while immersing myself in the drama of 17th and 18th century ideas, especially in France. Hence I do not speak for "American philosophy" nor as an expert on contemporary French thought. Over the last fifteen years I have spent a good deal of time in France, have known many of the professional philosophers there, but have not really participated at all in contemporary intellectual concerns. I have been concerned with historical interpretations and reevaluations of ideas from philosophy's modern Golden Age, that is, from Montaigne to Kant.

With this much said, let me turn to Professor Derrida's paper. I found his initial comments on the assumptions underlying the possibility and the occurrence of international philosophical conferences insightful. One could also raise the question of the purpose or function of these conferences and the role they are starting to play. I believe that it was a French thinker, Xavier Léon, at the beginning of this century, who first organized an international philosophical congress. In the days when the Republic of Letters really existed, such meetings were hardly needed. The free exchange of ideas took place through the mails, through personal travels, and through such self-appointed intermediaries of the intellectual world as Father Mersenne and Henri Justel. The breakdown of Europe into national spheres, the rise of national educational systems and national philosophies finally required the serious efforts of people like Léon to bring thinkers together again.

The role of conference in the sciences, especially since the war, may be creating the view that this is the way the intellectual world *ought* to go on. As Professor Derrida points out, such conferences are "feverishly" proliferating day by day. As some of us know only too well, the contemplative life is being transformed into a hectic one, in which one utilizes the few idle moments between conferences to write the paper for the next one, on whatever topic is proposed, whether it is one that one cares seriously about or not. These "talks" are rushed into print before one can catch one's breath or reflect, or reap whatever intellectual benefits may have come from the conference.

The conference is also a political event, both on a large and small scale. A significant measure of one's professional worth is the quantity and quality of the conferences one participates in. In the sciences, the conference as a way of intellectual life may be important and productive as a way of exchanging and developing results and ideas, and may be as important or more important than the publication and dissemination of them. It may be, and this *ought* to be carefully weighed and analyzed by those who are constantly encouraging more and more of them. Philosophers, whose progress is much slower and more deliberate, *ought* to give careful consideration to the effect the imitation of the *modus operandi* of the sciences is having on our profession. Many of us like to travel, enjoy seeing old intellectual friends and making new ones. But we are paying a price, an important one, in becoming captives of an open-ended system that consumes our time and our energies, and dictates the character of our work and the acceptable sorts of solutions.

Professor Derrida stresses the political character of international conferences, and the fact that they are endorsed and encouraged as long as they do not disturb. But, a troublesome aspect, from the point of view of the authorities involved, is that they do sometimes disturb, though perhaps less among philosophers than among scientists. At an international mathematical congress in Moscow, Professor Smaele of Berkeley denounced American policy in Vietnam and Russian policy in eastern Europe from the steps of Moscow University. This, as Professor Charles Frankel knows from personal experience, greatly disturbed the American and Russian political and congress worlds. I recently attended an international congress of historians of science in Paris which disturbed the Russian delegates by its attitude of condemnation of the invasion of Czechoslovakia.

The congresses, as Professor Derrida points out, develop in the context of political events: the papers are written while they are going on; the meetings take place in historical time. The conferences do disturb, but only a little bit. There is probably a range of tolerance, smaller for philosophy than for the sciences, in which the disturbance will be tolerated, and so our meetings go on within the *form* of democracy, but not necessarily its substance.

To turn from this to the main matter of the paper, Professor Derrida offers us a "report" on where France stands with regard to man. His report is actually a deep analysis of the philosophical background of a major trend within French thought in its movement away from Sartrean humanism. It centers on the roles of Hegel, Husserl and Heidegger in providing the original basis for humanism, the realization of the critique of humanism in the writings of these thinkers, and the recognition that there is still a kind of humanism remaining — not humanistic in the sense that truth is man-created, but still humanistic in that man, human nature, or human-reality, is basically involved in the approach to truth, or the realization of truth. Professor Derrida only briefly indicates what is following from this in French structuralism today.

Professor Derrida's intricate analysis raises many intriguing questions for an historian of philosophy. One concerns the role of Hegel's thought in the last century and a half. The tracing and analysis of this role is one basic way of seeing what has happened to philosophy in the Western world. National philosophical histories have been influenced and determined by when and how Hegel's thought affected them. Paradoxically, American and English thought were influenced by Hegel a long time before German and French thought. The Hegel who made such a great impact in the United States was far less humanistically read than the one who struck France in the mid 20th century. The Hegel of Brokmeyer, W. T. Harris, Royce and Loewenberg, the logical and formalistic Hegel of England, of Bradley, Bosanquet and McTaggart, led to a wave of reaction in which we in the English speaking world are still living. Pragmatism and the empiricism and the common sense philosophy of Moore and Russell came from a deeply-felt need to reject the whole kind of formal metaphysical complex that this Hegel represented, and the strange hold his interpreters had on certain levels of institutionalized thought. We are still living in this world in which Hegel is the enemy, the force of darkness constantly to be rejected in favor of the clear light of pragmatism, empiricism and common sense.

The Hegel who began to breathe in Germany in the 20's due to the efforts of the Lassons, Franz Rosenzweig, Karl Löwith and others, has hardly touched us, though Löwith and some of the others have lived and taught in America. The early Hegel has been translated, has affected some theologians, but few philosophers. The Marxian Hegel is just beginning to be taken seriously in the form of the current Marcuse boom. We have had perhaps more direct contact with this vibrant, humanistic Hegel than France has had, since many of the leading figures in German thought of the 20's fled to America, or fled to France briefly and then to America. But, for better or worse, they have as yet had fairly little influence on our philosophical scene. (The same, I think, is the case with Husserl, many of whose students came to America, and who now at the end of their careers are just beginning to get a hearing of sorts.) We must await further generations to trace the impact of the German and Austrian refugees on our philosophical culture. The affair was idiosyncratic, in that chance events determined who came, where they went, and what influence they had. The prevailing trends favored the logical positivists. Our anti-Hegelian phase drowned out any form, manner, or shape of 20th century Hegelianism. Our anti-Communism led to a too-easy rejection of the early Marx (or turned him over to the political scientists). Our unfamiliarity with the trends in Germany up to 1933, and in France up to 1940, made the messages of many of the refugees unintelligible to much of the philosophical audience. They spoke of strange, unknown thinkers who didn't fit in our canon and who seemed (and some like Heidegger still seem) untranslatable into our philosophical world. Phenomenology and existentialism are gradually, slowly, beginning to be accepted as movements to be studied, and if possible, understood. Marvin Farber and others have valiantly tried to make Husserl and recent French thought part of our philosophical consciousness, and now various schools, immersed in philosophical analysis, are desperately seeking for teachers of these movements, to explain them to the students, though the faculty still remains aloof.

The career of my colleague, Herbert Marcuse, is indicative of our situation. He has been here for 35 years. He, and his associates, Adorno and Horkheimer, though working in America, were hardly known to philosophers. Marcuse only began to teach here in the 1950's in a new institution, Brandeis, which was willing to employ off-beat intellectuals. Only in the last year have people in the dominant American philosophical community begun to read him, and many are probably still not convinced that he is a philosopher.

France was affected by Hegel almost a century after America. From Wahl to Kojève to Hyppolite, a humanistic Hegel, a Hegel seen often in terms of the Marx of 1844, has played a vital role. The texts read, and the way they were read, greatly influenced the philosophical scene. I remember going to a meeting in Paris in 1952 when Hyppolite spoke, and the tremendous excitement and enthusiasm with which he was received. The same was the case with those who went to Kojève's lectures, with those influenced by Lukacs. Then, as Professor Derrida points out, when Hegel was studied further a new phase occurred. A Hegel beyond humanism, a Hegel closer to the Anglo-American one of the last century, emerged as a critic of the humanistic Hegel. Similarly the late Husserl, the transcendental Husserl, came to the fore as a critic of the humanistic phenomenology. And, the Heidegger of the *Letter on Humanism* came to haunt the Sartrean rendition of *Sein und Zeit*. (The Heidegger case is most interesting for Heidegger was still alive to fight his interpreters). The time and the situation when Hegel and Husserl and Heidegger made their impact in France, and when Hegel did (since the others have not yet) in the United States perhaps offer one way of gaining insight into our philosophical differences.

The question of who has misread Hegel, Husserl and Heidegger is also fascinating. The battle goes on and no doubt will continue for centuries, as to what is a reading and what a misreading of these authors. I have no expertize in this matter, and hence will avoid any judgment on the question. The misreading of philosophers has been one of the main means by which the history of philosophy has proceeded. Philosophers always see their predecessors through their own categories, desires and aspirations. We have profited greatly from Aristotle's misreading of Plato (if such it was), from Kant's misreading of Hume, and so on. The value of philosophers is not denigrated by showing that in some one else's eyes, they have been misreading others. It sometimes leads, as apparently it has in France today, to a reason for rejecting certain views.

There is also the question of how seriously an author like Heidegger should be taken as the best interpreter of his own views. He probably has various reasons for wanting to insist that, in terms of his present views, his past ones should be interpreted in a certain way. Because of his present concerns, he may be too prejudiced to see certain things that others can discern. The fact that Husserl, as Professor Derrida points out, read *Sein und Zeit* much as Sartre did, may be more significant than Heidegger's later comments.

Perhaps the most interesting part of Professor Derrida's analysis is his placing in relief the kind of humanism that is, at bottom, involved in Hegel's Husserl's and Heidegger's thought. What I wish he had done after this is to indicate more sharply how this journey through humanistic interpretations of Hegel, Husserl and Heidegger, to their critiques of humanism, to the revealing of their remaining humanism, is related to Professor Derrida's own views.

Finally, I should like to turn to a matter Professor Derrida mentions early in his paper, which I think throws some light on the difference in our philosophical situations, and the difference between what I read as an extremely pessimistic conclusion to the paper, in contrast to a kind of desperately optimistic mood that I think is presently arising in America. Professor Derrida says he could only participate in this conference if he were assured that, "je pourrais témoigner ici même de mon accord et jusqu'à un certain point ma solidarité avec ceux qui, dans ce pays, luttaient contre ce qui était alors la politique officielle de leur pays en certains points du monde, notamment au Vietnam." As one who has been involved in this struggle in a minor way, I am heartened to be here with a kindred spirit. I think also that this struggle is giving rise to a new philosophical climate and context in America, that is forcing us to rethink our assumptions about the nature and destiny of man.

The American crisis symbolized in Vietnam and in the racial dilemma has regenerated the classical American optimism, that *we* can arrive at a better world, at a world in which human existence has a meaning and in which human beings can achieve some significant fulfillment and purpose. The very absurdity of the situations — Vietnam, and the black man dehumanized in America — have inspired some contemporary intellectuals with a passion to overcome the absurd evils of the present. The passionate rejection of Imperial America, bourgeois America, materialist America, Puritanical America, White Anglo-Saxon America, anti-Communist America, born of the student revolts of Berkeley, the marijuana smokers, the hippies, the civil rights movement, the anti-war movement, the McCarthy movement, has cried out for a philosophy worthy of its aims. Some of the young rushed off to the Orient, others to the anarchists, the non-Russian Communists, the non-Communist Marxists, or the black revolutionaries. The sterile, even antiseptic, legacies of empiricism, logical positivism, logical analysis, ordinary language analysis, and their more sterile political and social views, liberalism in either British or American dress, have proved totally inadequate to provide serious guidance or meaning. The meliorist pragmatic theories of William James and John Dewey appear to have failed, or to have become justifications for allowing the absurd to flourish in our midst. Pragmatism could become the name for the policies of our recent leaders, politics without principles, reacting to problems without any meaningful direction.

Some American intellectuals, American philosophers, are, I believe, in a state of crisis. A number of them are being transformed by the events they are presently living through. Their intellectual gods, Hume, James, Dewey, Russell, Wittgenstein, are dead or dying. Intellectuals are groping for new insight and inspiration. Marcuse's rapid rise to prominence, and even to being read by members of the philosophical establishment, is the most overt sign of this. This may in time make it respectable to mention even the names of Hegel, Husserl and Heidegger in polite American philosophical society without scorn or laughter. The hope, the passionate hope, is there that philosophy can and must provide the basis and the rationale for the revolutionary ardor and aspiration now sweeping American academia. The absurd can be overcome by a new philosophy of man. Events have captured us and are compelling philosophy to be meaningful, relevant and revolutionary.

Back in the early days of these events, I was on a university committee in 1964 to investigate the crisis at Berkeley. When I first met the student radicals, I was deeply moved by their seriousness, their passion, their idealism, their hopes, their unshakeable conviction that a better and more significant world could and must be found. A significant number of my colleagues have been touched, captured by this new spirit of the age. Events have pushed them into an ever deepening dismay and horror of the present human condition in America. The revolutionaries, black, student, anti-war, anti-Establishment, have given them hope and given them a supreme intellectual task and challenge — to provide a philosophy for the world that is before us and for that which is to come. Fichte said, "We philosophize out of need for our redemption," and the tragedy of the contemporary scene has called us back to this — we must redeem ourselves and our world, or be crushed by the absurd. The catastrophic failure of technology, of American scientific and engineering genius, to redeem man — the horrifying application of it in Vietnam and the ghettoes — to repress and to extend the power of the absurd — is compelling us to philosophize anew.

The pessimism of Professor Derrida's conclusion goes contrary to this hopeful and desperate mood. I don't know if the Paris revolution of May and June of 1968 is having similar effects. But, whether foolishly or not, I don't think we are ready to adopt the stance of Nietzsche's dancer, dancing outside the house, dancing in active forgetfulness. We want to dance *within* the house, to make man's house joyful. We may be egregious optimists, and Professor Derrida's all-too-brief and cryptic analysis of what our alternatives are, either trying to rebuild within the same world, in which we succeed only in confirming, consolidating, and "relieving" what we are trying to overcome, or erupting outside of it, and ending up where we started after a "false sortie," may unfortunately turn out to be only too true. However, at this moment in American intellectual history, I don't think we have the choice. We have to try. The risk is great. We may merely, as has too often happened, become the justifiers of a bleaker, more absurd world. The vitality is present now, and I feel we must take advantage of it, hoping against hope, that we will succeed at least to some small extent. In so doing, we may possibly repeat what happened in France in the last 25 years, the movement from an optimistic humanism to its rejection, to a new formalistic period that may be as sterile as the logical positivistic one we are now leaving. But our intellectual legacy differs in many ways from that of France, and so we will probably take a somewhat different course. The reading of our philosophical tradition does not make one sanguine, since our philosophical road seems to have been blocked since the days of Hume and Kant. A new Hegelian or Hegelian Marxist period may provide some inspiration, but Marcuse's pessimism indicates this is not too likely. My own groping has been towards finding an intellectual center in the vital aspects of Judeo-Christianity. These have provided revolutionary inspiration and insight in past times, have given some of this spirit to secular humanistic movements from the Enlightenment onward. If we can suspend our rejection of it long enough to find what is still vital, we may find a basis for a view of man to lead us beyond our present plight, and we may find a future. In one of the lines from Professor Derrida's recent book, *L'Ecriture et la Différence*,[1] it may be the case that "plus étrangement encore, que l'avenir lui-même ait ainsi un avenir."

University of California,
San Diego and La Jolla.

---

[1] Jacques Derrida, *L'Ecriture et la différence* (Paris, Ed. du Seuil, 1967), p. 118

ON "WHO WE ARE" AS A PHILOSOPHICAL QUESTION: COMMENTS ON DERRIDA

Marvin Farber

Professor Derrida's essay is particularly concerned with the impact of recent German writers on French thought. But he is so greatly pre-occupied with the Germans that only a minor indication of the French reaction and his own view is possible. He raises a question about the nature and location of man (the "we"), and after a rather lengthy presentation he ends with the same question—unanswered. It is evident that subjectivism is not helpful; and also that Heidegger is no more satisfactory in the 1960s than he was in the 1920s, for he has not succeeded in emancipating philosophy from the limitations of subjectivism.

Citing Husserl's view, Derrida states that just as a consciousness can be imagined without a soul, so can, *a fortiori,* a consciousness be imagined without man. It is not a matter of "imagining," however, but rather a question of fact that is at issue. It is a fact that a human consciousness presupposes an existing human being. To abstract consciousness from physical reality for special philosophical purposes, and to treat it in isolation, is merely an artificial device of method. In actual fact there are only historically conditioned human beings that can be said to be conscious, and there is no such thing as a consciousness in or by itself.

When Husserl speaks of the constitution of "new ontical objects" for consciousness, it is necessary to determine how much is included in the meaning of "ontical objects," as well as the actual role played by consciousness when something "constitutes itself for consciousness." The answer also depends upon the meaning of "constitution," and it must be made clear whether it is taken to mean a creative activity or merely a descriptive account of processes displayed by experience. In other words, the alternatives are an interpretation leading to metaphysical idealism, for which reality is made up of ideas; and a strictly descriptive and non-assumptive treatment of experience. Transcendental phenomenology operates within the "reduced" realm of pure experience, and it is subject to a group of conditions for its procedure. It is possible to find state-ments and arguments supporting both alternatives in Husserl's own

215

texts. But there can also be no doubt about his ultimate preference for a thoroughgoing idealism, which includes an ontology for which to be real means to be involved in the stream of experiences.

All findings resulting from a phenomenological approach to the nature of man must be considered along with the results of a behavioral approach, from the perspective of a methodology embracing physical, biological, social, and reflective regions of inquiry. Because the science of man comprises a group of disciplines based upon the natural and social sciences, an ideally complete account would involve all of ontology. In comparing the different approaches and methods, one must consider the selection of facts and the nature of the questions for inquiry. Both descriptive procedures and explanatory devices must be employed. A phenomenological approach must have recourse to structural patterns in experience, of which ideal essences are an extreme, limiting case. There can be more variable patterns, however, with essential structures reinterpreted with reference to the natural and cultural events involved. This is seen in the description of perception, the self or ego, and individuality. Just as the relatively independent status of formal logic does not prevent it from being included in the collective totality of sciences dealing with the world of existence and culture, so may phenomenological description be included among the methods of inquiry. In both cases, the real origin of the pure sciences involved is to be traced to the natural and cultural world.

When Derrida speaks of the danger of a discussion "degenerating into cultural or journalistic chatter," it may be observed that the correct use of the knowledge of culture has an important bearing upon philosophic thought. The conclusion of his discourse is a surprising end to "The Ends of Man," when he asks, "But who, we?" The real man (or "we") must have been lost somehow in order to make such a question possible. Unless the discussion is based upon scientific knowledge the "we" remains problematical. To say with Heidegger that language is "the house of being" is misleading and at best trivial in an analytic sense, while being literally false if the natural world is involved. On the other hand, to locate the "we" in the world by scientific means is to proceed with truth and evidence, and to avoid the mass of vapid verbiage which has become so alluring to persons seeking an alternative to logical methods. In the more praiseworthy cases, what appears to be novel and profound insight may turn out to be merely a translation into the most difficult possible language of fairly obvious items in ordinary and scientific experience.

The logic of questions must be considered. Not every string of words can be made to be a justifiable question. There are "homeless" questions, which are not meaningful in terms of any logically organized system of discourse, nor in terms of ordinary discourse; just as there are "proper" questions belonging to organized systems of knowledge or to ordinary discourse. Furthermore, there are pointless and vacuous questions; even though they may be said to be meaningful with reference to a system of discourse, there may be no point in asking them, if they are devoid of real content and are without consequences in experience. This applies to the attempt to question man and the world from a purportedly more radical dimension of thought. The assumption of a philosophical ether under the name of spirit, self, or ego adds nothing ontologically. Neither does the introduction of the "Cogito" as a fixed Archimedian point for philosophy offer a sanction for questions not anchored in physical and cultural reality. The appeal to the "Cogito" provides at most for standpoint questions which are meaningful within the limits of a special procedure or on the basis of the premises of a particular point of view—say existential-phenomenological or idealistic in various versions, explicit or implicit. There should be no element of philosophical mystery superadded to the collective scientific account of man historically, structurally, functionally, and factually.

Philosophers have engaged in mutual criticism without giving sufficient attention to the consequences of established knowledge for philosophic thought. The question of the place of man in the cosmos has intrigued writers seeking an escape from nature—even a linguistic escape. But the evidence is overwhelming and conclusive: man is a part of nature, just as cultural evolution is an incident in universal evolution. Even the pure ego is a late emergent, arising as a fiction from the thought processes of subjectivistic thinkers, who are themselves historically conditioned bodies reacting to the social and natural world.

From one point of view, man is a complex of stresses and strains, of chemical elements, or of "midriff and guts." From another point of view, man creates values in relationship to nature; and man develops systems of thought, real and abstract in their reference, all the way to idealized conceptual structures. It would be a naive error, however, to suppose that man's ontology must include ideal features ascribed to the fictions he has engendered. A vision of eternity is not therefore an eternal vision, any more than the thought of consciousness without a body is therefore a distinct kind of being free from bodily relations.

Finally, it is important to think of man not only as a being with bodily organs, but also in the sense of a being in a historical form of society, as a serf, a proletarian, a capitalist, etc. The self or ego must be viewed as a variable in actual history. Only on that basis can we know "who we are."

A meaningful sociohistorical question is to be answered factually, and there is no place for an aura of mystery. In short, philosophy must be based upon the world of experience; and its questions should never violate the content of established knowledge.

STATE UNIVERSITY OF NEW YORK AT BUFFALO.

ON SELF-REFERENCE: COMMENTS ON DERRIDA

Peter Caws

The chief difference between contemporary philosophy in French and contemporary philosophy in English, and the chief obstacle to mutual understanding between French philosophers on the one hand and Anglo-American philosophers on the other, is that philosophy in English has never really come to terms with Hegel and his intellectual legacy, while philosophy in France has never really come to terms with the revolt against Hegel represented by pragmatism and logical empiricism and linguistic analysis. I overlook for the moment the flirtation with Hegel that occurred at Oxford and at Harvard around the turn of the century, and I ignore French philosophy before 1940, Hegel's chief impact having been felt since the war—directly through Hippolyte and indirectly (via Husserl and Heidegger) through Sartre and Merleau-Ponty. The Oxford Hegelians are not without a kind of negative importance, it is true: without Bradley, Moore would have had less to refute, and there might have been no early Russell for him to convert. But recent philosophy in England and America has not only forgotten Hegel, it has also forgotten the fact that it owes at least part of its character to the reaction against him. There are of course people working on Hegel in English; I speak of the dominant trend. For a whole generation of American students of philosophy Hegel has been known, if at all, only as an awful example of what not to become.

This situation is further complicated by a systematic ambiguity in the role of language as a source of philosophical problems. So-called linguistic analysis in England and America has proceeded in almost total ignorance of linguistics, whereas in very recent French philosophy de Saussure has been elevated almost to the status of a patron saint. When English-speaking philosophers talk of language they are usually thinking of particularities of use; when French-speaking philosophers do so they are usually thinking of generalities of structure—if they deal in particularities at all these are likely to be of etymology or style. There are exceptions, of course; the paper of Professor· Vuillemin in the present collection is one. (By contrast, the paper of Professor Sellars may be taken as a paradigm of recent linguistic philosophy in English.)

Professor Derrida is not always intelligible even to his compatriots; given these differences of tradition and attitude he may well seem totally opaque to American philosophers, who as a class react to opacity with impatience and even intolerance. But it may be worth while to entertain for a moment the possibility that somewhere between the lucid and the ineffable (whereof one must of course be silent) there may be a region in which there genuinely are important things to be said and it genuinely is difficult to say them. Clarity and distinctness are all very well, but ever since Pascal's criticism of Descartes the French have been accustomed to the notion that an insistence upon them may result in an impoverishment of philosophy. I do not wish to condone unnecessary fuzziness— American readers are tempted to suspect that French philosophy is *deliberately* obscure, and it must be admitted that a certain intoxication with style, a preference for the *bon mot* over the *mot juste,* sometimes overtakes French philosophers. But what Professor Derrida is trying to say in this paper, if I have understood it, does not lend itself to exactness of formulation, and that for a reason.

Apart from its preoccupation with the history of a philosophical tradition in which, as I have said, English-speaking philosophers tend to take a rather minimal interest (the question whether Hegel, Husserl and Heidegger have or have not been correctly represented as humanists), the basic concern of Professor Derrida's paper centers, it seems to me, on the problem of what happens when man addresses himself to the problem of man, when the subject questions the status of the subject, when language examines the sense of language. For the latter difficulty the analytic tradition has a ready solution: distinguish between use and mention, between language and metalanguage, and the problem vanishes. (The infinite regress thus opened up is not usually taken seriously.) But the metalanguage is still language; how do we, with only language at our disposal, illuminate the totality of the system of language? The enterprise must be undertaken from within, and the force of the "reduction of sense" of which Professor Derrida speaks is to deprive the system of language, taken as a whole, of any sense or significance at all. Not that any particular utterance ceases to "make sense"—it is just that this sense derives from the structure of language, and that this structure is closed and self-referential, not signifying anything apart from itself.

"The end of man" is the end of the attempt (moving now from the linguistic to the anthropological plane) to locate in man—or in the idea of the human—the significance of the philosophical enterprise.

Philosophy continues to be done by men, but they are within the system: they derive their significance from it, it does not derive its significance from them. Significance, for man, has always been an end also in the other sense of the term—a goal, perhaps a destiny. The fullest actual significance, this structural interpretation suggests, lies in an apprehension of the nature of the only possible significance, which thus becomes the apprehension of itself. And this is open to every man, but only if he follows the history of philosophy in turning his back on man as the bearer of significance.

Self-reference, as various well-known paradoxes show, is a logically perilous concept; English-speaking philosophy has been wary of it except under strict logical controls. The fact that the history of philosophy in English since the revolt against Hegel appears somewhat anecdotal and fragmented is not unconnected with this cautious attitude, for Hegel more than anyone is responsible for setting European philosophy on its self-referential track. Without suggesting for a moment that the undoubted gains in rigor and sophistication attributable to the self-imposed limitations of analytic philosophy should be given up, we may profitably be reminded by reflections like those of Professor Derrida that the question of the direction and purpose of the whole enterprise can at least be legitimately raised, even in the context of contemporary history in the wider sense (as suggested at the beginning of his paper). Most of us, confronted with such a challenge, would be tempted to fall back on some more or less vague form of humanism; Professor Derrida shows that it cannot be as simple as that. We might of course refuse to entertain the question at all. But if it should come to perplex us, we might do worse than take a second (or even a first) look at Hegel. The worst that could follow would be a better understanding of the preoccupations of our French colleagues, even if we did not, as we might, come to share them.

Hunter College
City University of New York.

COMMENTS ON DERRIDA

WESLEY C. PIERSOL

What is man? Is this still a valid question? Was it ever? And if so, was the question ever properly formulated? What is the language of its formulation? Since one of the topics of this conference is philosophical anthropology, Professor Derrida considers: "Where, then, does France stand with regards to man?" Viewed historically, in the ten years after the second world war, the *anthropological* reading of Hegel, Husserl, and Heidegger, which supplied the best resources for French thought was a misreading of them. Even in the current anti-anthropological thinking in France, this misreading had not been rectified.

By passing Derrida's acute re-evaluation of Hegel, Husserl and Heidegger, we will reflect briefly on some of the themes in "The Ends of Man:" 1) *telos,* 2) the phenomenological metaphor, 3) the need for a changing of terrain and of style (un ebranlement radical).

I

The end of man is both his *telos* and his *eschaton,* both his death, the mortality, and finitude, which are the very condition of the ideality of thought, and his fulfillment, as "man," as "we" or as the place of unfolding of teleological reason—history. A reflection on the ends of man becomes a reflection on language and on conceptual thought. Hence the citation from Michel Foucault's *Les mots et les choses:* "Man is an invention whose recent date and whose nearing end perhaps, are easily shown by the archeology of our thought."

"The unity of the two ends of man, of his death, of his termination, and of his fulfillment is enveloped in the Greek thought of *telos,* in the discourse on *telos* which is also discourse on *eidos, ousia* and *alethia.* The end of man is written into the thought and the language of being. The equivocality of the two meanings of the end of man goes as follows: the end of man is the thinking of being. Man is the end of the thought of being. The end of man is the end of the thought of being. Man has always been his own end, that is, the end of himself (de son propre).

222

Being has always been its own end, that is, the end of itself. Humanism and metaphysics are inseparable from the language in which we express them. How, then, can we take a distance from our own Indo-European linguistic milieu?

II

Heidegger undercuts whatever the metaphysical predicate "human" can name, in his radically archeological questioning of humanism, of the "genesis of the concept and of the value of 'man' (a renewal of the Greek paideia in Roman culture, the Christianization of the Latin humanitas, a renaissance of Hellenism in the XIVth and the XVIIIth centuries, etc.)" ". . . Man must learn to exist in that which has no name." In Heidegger's discourse, with the interplay of implicit/explicit, near and far, nearest and farthest, the phenomenological metaphor replaces the humanist or metaphysical statement. Heidegger has deconstructed the authority of the present over metaphysics, to lead us to think the presence of presence, hence the interplay of all the varieties of phainesthai, of brilliance, of openings, of Lichtung, which open onto the space of the presence and the presence of space.

The value accorded presence to self as absolute presence (preceding—again—the predicate "man") leads to a valorization by Heidegger, and by Derrida, of spoken language, of voice, of listening.[1]

III

A changing of style and of terrain is necessary. What is to give us the needed shock and impulse, since it will not come from within our language, literature or philosophy? A recourse to Nietzsche is particularly insistent in France (and of course most recently we have Professor Danto's excellent work on Nietzsche). Nietzsche's super man (as opposed to superior man) will dance outside of the house, in this "aktive Vergeszlichkeit," this active forgetfulness and this cruel feast spoken of in *Genealogy of Morals*. Is this guard mounted around the house a wake or is it an awakening? Derrida concludes: "We are perhaps between these two vigils which are also the two ends of man. But who, we?"

These questions are to be taken literally. They imply a distance to be taken in regard to some of our most familiar words and concepts: "man," "nature," "culture," etc. We will conclude with two brief remarks:

---

[1] See for example Jaques Derrida's *De la grammatologie* and his *La voix et le phénomène*.

1) This distance can, on one hand, be a curious reversal, come from an accepance of what presents itself *as it manifests itself*. One of Ludwig Wittgenstein's "positive achievements," although according to Paul Engelman it has so far met with complete incomprehension, is "his pointing to what is *manifest in a proposition*. And what is manifest in it a proposition cannot also state explicitly."[2] "The poet's sentences, for instance, achieve their effect not through what they say but through what is manifest in them, and the same holds for music, which also says nothing."[3] In Wittgenstein's letter of 9/4/17, he says "The poem by Uhland is really magnificent. And this is how it is: if only you do not try to utter what is unutterable then *nothing* gets lost. But the unutterable will be—unutterably—contained in what has been uttered."[4]

2) How to go about effectuating this change of terrain, or change of style, or both, no longer from within our Indo-European linguistic milieu, but rather that of the "anonymous depths" from which Derrida as well as some of the French "structuralists" speak. Their anti-anthropological methodology furnishes a tool for problems such as (1) the relation of nature and culture (which as J. B. Fages points out in his useful little book on structuralism: *Comprendre le structuralisme*,[5] is identical with the debate unconscious-conscious), as well as (2) the relation of "coded systems" with phenomenological hermeneutics[6] (3) that of *structures* (language, family relationships, etc.) with praxis,[7] and finally (4) of history (as inevitable progress in time) with diachronic structure.[8]

Professor Derrida's scholarship and style give an impetus toward bringing about the "ebranlement radical" of which he speaks.

UNIVERSITY OF MARYLAND
BALTIMORE COUNTY.

---

[2] Paul Englemen, *Letters from Ludwig Wittgenstein with a Memoir* (New York, Horizon Press, 1968), p. 83.

[3] *Ibid.*, p. 83

[4] *Ibid.*, p. 7 and p. 83

[5] Paris, Privat, 1967, p. 111

[6] *Ibid.*, p. 111-113

[7] *Ibid.*, p. 113-115

[8] *Ibid.*, p. 115-118

Section 6

COMPLEX EVENTS *

Arthur C. Danto

> Action seems like a leak from another realm or world into
> this world — an intervention such as God would bring about
> were he able to bring about changes in the world without
> transgressing the laws of nature ... We stand within and
> without Nature.[1]
>
> Brian O'Shaughnessy.

The purpose of this paper is to describe a structure which logically
defines the nature of man, so that any theory of what man *is,* if I am
right in what follows, must be consistent with this structure. I shall
propose that men are *complex* entities in a specific sense of complexity
to be elaborated below, and that our philosophical understanding of
human nature will be exactly proportionate to the degree of clarity we
may attain with regard to complex structures of this sort.

I

Some Preliminary Notions

It will be useful to introduce and briefly to comment upon some
general philosophical notions which will be drawn upon in constructing
a theory of complexity.

(1) An action α is a *basic action* of an agent m only if (i) m performs
α; and (ii) there is no action β, distinct from α, and such that m performs
α by performing β. Basic actions are crucial for the theory of action in
that it can be argued, I believe conclusively, that unless there are basic
actions, there are no actions whatever. More specifically, if m performs
an action γ, then either γ is a basic action or there is some basic action

* This paper is part of an inquiry supported by a grant from the Columbia
Council for Research in the Humanities.

[1] Brian O'Shaughnessy, "Observation and the Will," *Journal of Philosophy,* LX,
14, July, 1963, p. 368.

performed by m as part of his performing γ. *Raising an arm or closing an eye* are standard examples of basic actions for normal agents.[2]

(2) Let α be an action of m's and let b be an event distinct from α, and let α cause b. If (i) m believes that there is a causal connection between α and b and (ii) m applies this belief, then m has performed the *non-basic* or *derived* action β of *causing b to happen*. It is a mark of a non-basic action β that m performs β only by performing a distinct action α, itself basic. A standard example of a non-basic action for normal agents is *moving a stone*.

(3) There is an interesting analogy in the theory of knowledge to these notions in that a sentence s is a basic sentence for m if m knows *directly* that s, that is (i) m knows that s and (ii) there is no sentence r, distinct from s such that m knows that r and m knows that s only because he knows that r. If, by contrast, m knows that t only because m knows that r, where r and t are distinct, then m knows indirectly that t, and t is insofar a non-basic sentence for m. And just as non-basic actions require that m know and apply the knowledge of a *causal* connection between, say, a and b, so does non-basic cognition require that m knows and apply the knowledge of an *inferential* (in fact, I believe, an entailing) relation between, say, r and t. This *limits* m's performative and his cognitive liabilities only to *some* consequences of his direct actions and of his direct cognitions respectively, that is, not every consequence of an action is an action, and not every consequence of something that m knows is a further piece of knowledge for him. Meanwhile, it may be argued in a manner perfectly analogous to the way alluded to in (1) that if there is no direct knowledge, there is no knowledge. But while it is impossible that there should either be action or knowledge without direct action and direct knowledge, there are radical but otherwise unattractive positions in the theories of knowledge and of action alike, according to which we know *only* what we know directly, and do only what we *directly* do.

(4) I subscribe to and shall presuppose but not argue for an essentially Humean account of causality as a relation between ordered pairs of *distinct* events. The event e-1 is described as a cause only if it satisfies positionally the relation Causes (e-1, x); [3] and as there is an absolute distinction between absolute and relational properties, nothing about

---

[2] I have elaborated a theory of action with essential reference to basic actions in a number of papers. See "What We Can Do," *Journal of Philosophy,* LX, 15 July 1963, pp. 435-445; "Basic Actions," *American Philosophical Quarterly,* II, 2 April, 1965, pp. 141-148; "Freedom and Forebearance," *Freedom and Determinism,* ed. Keith Lehrer (New York, Random House, 1966), pp. 45-63.

[3] This view is brilliantly vindicated in Donald Davidson's "Causal Relatons," *Journal of Philosophy,* LXIV, 21, November 9, 1967, pp. 691-703.

e-1 as such, i.e., absolutely, will (as Hume famously noted) enable one to deduce that e-1 satisfies the causal (or any) relation. So that experience alone enables us to tell what descriptions, which presuppose satisfaction of a relation, are true of e-1.

When e-1 is an event in the history of an individual m, then if e-1 causes e-2, we may derivatively speak of m as causing e-2. Of immediate relevance to our topic is the case where m is said to cause b when m does a, and "Causes (a, b)" is true, and when, finally, m's causing b to happen is the derived action β of m. It *is* a derived action if m knows that Causes (a, b), applies this knowledge, and, of course does a. Obviously α is a basic action of m in case, when Causes (x, α) is true, x is not an action of m's. I mention this because I wish it to be open that basic actions should be caused. Their being basic rules out only a certain *class* of causes. And the epistemological analogue to this is instructive. It is, thus, an explanation, even if it is also a justification in certain instances, for m's knowing that t, that m was *caused* to know that t by his having *inferred* t from s, when he knew that s. But there are other ways in which a man can be caused to know something. He could have knowledge innately planted in him, or could have gotten it adventitiously, and it is compatible with my concept of direct knowledge that m may have been caused to know that which he knows directly, providing only that it was not caused by his first knowing something else, from which he inferred it. It is a thesis of empiricism that m knows that s only if m has been caused to know that s, and nothing I have said is incompatible with this. There is an analogous thesis (held in a way by Hobart) that I can be said to have done something only if I have been *caused* to do it. But again, nothing I have said about direct action is incompatible with this. Knowledge (or action) being in any instance direct, rules out only a class of causes, not the class of causes *uberhaupt*.

(5) The event e is an *event of the lowest order* — a basic event, so to speak — if there is no distinct event f which is a proper part of e. An event then is of a *higher-order* than e if it contains some distinct event as a proper part. Thus, if Causes (e, f) may be counted an event, it conspicuously belongs to a higher-order.

One can in principle give a complete description of the universe in terms of lowest-order events, and there is a sense in which this description would cover everything that happens, since it is obvious that there are no higher-order events if there are none of the lowest-order. Now there can be a position of Radical Atomism which holds that nothing takes place *save* events of the lowest-order. That of course would require us to say that Causes (e, f) is not (really) an event, but (perhaps) an imposition onto the mosaic of events by our minds, a view held (roughly) by Hume and (more roughly still) by Kant. And Radical Atomism would be a correct and plausible theory of the universe if in fact every so-called higher-order event sundered neatly and non-residually into constituents, each of which was an event of the lowest-order. Then all the relational apparatus would be swept, by default, into the mind (that convenient philosophical dustbin), which reads conjunctions as connections, and in general takes the structures it imposes for structures it discovers in the world. Such dissolutive strategies are overfamiliar in philosophy, but the decision as to what belongs to the world, and what belongs to *our* (mere) ordering apparatus, is one not to be lightly made, and I should propose the following criterion: a Radical Atomism of events is untenable if we are constrained to countenance higher-order events, i.e., events which do not sunder neatly and non-residually into constituent lowest-order events. For these, if such there be, we are constrained to Realism.

Reference to events of various orders may appear arbitrary or bizarre, but this will be only because the notion of an event is largely unstructured in philosophical discourse: like the notion of a *thing*. Indeed, exactly comparable questions arise for individuating things, and of demarcating higher- eq and lowest-order things by the criterion of whether or not they contain things as proper parts. I, however, shall employ a somewhat different model, since any reservations a reader may have regarding events are not likely to be alleviated through recourse to things. So let me point out that in language we have some intuitive basis for effecting distinctions of the sort I have been sounding, namely, we can identify a class of lowest-order or atomic *sentences* as those sentences which contain no further sentences as proper parts. The flow of language is sententially articulated, and we are able with no great practical, although no doubt with considerable theoretical difficulty, to mark the points of sentential join and segmentation. We have comparable intuitions which enable us to mark the boundaries of things and events — of where things begin and end, and when events are over — and, as with events and things, we have an intuitive sense for *completeness:* in primers of grammar, a sentence is complete if it expresses a "complete thought." But to have a concept of completeness is also to have a concept of *incompleteness,* which for my purposes is especially useful: for just as an incomplete sentence fails to be a sentence, I shall wish to say that an incomplete thing is not a thing (but a fragment) and, more immediately relevant, an incomplete event is not an event.

II

The Concept of Complexity

Sentences, however intricate, are atomic when they contain no sentences amongst their proper parts; compound sentences contain proper sentential parts conjoined by truth-functional connectives. A philosophically crucial class of sentences is neither of these, and on the model of the grammatical distinction between compound and complex clauses, I shall term these *complex sentences*. A crucial example is (*A*) "*m* believes that *s*," in that (i) (A) contains *s* as a proper sentential part; (ii) the whole sentence (A) is truth-functionally independent of the truth-value of *s*; and (iii) if we subtract *s* from (A), we are left with a non-sentential remnant, "*m* believes that . . ." Though grammatically a conjunction, "that" hardly can be taken as truth-functionally a conjunction, viz, as joining "*m* believes" with *s*; for then, by the common rules of conjunction, there could be no false beliefs.

The logical parsing of complex sentences is, at present writing, moot. Thus "believes that" has been taken as a relational predicate (taking as arguments names of believers and of 'objects of belief,' e.g., by Plato); as a propositional attitude, by Russell, and, more narrowly, as a statement-forming operator upon statements in a system of epistemic logic, by Jaakko Hintikka; and as a portion of a predicate, viz, "believes-that-*s*" which is then taken as true of individuals one at a time, by Quine.[4] I favor the latter analysis of "believes-that-*s*" [5] as what I term a *sentential predicate,* for there are immense philosophical advantages in treating "believes that" (and co-logical expressions) in this way. But I cannot argue the matter here. My immediate concern is to employ the concept of complexity as a structural guide for the articulation of what I shall call *complex events*.

An atomic or lowest-order event, however otherwise intricate its structure, contains no distinct event as a proper part; a compound event contains proper eventival parts externally conjoined by whatever may be the connectives for an elementary logic of events, e.g., perhaps purely temporal connectives like "then" — in "e-1 then e-2"; or "while" — in "e-1

---

[4] W. V. O. Quine, *Word and Object* (Cambridge, M.I.T. Press and John Wiley, 1960), pp. 215-216. For relevant criticisms — though not, I believe, insuperable ones — see Donald Davidson, "Theories of Meaning and Learnable Languages," *Proceedings of the 1964 International Congress for Logic, Methodology, and Philosophy of Science* (Amsterdam, North-Holland Publishing Company), pp. 391-392.

[5] See my *Analytical Philosophy of Knowledge* (Cambridge, Cambridge University Press, 1968), Ch. IV *passim*.

while e-2." A *complex* event then will contain at least one distinct event as a proper part, without being non-residually resoluble into events of the lowest-order externally conjoined by event-connectives. Rather, in addition to its atomic proper parts, the complex event will contain a non-eventival remnant.

I hasten to illustrate. The event described as "m does a" (hereafter notationally abbreviated as $m\mathrm{D}a$) — an action performed by m — is a complex event. It is, to begin with, an event. It contains another event as a proper part, namely a. Finally, if a is subtracted from $m\mathrm{D}a$ there is left a non-eventival remnant in the respect that there can *be* no event which can stand on its own and be truly described with $m\mathrm{D}$: there is no doing which is not the doing *of* something, as there is no believing which is not a believing *of* something: no *atto puro,* mental or otherwise. The non-eventival "m does . . ." corresponds, in a structural sense, to the non-sentential fragment "m believes that . . ." (which could in turn be described as a non-eventival remnant of a complex event, if m's believing that s were a complex event.)

Consider now the case in which m knows that s (hereafter notationally abbreviated as $m\mathrm{K}s$). It is not altogether clear whether the sentence $m\mathrm{K}s$ is a *bona fide* member of the class of complex sentences of which "m believes that s" is the paradigm. There are, on the one hand, most (perhaps all) of the opacities of reference, meaning, and quantification which notoriously characterize the members of this class, which (the reader may verify) are shared by $m\mathrm{K}s$. But on the other hand, $m\mathrm{K}s$ is to *some* degree truth-functional. It is a commonplace of epistemic analysis that $m\mathrm{K}s$ entails s, so if s is false, likewise it is false that $m\mathrm{K}s$. Of course the *truth* of s is compatible with the falsity of $m\mathrm{K}s$, there being few if any sentences such that, if *they* are true, it must also be true that we *know* them (a candidate for such a sentence, curiously, would be $m\mathrm{K}s$ itself, for there are philosophers who hold that we cannot know without knowing that we know.) So, although we can know nothing which is not the case, much can be the case without our knowing it to be.

Now there is a very strong analogy between our concepts of knowledge and of action in connection with the features just mentioned. Let 'a' have the meaning: "m's arm rises at time t." I shall suppose the latter describes an event of the lowest-order. Well, just as $m\mathrm{K}s$ entails the truth of s, so does $m\mathrm{D}a$ entail the occurence of a, where $m\mathrm{D}a$ here has the meaning: "m raises his arm at time t." If $m\mathrm{D}a$ takes place, a must happen, and if a does *not* happen, neither does $m\mathrm{D}a$: m cannot raise his arm at time t if his arm does not rise at time t. Again, there are very few events of the lowest order such that, if they happen, then they *must* have been *done,* i.e., must occur in a context specified as $m\mathrm{D}$ . . . Rather, most if not all lowest-order events could take place without our having done any of them. For m's arm may rise at time t without m raising his arm at t; and in general, the happening of a does not entail the happening of mDa. If, as O'Shaughnessy suggests, action is like a leak from another world into this one, we might take *this* world to be: the world of lowest-order events. Then, if there are actions, we should have an extraordinarily complex universe. It is a universe in which some events which are parts of this world are *contained* in high-order events, only parts of which are parts of this world. This sounds Idealistic, but it is only partially so, for plainly, if a fails to happen, so does mDa, and if the events of this world did not exist, no higher-order events would either. But since in principle all the lowest-order events could take place indifferently as to whether they were embedded in contexts exemplified by mD . . ., the distinction between those lower-order events which are done, and those which happen but are not done, is not a distinction which can be made at the level of lowest-order events as such. So conceived, the world would be just the world it is, whether there were actions or not, that is, whether or not the universe were complex. We are within and without the world, but the sense in which we are in the world would not enable anyone to know that we were also without the world. The existence of actions casts not a differentiating shadow on the world of lowest order events.

III

Some Philosophical Implications

I shall suppose that if there are actions, they are complex events, in that they contain at least one distinct event as a proper part. For simplicity I shall restrict my discussion to basic actions. If mDa describes a basic action, we are dealing with two distinct events, mDa and a, where there are of course some asymmetries of identification, in that we may identify a without mDa, although not the other way round. I shall now sketch out some philosophical features of my concept.

(1) The event a is in a causal series of atomic events at the physical-physiological level. Arms rise naturally only when muscles flex and neurons fire. The detailed accounts of this are to be found in science books, and as philosophers we are obliged to respect them. But just because these are accounts in terms of events of the lowest-order, it is not to be expected that we shall find in them reference to actions: for at this level there are none. The case, indeed, is not unlike what we encounter in the physiology of perception. There is a compact series of events, beginning with the vibration of a string, which sets up perturba-

tion of a medium, which in turn sets up vestibular agitations, which are translated into nervous impulses, and so on. We could describe this entire series without knowing what *sounds* are, we could know the world was full of vibrations and not know it was filled with *noise*. For perhaps sounds have no location in the compact series just sketched. It is only that when the series occurs, a man hears sounds. And it may also be that when there is the innervation and flexing of a muscle, a man raises his arm — but the latter is not an event in that series. To attempt to *insert* actions into the series of events at the lowest order is in effect to attempt to collapse mDa onto a. But when one does so, some exceedingly paradoxical results occur. Thus, I only can cause a certain brain event b in myself by raising my arm. But then I cannot raise my arm unless b occurs. So if we collapse mDa onto a, we appear to get causality running in two directions, from a to b and from b to a. There may be two-way causality, but since we are obliged to make some adjustment to the facts, conceptual conservativism suggests that we retain our asymmetric concept of causality by acknowledging that it is the distinct event mDa which causes the brain event b, and the brain event b does not cause mDa but rather the distinct event a. And while there may be problems here, we may face them with our causal structure intact.

Meanwhile, let us note some of the connections which we are permitted under this scheme. If mDa and a are distinct, then in general the causes of mDa will not be the causes of a, nor conversely. Thus it is generally false to say that b causes mDa, viz, causes m to raise his arm. Rather, it causes a: the arm rises when the brain event occurs. Again, the causes of mDa need not be the causes of a. Explanations of the raising of the arm, and explanations of the arm's rising, will typically make reference to disjoint sets of causes. It is perfectly compatible with mDa *not* being caused (if that should be the case) that a itself should be caused, e.g. by physiological events. Philosophers have latterly been stirred to draw a distinction between causes and reasons, but I see no serious argument against regarding reasons as a species of cause, so that the concept of causality requires no essential modification through happening to have, as a species of cause, what philosophers have termed reasons. It is only that a member of this species could not cause a, although it might plausibly cause mDa. Finally, there may be (there almost certainly must be) a physiological series of causes for a such that only when a is so caused is it true that mDa. But differentiated series of causes for the event a would not as such enable us to know *which* such series went with actions, for, at the level at which we marked out these series, there would be no room for actions at all.

(2) Let me stress that the Logic of mDa is rather more like that of

mKs than of "m believes that s." For the truth of the latter entails nothing regarding the truth-or-falsity — or even the *sense* — of s, whereas mKs entails that s is true and *a fortiori* meaningful. Knowledge, like action, therefore puts us in contact with the world, since it is the world which commonly makes s true and in which a takes place when mDa.

Against this background, it is useful to note that we need not be struck dumb by the celebrated koan of Wittgenstein, namely, what remains over when we subtract *m's arm goes up* from *m raises his arm*. In one respect, nothing of course remains over, inasmuch as, if a does not occur, neither does mDa. But in another way of looking, something is left over in that a only is contained in, and does not completely constitute, mDa, viz., and a crucial question for the philos-

ophy of action concerns the interspace between a and mDa. Concerning this I am reluctant to offer any specific theory, but I believe I may make one or two negative suggestions, based upon distinctions I have introduced. Since mDa is a basic action, containing a as its constituent lowest-order event, the interspace must be counted as non-eventival, and hence does not contain any *events*. So there is nothing in the interspace which may stand to a in the ordinary causal relation if we persist in regarding the latter as holding between ordered pairs of events. Now suppose some philosopher wishes to rehabilitate the old notion of volitions, analyzing thus mDa as the volition-that-a plus a. Then the volition-that-a at least could not be an event nor *a fortiori* an action in its own right. Nor could it be a cause of a: if anything, it would be a formal cause of mDa being an *action*. So conceived, the destructive arguments against volitions invented by Ryle [6] would have no application, for they work only on the assumption that volitions are actions in their own right, as well as being non-contingently related to actions as causes. No: volitions would now not be something we *do* but something we *have: states* of agents rather than events.

The analysis of volitions would yield more or less the same structure as that found through the analysis of beliefs, e.g., there would be just the same intentionalities and opacities and the rest. Belief-that-s, in contrast with knowledge-that-s, does not entail that s is true. Comparably, the volition-that-a entails nothing regarding the *happening* of a, although

---

[6] Gilbert Ryle, *The Concept of Mind* (New York, Barnes and Noble, 1949), Ch. III *passim*.

mDa does entail that a happens. There is a natural inclination to analyze mDa as the volition-that-a plus a since there is an analogous analysis of mKs, almost standard in the theory of knowledge, as the belief-that-s-plus s. *Both* analyses are defective, for plainly, I may have the volition-that-a and a may happen, and yet not happen because done by me, just in the way in which I may believe because I have adequate evidence for s that s, and s may indeed be true, but its being true may be for reasons having nothing to do with the evidence I possess. It will hardly do to tighten the connection by suggesting that a happens *because* of the volition-that-a for, apart from elevating volitions to the status of causes, no room is left for actions, viz, for *executing* our volitions. I have no interest in advocating a theory of volitions as such, but only in pointing out some negative features which must govern any positive proposal for a candidate for occupancy of the theoretical space between a and mDa.

(3) Unlike belief and (say) volition, knowledge and action connect us with the world. For when we know that s, s must be true, and when we do a, a must happen. Let us at this point ponder *direct* knowledge, i.e., where m knows that s but not because m has evidence that s. And this, of course, corresponds to direct action, where m does a, and a does not happen by m doing something distinct from a through which a happens. Now I believe that the analysis of direct knowledge must have the following form: there must be a pair of relations R and R' such that m knows directly that s only if m stands in the relation R to the very thing to which s stands in the relation R', so that, as s is true only when R' is satisfied, m knows that s only when R is satisfied (and naturally the satisfaction of R' does not entail the satisfaction of R!). We might speak of R' as the truth-relation and R as the knowledge-relation, and while I cannot dilate upon either of these here,[7] let me say that they are relations of a different order than any relations which hold amongst events of the lowest order, or amongst sentences as such, for the truth relation holds between sentences and the world, and the knowledge relation between *us* and the world (and to know oneself is *ipso facto* to be within and without the world). As knowers, we stand to the world in a relation something like that in which language stands to the world when units of it are *true*.

Now I should propose that much the same is so when we are considered as agents, for it is plausible to suppose an analogous structure here as well, namely, that when mDa is true, m must stand in an actional relation to the very event to which 'a' stands in the descriptive relation.

---

[7] This account of direct knowledge is defended in *Analytical Philosophy of Knowledge,* esp. Ch. VI.

So again, action is, as with knowledge, a relationship between us and the world, rather than (merely?) another intra-worldly relation. I note in passing that any number of sentences may stand in a satisfactory truth-relation to that to which m stands in the knowledge relation, without it following that m knows *all* of this; and similarly there may be any number of descriptions of the same event to which m stands in the action relationship, without it following that he *does* all these things, i.e., as an action. What Chisholm and others refer to as the descriptive element in actions [8] enters at this point, and at a corresponding point will be found the descriptive element in knowledge. But while the one term in the relation — a, thus, in the action relation — may be clear, since it is fairly clear what it means to say, for example, that m's arm rises at t — the other term in the relation, namely m, may remain perplexing. Given that m may be you or me, the question we now are asking is what is man, considered as a knower or a doer?

IV

What we Are

Were I writing a *Meditation,* I should propose at this point what my master Descartes would have said: *sum res complex.* And indeed, that far more plausibly and less misleadingly than *sum res cogitans* would be licensed by an astutely appreciated *cogito.* Man is a complex entity in that complex events typically constitute portions of his characteristic history.

Consider one last time the lowest-order a, and suppose $m\mathrm{D}a$ true. Then a will stand in two different sorts of relations at once: its horizontal relations with other events in the world, and its vertical relations with m. But it is just for this reason that we ourselves, as complex entities, are within and without the world. If, of course, you subtract the world, you subtract a and hence $m\mathrm{D}a$ is false. So without a, m does and so, as agent, *is* nothing. But then neither is m only a 'and nothing more.' It is only that, whatever more we are in excess of a, this is not something which could be if a were not. So m exists only as a complex entity, even if we refer to m as the other relatum in the relation $m\mathrm{D}a$.

Let me stress that m would be a complex entity even if the event a were a mental event, viz, the occurrence of an image. Our complexity then would be invariant to any distinction between the mental and the

---

[8] Roderick Chisholm, "The Descriptive Element in the Concept of Action," *Journal of Philosophy,* LXI, 20, October 29, 1964, pp. 613-625; and his "Freedom and Action," in *Freedom and Determinism, op. cit.*

material; and relative to the difference between complex and non-complex entities (or events), the familiar distinction between the mental and the material may be counted as negligible. So even if the Identity theory should go through, this would entail no collapse of the distinctions I have been concerned to frame. Our distinction is virtually at right angles to the distinctions which it is the task of the Identity theory to overcome, and so we require a view of man which virtually is at right angles to all those standard views based upon the customary dualisms and their alternatives. I have made at best here a mere beginning towards the articulation of a correct philosophical anthropology.

Columbia University.

COMPLEXITY AND AMBIGUITY:
SOME OBSERVATIONS ON PROFESSOR DANTO'S
"COMPLEX EVENTS"

Gilbert Varet

This joint meeting of American and French philosophers is the first of its kind, and for this first time we perhaps could not hope to reach a complete level of philosophical dialogue. Perhaps what we have had in its place is only an alternative succession of tentative positions. In my opinion, this is only natural, and we need not regret it. Each of us is already restricted in his thought by his basic presuppositions which we rarely have the opportunity to reflect upon or be more fully aware of. But in this regard, this philosophical meeting is a challenge of alternative possibilities: several problematical positions are presented on each side. It is such confrontation and dialogue that we surely need. My task in this paper cannot be to examine the philosophy of Professor Danto in its entirety. It would be enough if I can make clear his initial system of propositions by way of contrast, and by the same means, if I can express my own set of philosophical judgments, at least, if I dare say, as an instance of "French" philosophy.

In his *Philosophical Investigations,* Wittgenstein wrote:

> Let us not forget this: when 'I raise my arm', my arm goes up. And the problem arises: what is left over if I substract the fact that my arm goes up from the fact that I raise my arm?.[1]

I don't know the exact position of Professor Danto regarding Wittgenstein's theory. But I suppose that it is in the Wittgensteinian context that Professor Danto's viewpoint has its initial inspiration.

What is of first interest in Professor Danto's paper is its general aim. Its immediate task is not to describe man's specificity by means of more or less complicated propositions that one could deduce from a set of basic axioms, but to justify the principles which render possible all descriptions of this kind. From this point of view Professor Danto's purpose is to force us to take into account an initial complex structure

---

[1] Ludwig Wittgenstein, *Philosophical Investigations* (Oxford, Blackwell, 1958), p. 161e, No. 621.

that had not been recognized heretofore in our fundamental axioms, but which permits us to express every state of fact in the domain of human events.

Of course, it is the property characteristic of human action that requires us to make such economic modifications in our logical habits. This is not without some precedence in the schema of knowing, with which we are most familiar. However, this involves a very little "complication" at first: it requires us only to realize the immediate implications in the axiomatics of knowledge, and then *mutatis mutandis* to apply these to the parallel domain of free will, which directs all events in history, morality and value — in other words, to interpret the human, and to bridge the hiatus between human emergence and nature.

Such an attempt is attractive and suggestive. It is also characteristic of a general aim of philosophy in the United States. Every American philosopher has something like a national vocation to build a great George Washington Bridge over all abysses of dualism: in this case between man and the world.

In proposing his initial philosophical distinction of complexity, Professor Danto wishes to save the monistic basis of every empiricism, positivism, realism, naturalism, and so on. But this presumed *dualism,* in the case of human events, is simply what many Continental philosophies call "dialectics" — for instance, the "dialectical nature" of man. And so, from this side of the ocean river, it is my old-cultured, historical, philosophical Europe that Professor Danto's George Washington Bridge is now attempting to reach. I am surely not the man to say "No!" in principle. Willingly, I was going to extend a hand, and to raise an arm, too, in the direction of Professor Danto's effort. But there are many problems. And to begin with, they are not exactly the same on this side and on the other side of the projected Bridge.

For example, I have just said: this presumed dualism is "simply" what we call dialectics. But, to be more precise, Professor Danto's proposals are not minor logical modifications; they involve, I believe, an excessive *over simplification.* Insofar as Professor Danto's aim was to bridge our distances — and I recognize that it is not his first interest — his proposal unfortunately is incapable of convincing a Continental philosopher. For "dialectics" is *not* "dualism." Dualism is a mere juxtaposition of two unchanged monisms. And to be sure, there is a very frequent juxtaposition of cosmic naturalism and personal spiritualism throughout the English speaking philosophical literature. On the contrary, the word "dialectics" implies that each structure modifies its opposite; and therefore there are not at all two juxtaposed structures, but only one *process* in perpetual internal tension.

When Sartre says — it is the most "simple" instance of dialectics — that "human reality is what it is not and it is not what it is," he doesn't express a dualism of substances, "Being" *and* "Nothingness," but a kind of original relationship which is a relationship of ambiguity. Or when Sartre summarizes his whole dialectics in saying: "to be within the world and not to be without the world," this "not to be" is *a definite one* at each time, and only a "Nothingness" by algebraical addition. I recognize that in writing his paper Professor Danto probably did not have these precise quotations of Sartre in mind. But we do have a quotation from Brian O'Shaughnessy, which curiously is almost equivalent: "We stand within and without Nature" — as a bridge. This quotation parallels almost literally the formula of Sartre I have just quoted. So my present comparison is authorized by Danto's paper.

And my personal opinion is that Professor Danto could not succeed in his task without some ambiguity and dialectics. His own tentative attempt to modify the "identity theory" is nothing else than such an attempt; that is, an attempt to introduce a little dose of initial ambiguity into its closed system. Most likely I shall be unable to convince Professor Danto and to obtain his assent. To agree with my proposal would be to abandon, not only the particular monism of the "identity theory," which is nothing but a derivative consequence, but the general monism implicit in his logical structure.

It is on this side of the ocean that Professor Danto is beginning his Bridge. And the basic stones of the whole framework are to be found at the lower level, i.e., in the first part of his paper. The first part is very long and very clear. May I say in appreciation, that this first part seems to be required in many papers in American philosophy of this sort. I suggest that each of us should have his own system of logical symbolism printed on the back side of his "carte de visite": it would save a lot of time. So, I shall not discuss this first part. It is of domestic American interest. Professor Danto has said nothing which is incompatible with empiricism, realism, monism and naturalism in this first part.

Possibly, my only question here would be about the exact position of Professor Danto regarding *logical atomism.* I do not understand or appreciate its role in his thought. Perhaps I do not understand it because I have never understood what an "atomical sentence" could be. In my opinion, the smallest sentence is already molecular, a *complex* sentence. A pure atomic sentence would be totally empty and without reference to the world. For if it has *meaning,* at this very moment it refers to *something else,* and it is no longer an *atomically simple* one. So the smallest sentence lies at the crossing point of two processes:

a) it refers horizontally to the previous and subsequent surrounding "world of discourse," the linguistic context;

b) and vertically, it refers to the transcendent "world of things," the realistic context.

But this is also the *minimal* structure of consciousness; that is to say, of the "human event," according to Professor Danto's terminology.

I mention this because in the third part of Professor Danto's paper, he does use the Husserlian-Saussurian scheme in distinguishing and connecting the two series: R and R'. In my opinion, he is right here; and this connexion is relevant to every possible meaning-process. But what about monism? What about logical atomism?

I agree with Professor Danto in the second and third parts of his paper. But is he still agreeing with himself?

In any case, I should like to discuss the problem of an "inter-space of non-eventival remnance." To my idea, rather than being any Humean hiatus in the causal relationship, this is exactly the place of *Nature* — and for the silence of the sea. In the same direction, one might say that from the wave to the brain, there is a long fairy tale. I agree that we must *respect* scientific truths, but there is nothing that obliges us to *begin* with them. If a sound from the very first is not yet a sound, *it would never be*. If a sound doesn't possess *meaning* from the very first, it will never do. One can never explain the meaning or beauty of Beethoven's *Opus 127,* for example, with only physico-physiological objects in a Humean space of "non-eventival remnance"; that is to say: one can never constitute a philosophical aesthetics, an ethics, a politics, and so on *on this basis*. But, to be sure, *first* you must hear the sound, and immediately you know whether it was the thunder of the ocean or the human voice. Only *afterwards* do you ask about its "how?." Only *mediately,* little by little, do you learn to decipher the successive "how" of the physico-physiological production of a sound in the "interspace."

As a last point I should like to show that Professor Danto's system of sentence is not free of ambiguity.

To begin with, in my judgment, there is certainly a major ambiguity in Professor Danto's constant parallelism between *to know* and *to do*. For there are ambiguities in each of the concepts, to know and to do taken independently:

1. For example, the statement mKs is ambiguous both in itself and in Professor Danto's use of it. First, *in itself,* for it is obvious that every knowing as such has two sides, an objective and a subjective side. I agree that between belief, opinion, faith and so on, on the one hand, and *knowledge* on the other, there is a radical difference — *in the mind of the knower*. But that doesn't make knowledge something totally objec-

tive: there is always a knower. Perhaps a truism is here relevant. "It is well known that *a*" means that "people *know*." In *true* knowledge, the knower and known are in some kind of *equality,* and this is the moment of Truth. The difficulty is not reduced by using logical symbolism; it is only emphasized. In the sentence *m*K*s,* now the knower *m,* now the known *s* are stressed; by turn we are either in the inner world of the subject or in the objective world of things. Thus by writing *m*K*s* Professor Danto is both "within and without the world" at one and the same time. Evidently this makes it easier to go beyond, from knowing to doing. Otherwise, why say *m*K*s,* and not only *s*? And if *s,* then *s*?

2. An ambiguity again appears with *m*D*a*; but it is not exactly the same and the two cases are not parallel. For use is made here of a specific property of the English verb *to do,* which is not easily translatable into any other language. And perhaps the ambiguity here is not only double; it is, so to speak, threefold. For in "*m.D* . . .":

either (1) 'D' may be the auxiliary verb as it is normally needed in English for negative and interrogative sentences: "He doesn't come," "Does he leave?", etc. But I suppose that in the examples given by Professor Danto, *m*D*a* is not reserved for such interrogative or negative instances, for this would be contradictory with his own system of notation; or (2) 'D' only emphasizes the action, and therefore it is useless for the logical expression of the verbal function, because it only points out that the action is really, or has been really, made, as in the example, "Yes, he *does* believe so!"; or (3) 'D' signifies in the strong sense and independently a verb expressing action in general; and in this case it is itself an *a.* But in no case would "does" be appropriate to express a mere *intention* to do. As a matter of fact, it is not 'D' as such, which expresses the intentionality here, but it is only the interruption of the sentence, as stressed by the suspension points after "mD . . .", that expresses the intention. "What is left over if I subtract the fact that my arm goes up from the fact that I raise my arm ?", has already been asked by Wittgenstein.

Accordingly, the exact logical scheme of action is not "*m.D.a.,*" but only "*m.a.*" However, and there lies the essential difference between knowledge and action, you can *never* say only *a,* as you can say *s.* I can say, and surely it is a truism: if need be and if it is well known, a fact can be isolated from every knower (*s,* but if *s,* therefore *s*); but an act always has an agent. And really, it is not enough to say: for *m.a,* but if *m.a.,* therefore *n* . . . (the name of my nearest neighbour) shall be happy or on the contrary suffer. In other words, an action always has at least one agent and one or more patients or recipients. And here is where the Great Bridge of Being, the Inter-space of eventival remnance, or the inter-space of human communication can be found.

Professor Danto's theory of "doing" attempts to justify the lower world of volitions, intentions and possibilities in human action. What he is searching for, is the *complementum possibilitatis* of both scholasticism and contemporary philosophy. What he needs is to supplement his account with the "complement d'origine," the "difference originaire," as our colleague Derrida would say, and as would Heidegger, Hegel, Maimon, indeed each of us. Although I have raised some difficulties that I have found in Professor Danto's paper, I appreciate fully the significance of the philosophical problem that he is dealing with and the complexity of his attempted solution, both of which bear careful study.

UNIVERSITÉ DE BESANÇON.

COMMENTS ON DANTO

Edouard Morot-Sir

I agree basically with Arthur Danto, first when he makes philosophy a research into human nature and when he refuses implicitly all generalization based on the results of a scientific anthropology, and then when he calls up the idea of *complex entities,* which he specifies immediately in speaking of *complex structures.* And in his conclusion I note this revealing formula: "We ourselves, as complex entities, are within and without the world," which thus defines the idea of complexity in man by a theory of action which is irreducible to a theory of event, such as the latter is formulated by a physicalist logic. However, my philosophical solidarity with these themes is not without some interrogations which I would like to submit to Professor Danto.

In the first place, this effort of determination of human nature, which is in itself legitimate (the demonstration offered by A. Danto seems to me difficult to refute) is new in its style, but not in its intention. It is in effect immanent in all Cartesian metaphysical reflection; it is later taken up again by Kant, who makes man a being apprehended on the two planes of phenomenon and noumenon; and Sartre gives a new interpretation of this philosophical anthropology with his theory of consciousness characterized by the relation of the in-itself with the for-itself, and by the concept of project in opposition to that of situation. We know what difficulty this inevitable decision concerning human complexity entails. If the world is defined as a set of events which are decomposable into units of events yielding to a causal determinism, how is this logic reconciled with what could be called a logic of morality, according to Kant or Sartre? My impression is the following: in renewing philosophical anthropology, Descartes brought to the fore a problem to which he himself admitted the absence of a solution when he made the union of the soul and the body an obscure idea. Kant and Sartre have tried to clear up this "complexity" by referring us to the absolute of an ethical experience. A. Danto does the same, as his logical demonstration establishes again the irreducibility of action to a certain type of naturalism. But then why not recognize this fact as the ultimate situation of a negative anthropology (in analogy with the process of negative theology)? And this leads me to a second remark:

What meaning can the proposition "Man is within and without the world" have? It must be specified whether he is this way alternately or simultaneously. If he is alternately so, the proposition brings us back to a dualism or parallelism, a model of which Spinoza could give us (Spinoza having refused the substantial union of the soul and the body as Descartes posited it in its obscurity). But we know that this position is the very negation of anthropology as the ultimate goal of philosophical reflection. We can therefore only admit the simultaneousness of the fact of being within and without the world. This is to admit the fact of a contradiction in itself irreducible. But is this not then to recognize a fact admitted by dialectic philosophies? I am speaking of the coexistence of contradictories or opposites. And so I wonder if Professor Danto's idea of complex structures is not another term for dialectics, so that human entity equals complexity equals structure equals dialectics. It is the series of these identities which should be the object of philosophical reflection.

There remains the question of the why of this complexity or dialectics. One could perhaps say, leaning on the naturalistic tradition, that this is a false problem provoked by a certain definition of the world. And the difficulty could disappear if I gave the world a definition which is not in contradiction with the concept of action. However, I feel that to limit the discussion to an argument of definitions is not to recognize its gravity. And I would like to suggest an avenue of reflection: is there not a similarity of problematics between anthropology and theology, the latter having tried to maintain the simultaneousness of the two propositions, God is without the world, and the world is within God? And if this type of thought is carried to its conclusion we arrive at theodicy or anthropodicy: what is the world in relation to God or in relation to man? And we see that the proofs of the existence of man pose no fewer difficulties than do the classic proofs of the existence of God.

This leads me to a final suggestion. Have we the right to juxtapose, as seems to be the case in Professor Danto's philosophical anthropology, a dialectic concept of man and a naturalistic concept of the world? I personally would be in favor of a univocal problematics of man and the world, and thus of a first philosophical step requiring the passage from logic to dialectics. In brief, I do not believe that a philosophical anthropology can be elaborated and thus justified by a logical methodology, if, that is, we accept the definition most logicians give logic today.

NEW YORK CITY.

CONCILIATION

GERARD DELEDALLE

In memory of J. M. Baldwin, the conciliator of
"French and American Ideals."

Professor Polin and Professor Danto both deal with the human, but their manner of speaking of it is so different that their papers might be taken for the expression of the two types of philosophy that the Conference was intended to confront: French philosophy and American philosophy. Polin belongs to the humanistic and even moralistic tradition, whereas Danto has chosen to follow in the steps of linguistic analysis. However, if Derrida is equally representative of a certain French tradition and Wilfrid Sellars is on the side of Danto, Vuillemin follows, continues and thoroughly explores the analyses of Wittgenstein and Austin; and one can hear in the defense of the *ego,* proposed by Chisholm in opposition to Sartre and the linguistic analysts and to Hume and Kant before them, a kind of humanistic echo in the analytical cave.

Even if one asserted, moveover, that an anti-humanistic movement is taking shape in France and that a humanistic movement exists in the United States, one of whose most famous exponents is Roy Wood Sellars, the father of Wilfrid Sellars, one would prove only that, over and above national differences, there are today two antinomic ways of philosophizing. We shall try to show that this is not so.

I

First, there is not, as Derrida suggests, "France" or French thought, on one side, and "America" or American thought, on the other, all the less so as the manner of philosophizing now employed by a number of American philosophers is "English," and even "Austrian" through its father Ludwig Wittgenstein. Of course, there are problems which are particular to a given historico-geographical area, and the solutions to them, when compared with others, may give the impression of being quite different or even opposed[1]. For my part, I think this is simply because of a historical time-lag in the solution of identical problems, the consequence of which is to provide philosophers who consider these problems later with different methods, or because of a geographical "space-lag," which has exactly the same consequences. The anti-idealistic reaction of Russell and Dewey, the pragmatism of Schiller and the American pragmatists, the new realism of Russell and the American new realists illustrate by their differences the existence of this "space-lag." On the other hand, what can be closer in spite of appearances and labels, than William James's radical empiricism and the transcendantalism of his father[2], and the analytical philosophy of W. Sellars and the humanistic naturalism of his father? Wilfrid Sellars himself testifies to this and his testimony is worth quoting: "A discerning student of philosophy, familiar with the writings of Sellars *père,* who chances to read Sellars *fils,* and is not taken in by the superficial changes of idiom and emphasis which reflect the adaptation of the species to a new environment, will soon be struck by the fundamental identity of outlook. The identity is obscured by differences of terminology, method and polemical orientation, but it is none the less an identity."[3] So much for the time-lag.

Derrida links up Sartre and existentialism to a humanistic (also called anthropologistic) interpretation of Hegel, Husserl and Heidegger, to which he opposes a new anti-humanistic interpretation which had not yet been made, since today Sartre, Husserl and Heidegger, and Marx too, are "amalgamated" "with the old humanistic metaphysics." As the problem now concerns ways of philosophizing, beyond historical and geographical contingencies, I should like to make two suggestions. If this second interpretation in which it is less a question of man than of the "relief" of man, has not been made, is it not because after the Second World War symbolic logic and linguistics provided the philosopher with new tools for analysis? Tools as yet little used in France, but which French philosophers will soon no longer be able to neglect. The "space-lag" will no longer serve as an excuse for the disdain hitherto shown for them. For once again, it is not merely a question of means of expression or

---

[1] In my *Histoire de la philosophie américaine* (P.U.F.), I myself have described the general characteristics of American philosophy by opposition to the general characteristics of European philosophy.

[2] See my paper, "William James et son père," *Les Etudes philosophiques* Oct.-Dec. 1955, pp. 634-646.

[3] Physical Realism, A Symposium in Honor of Roy Wood Sellars, *Philosophy and Phenomenological Research,* 1954, XV, p. 13.

of working tools. This philosophy is already here, it seems to me, "naked under its clothes," to use Wittgenstein's expression, in Sartre and Heidegger. They wear old-fashioned clothes because of the time-lag, but they belong to the movement disagreeing at one and the same time with the idea of the precedence of knowledge and particularly of perceptive knowledge, and with what Russell, quoting General Smuts, calls "holism"[4] by which linguistic analysis can be negatively defined. What is first is no longer knowledge for Sartre, it is the non-reflexive, which is not sensorial knowledge, but the being of the existent, existence, the existence suddenly revealed to Sartre in *La Nausée,* the existence which is "the very stuff of things."[5] It is the firstness of C. S. Peirce, the "situation" of John Dewey and the "Sachverhalt" of Wittgenstein, which has been wrongly called "état de choses" in the French version, and of which the no more appropriate English translation "atomic fact" has tried to express the non-elementary unity. Dewey once remarked to Sidney Hook who was explaining the philosophy of Heidegger to him, that he could see in it only a description of the idea of "situation" in transcendental German.[6] So it is not monism nor atomism which is to be opposed to "holism," but contextual pluralism. Who would deny today that the one is not opposed to the multiple, that the one has meaning only in the multiple, the one of a situation in the multiplicity of situations—the one of the rules of a game in the multiplicity of language-games?

Russell realized all that and has never ceased to insist on it. In his view philosophical oppositions depend only on the choice of premises in a given discourse or language game. Russell wrote in a letter to Gilbert Murray in 1902: "In all our discussions on ethical subjects, I observe a difference as to premises, a real divergence as to moral axioms."[7] Comparing his own philosophy to Dewey's, Russell was to write again 37 years later in 1939: "In every writer on philosophy there is a concealed metaphysics, usually unconscious; even if his subject is metaphysics, he is almost certain to have an uncritically believed system which underlies his explicit arguments. Reading Dewey makes me aware of my own unconscious metaphysics as well as of his. Where they differ, I find it hard to imagine any arguments on either side which do not beg

---

[4] In *The Philosophy of John Dewey,* Schilpp, ed., 1951, p. 140.

[5] Sartre, *La Nausée* (Paris, Gallimard), p. 140.

[6] Sidney Hook, Some Memories of John Dewey, *Commentary,* Vol. XIV, Sept. 1952, p. 246.

[7] *The Autobiography of Bertrand Russell,* (New York, Bantam Books, 1968), p. 208.

the question; on fundamental issues perhaps this is unavoidable."[8] But the liberalism and the democratic spirit of Russell (who presided over the Vietnam War Crimes Tribunal in Stockholm in 1967) and of Dewey (who presided in Mexico in 1938 at the Commission of Inquiry into the Charges Against Trotsky at the Moscow Trial) show clearly that one of the "fundamental issues" about which Russell and Dewey do not disagree is humanism.

Many misunderstandings which have become apparent in the course of the discussions during the Conference could be cleared up if it were admitted that everything which unites and separates Dewey and Russell depends on the very principle set forth by Russell and which they both apply to their own philosophy, each in his own "situational" way: a fundamental humanistic *a priori* common to both, biologico-Darwinian axioms in Dewey's case and logico-mathematical axioms in Russell's. We shall confine ourselves to a few remarks concerning Jack Kaminsky's reply to Raymond Polin, because it so happens that Polin's creativistic humanism is very much like Dewey's—which Kaminsky seems to reproach him with—and that the American analysis which claims Russell and Wittgenstein as its originators possesses in Dewey a philosopher whose analytical pluralism is inseparable from his humanism.

Polin's metaphysical position seems to me essentially the same as Dewey's: there is the same concern with man, the same precedence of value, the same creativistic conception of man and value.[9] Polin might say that the comparison must not be carried too far, for there are two contradictory axiological attitudes in Dewey: a "humanistic" attitude and a "pragmatistic" attitude.[10] No doubt, one could reply that Dewey escapes from the contradiction if one likes to consider that only his humanistic attitude is axiological, his pragmatistic one being in fact methodological. However that may be, there is in Polin as in Dewey a humanistic *a priori* which is not justified and has no need to be. Is it affective or rational? Perhaps the problem is badly stated—and perhaps it is not a problem for us. In the broad context of the "situation" of Western man, there is perhaps no other possible assumption than that: the value of man. Kaminsky reproaches Polin with not justifying his creativistic conception of man and value. Why should creativity be

---

[8] In *The Philosophy of John Dewey*, p. 138.

[9] See Polin, besides his contribution to the Conference *La création des valeurs* (Paris, P.U.F.) and *La compréhension des valeurs* (Paris, P.U.F.). On Dewey, see my book *L'idee d'expérience dans la philosophie de John Dewey* (Paris, P.U.F.) and especially concerning value, pp. 369-378 and 453-461.

[10] See Polin, *La compréhension des valeurs*, pp. 88-91 and 121-124.

better than non-creativity? To my mind Polin is right not to give any demonstration of it, even from Kaminsky's point of view, for that would turn this fundamental axiom into a theorem of another metaphysics. Dewey who affirms that the creativity of man is the same as that found in any living organism has no need to reply to this other question either: Why is life better than death? The West has chosen life, and Dewey— and Polin—too.

Given this, Polin's system differs from Dewey's because their definitions of creativity and value are different, although these differences are more apparent than real, more a question of language than of principle, of expression than attitude. I mean by this that because Polin's conceptual system is ethical it is of the same order as Dewey's, whereas they are both different from Russell's which is of a logico-mathematical order; in other words, there is a conceptual link between the philosophies of Dewey and Polin and their humanism, whereas in Russell's case there is not. At this point we might remark that Russell's humanism is an affective *a priori* and Dewey's and Polin's a rational one.

Let us examine three points raised by Kaminsky:

(1) It is a fact that men are creative: they produce works of art, elaborate imposing scientific theories, and struggle to make the world a place where life is pleasant. Does this fact imply the obligation for every man to struggle rather than do nothing? We have partly replied to this question. The reply follows directly from the basic axiom that it is better to be than not to be, better to be living than dead, better to act than to do nothing. Dewey, because he is a naturalist, goes further and affirms that the obligation to create is not implied by the fact that there are creators but on the contrary and more profoundly by the fact that the nature of all life being dynamic, a "process," that is to say an obligation to create in order to live, it is the fact which is implied by the obligation.[11]

(2) Moreover Polin tells us how we can recognize creativity: it is intelligible to everyone. Pretending to believe that this intelligibility is an objective universal one, Kaminsky rejects this definition as unintelligible. It seems however that Polin, like Dewey, means that intelligibility is situational, all the more perfect certainly as it is universal, but within the limits of the situation, limits which may have the narrowness of esoteric language or the breadth of the language of "use and enjoyment," to use Dewey's expression. The problem of an objective intelligibility out of context does not arise. Our world is a civilized one, and, in

---

[11] See especially, the article of 1903 entitled *Logical Conditions of a Scientific Treatment of Morality.*

virtue of this forms one situation which is intelligible for all those who participate in this situation. We have known that for a long time and the *Philosophical Investigations* have only reminded us of it. What Polin says is no different. (3) The third point raised by Kaminsky relates to the notion of order linked to that of creativity. Polin says: "A creation is not recognized as such except when it is the creation of an order." How can we distinguish order from disorder? Kaminsky first asks. Polin replies: "An order without meaning would not be received as an order." Through meaning order therefore appears as being necessarily intelligible, which eliminates all possibility of confusing order with disorder. Such is also Dewey's position. But how to distinguish "good" order from "bad" order? "Is Communism more orderly than democracy?" The answer is no, because, says Polin, order is disorder when imposed *ab extra*: disorder is discontinuity. It is, in short, Dewey's very criterion: democracy is more orderly because it is a continuous reconstruction of experience. Polin writes: "It depends on man to realize effectively this order, either continuously by each of them in the City [. . . .], or in the gradual development of the history of men [. . . .]".

II

Does that mean that Kaminsky is opposed to the human? Certainly not. He does not reject Polin's humanistic thesis. He is ready "to dream the impossible dream," but wants to be given the proof of it. Russell and Wittgenstein and analytical philosophy are not so hard to please and would be quite satisfied with Polin's *a priori*. All things considered, humanistic philosophy and analytic philosophy, far from contradicting each other, are reconciled: *they are both contextual*. The one starts from the great principles of the language-game, Western philosophy whose object and subject is man, and the other distinguishes in that wide game, whose principles and rules it does not question, those situation-games which are the daily lot of the philosopher and of the man in the street. While reading and listening to Danto, Kaminsky, Melden, Sellars and Vuillemin, one does not have the impression that playing the analytical game means denying the value of man. Might it not be rather the proof that Polin and Dewey are right: man is defined by his creativity?

In his letter to Gilbert Murray, which we have quoted above, Russell proposes a solution to philosophical divergences: "As I am very anxious to be clear on the subject of immediate moral intuitions (upon which, as is evident, all morality must be based), and as a divergence upon fundamentals raises doubts, I should like to make an attempt to discover precisely what our differences are, and whether either of us holds at the same time mutually incompatible axioms."[12] It is with this suggestion that I will conclude, letting each one apply it in his own way to the discussions of the Conference: conciliation does not mean resolving divergences that the axioms and rules of the language game cannot by description resolve; conciliation means understanding how a theorem follows directly or indirectly from a set of given axioms. It is the lesson we can learn from this Conference, a lesson taught us by analytical philosophy, and it is a lesson of humanism—humanism in action.

UNIVERSITE DE TUNIS.

---

[12] *The Autobiography of Bertrand Russell,* p. 208.